NETWORKING THE BLACK CHURCH

RELIGION AND SOCIAL TRANSFORMATION
General Editors: Anthony B. Pinn and Stacey M. Floyd-Thomas

Prophetic Activism: Progressive Religious Justice Movements in Contemporary America
Helene Slessarev-Jamir

All You That Labor: Religion and Ethics in the Living Wage Movement
C. Melissa Snarr

Blacks and Whites in Christian America: How Racial Discrimination Shapes Religious Convictions
James E. Shelton and Michael O. Emerson

Pillars of Cloud and Fire: The Politics of Exodus in African American Biblical Interpretation
Herbert Robinson Marbury

American Secularism: Cultural Contours of Nonreligious Belief Systems
Joseph O. Baker and Buster G. Smith

Religion and Progressive Activism: New Stories About Faith and Politics
Edited by Ruth Braunstein, Todd Nicholas Fuist, and Rhys H. Williams

"Jesus Saved an Ex-Con": Political Activism and Redemption after Incarceration
Edward Orozco Flores

Solidarity and Defiant Spirituality: Africana Lessons on Religion, Racism, and Ending Gender Violence
Traci C. West

After the Protests Are Heard: Enacting Civic Engagement and Social Transformation
Sharon D. Welch

Ecopiety: Green Media and the Dilemma of Environmental Virtue
Sarah McFarland Taylor

Catholic Activism Today: Individual Transformation and the Struggle for Social Justice
Maureen K. Day

Religion, Race, and COVID-19: Confronting White Supremacy in the Pandemic
Stacey M. Floyd-Thomas

Networking the Black Church: Digital Black Christians and Hip Hop
Erika D. Gault

Networking the Black Church

Digital Black Christians and Hip Hop

Erika D. Gault

NEW YORK UNIVERSITY PRESS
New York

NEW YORK UNIVERSITY PRESS
New York
www.nyupress.org

© 2022 by New York University
All rights reserved

References to Internet websites (URLs) were accurate at the time of writing. Neither the author nor New York University Press is responsible for URLs that may have expired or changed since the manuscript was prepared.

Library of Congress Cataloging-in-Publication Data
Names: Gault, Erika, author.
Title: Networking the Black church : digital Black Christians and hip hop / Erika D. Gault.
Description: New York : New York University Press, [2022] | Series: Religion and social transformation | Includes bibliographical references and index.
Identifiers: LCCN 2021011563 | ISBN 9781479805815 (hardback) | ISBN 9781479805822 (paperback) | ISBN 9781479805860 (ebook) | ISBN 9781479805839 (ebook other)
Subjects: LCSH: African American churches—History—Research. | African Americans—Religion—Research. | United States—Church history—Research. | Hip-hop—Religious aspects—Christianity. | Technology—Religious aspects—Christianity. | Digital media—Religious aspects—Christianity.
Classification: LCC BR563.N4 G38 2021 | DDC 277.30089/96073—dc23
LC record available at https://lccn.loc.gov/2021011563

New York University Press books are printed on acid-free paper, and their binding materials are chosen for strength and durability. We strive to use environmentally responsible suppliers and materials to the greatest extent possible in publishing our books.

Manufactured in the United States of America

10 9 8 7 6 5 4 3 2

Also available as an ebook

To Dad and Mom

To Ntare Ali Gault and Hazel Irene Elise Gault

CONTENTS

List of Illustrations ix

Glossary xi

Preface: My Life as a Digital Black Christian: An Autoethnography xv

Introduction: Performing: Black Christianity in the Digital 1

1. Turns: The Story of Lecrae Devaughn Moore 41

2. Race: The Story of Propaganda and Joseph 69

3. Body: The Story of Jackie 107

4. Work: The Story of Natalie and Beleaf 138

5. Church: The Story of Jamaica West 180

Epilogue: Generations "Birthed in Flickering Lights" 209

Acknowledgments 221

Notes 227

References 247

Index 265

About the Author 279

ILLUSTRATIONS

I.1.	Joseph Solomon, Instagram post	33
I.2.	Legacy Fest, with DJ Wade-O	36
I.3.	Legacy Fest, Joseph Solomon performing	36
I.4.	Rapper Da Truth and DJ Wade-O	37
1.1.	Lecrae, Twitter post	65
2.1.	Performance poster for Propaganda	71
4.1.	Natalie Lauren Sims, Twitter post	171
4.2.	Catalina Bellizzi, Twitter post	173
4.3.	Catalina Bellizzi, Twitter post	174
4.4.	Jamaica West, Twitter post	174
4.5.	Catalina Bellizzi, Twitter post	175
4.6.	Catalina Bellizzi, Twitter post	176
5.1.	Jackie Hill-Perry and Preston Perry	194
5.2.	Meme	198
E.1.	Meme	210
E.2.	Meme	210
E.3.	Meme	211
E.4.	Heather Lindsey, Cornelius Lindsey, and Bishop T. D. Jakes	214

GLOSSARY

BLACK CHURCH, THE: First referred to as the "Negro Church" by W. E. B. Du Bois (1903) in *his book of that title*, in scholarly and religious writings of the twentieth century, the term came to refer to the seven largest predominantly Black denominations. In popular discourse, the "Black Church" refers to a variety of beliefs and practices identified with Black, mostly Protestant Christianity. In such discourse, its more enduring liturgical elements include embodied forms of worship such as shouting, whooping, and the singing of gospel music. More recent scholarship, however, emphasizes both the mobility and fluidity of the "Black Church." In this book, it refers mainly and broadly to a linguistic site for Black cultural expression and spiritual renewal. Digital Black Christians replicate the church's communal and liturgical practices (e.g., common phrasing, songs, and preaching) through their online discourse (meme-sharing, hashtags, etc.). I therefore leave the term in its capitalized form when it is used by young adult Black Christians in direct quotes. When I critique its historical usage and refer to its contemporary function within Black religious practices, it also appears as *the Black Church*. This is my attempt at preserving the conceptual framing of an institution as experienced and understood by digital Black Christians. Concurrently, my focus on the contemporary linguistic/textual practices of young Black adult Christians is meant to challenge the assumption that its terminology is an all-encompassing mode of Black Christian expression. This approach embodies a critique of the way institutional forms of the Black Church has influenced the scholarly study of young Black Christians, over the Black Church's rhetorical tradition.[1]

CHRISTIAN: Broadly defined, a self-identified affiliate of Christianity. Such affiliations are varied and have complex roots in each adherent's own beliefs and practices regarding the religion. This may include regular daily/weekly prayer times and attendance at a house of worship. Deeply held beliefs may also be expressed in more discursive ways such as meme-sharing, participation in online forums, informal meet-ups, or travel to artistic conferences or spoken-word events.

CREATIVE: A term that has received wide usage in the last decade, *creative* is used in this volume in the context expressed by interviewees. Many use it to denote an essential way of moving through the world as an artist and free Black person. For my guides, it is also linked to a particular God-consciousness, the notion that their own creative content both expresses and is given by God. Taking a justice-centered approach, in this volume I use the term *creative* on its own, without qualifiers, to refer to Black Christian creatives. When it refers to others (e.g., white creatives, Black woman creatives), it always carries a qualifier.

DIGITAL: Indicates the various ways young Black Christians engage with digitized forms of media (e.g., software, digital images, digital videos, video games, web pages and websites, social media, data and databases, digital audio).

DIGITAL BLACK CHRISTIAN: Used throughout this book as a more adequate identifier than *millennial*, the term privileges common experience over age in describing Black Christians concerned with young adult Black culture who have embedded digital technology and hip hop in their religious practices.

ETHNOGRAPHY/DIGITAL ETHNOGRAPHY: A methodological approach to understanding and writing culture through the use and study of digital communication. Techniques like data mining and online content-analysis are coupled with the physical-site observations and interview techniques that are traditionally used in qualitative research.

HIP HOP: Tricia Rose describes hip hop as "a locally inspired explosion of exuberance and political energy tethered to the idea of rehabilitating community" (Rose 2008, ix).[2] As such, hip hop can be understood both as a culture and a movement centered on music. Hip hop also represents a general way of being in the world oriented by the economic and social realities of late twentieth- and early twenty-first-century urban Black youth. The themes of hip hop music and discourse center on common experiences of poverty, the need for racial and gender uplift, ghetto life, police brutality, incarceration, working/hustling, survival/surviving, sexual desire, friendships/relationships, and carousing. Its aesthetic and musical practices are commonly associated with rap music, spoken word, deejaying (scratching, beatboxing, turntablism), break dancing, urban Black and brown youth fashion, and graffiti-writing.

MILLENNIAL: A term first developed by Neil Howe and William Strauss to describe children born in or after 1982, and thus graduating from high school at or after the dawn of the new millennium, around 2000.[3] Its use is deeply subjective and often precludes the diverse experiences and affiliations of the demographic it claims to encompass. Researchers and demographers use a myriad of other dates and methods to determine who they consider to be a millennial.

NETWORKS: The professional and personal encounters (from online to offline) that connect digital Black Christians in meaningful, albeit typically brief (religious) relationships.

PREFACE

My Life as a Digital Black Christian: An Autoethnography

My mother bought me my first writing tablet "for my thoughts" when I was about five or six. Even at that age, I felt the "call" to write. I wrote my first poem in the second grade for my teacher Mrs. Nesbit's going-away party:

> I want you to go
> I want you to go
> but before you go
> I want you to know
> I love you so.

Reading it, she bounded toward me with her arms flung open wide, enveloping my little brown self in her plump rosy arms. I was astounded. Till then, I had not known my words could inspire such emotion.

* * *

It was a small storefront church in South Carolina that ran along the shabby end of Sumter's otherwise picturesque downtown. Sandwiched between a barbershop and beauty salon, it was the holiness Pentecostal church that my father pastored. Each summer, just prior to the start of the school year, our church hosted a revival. I hated it. The revivalists always stayed in our home, taking over the bedroom my sister and I shared. Past and present transgressions would be uncovered and used as a cause for more tarrying—a process of mournful waiting and petitioning for the Holy Spirit's presence—and fasting. Though less intrigued by the latter, tarrying was of some interest to me. I had seen other child seekers on bended knees before the altar repetitively calling on the name of Jesus as missionaries whispered words of encouragement and admonition in their ears. They often leapt to their feet shouting, smiling, and testifying about having been made new. More than anything, I was curious to know what that felt like.

* * *

"Jesus! Jesus! Jesus!" I shouted, as loudly as my little lungs allowed.

"You got to call Him like you want Him!" the evangelist shouted into my ear just as loudly.

In the background, I could hear my father along with the other members of the congregation singing, "Come by here de Lo-ord, Come by here. Oh-oh-Lo-or-od come by here! Somebodies calling Lo-ord. Come by here. Oh-oh-Lo-or-od come by here."

I was six years old and I desperately wanted to be saved "with" the Holy Ghost like other children. I had been tarrying for a week and had decided that I would receive the baptism of the Holy Ghost that very night. Finally, I felt a break between the physical and spiritual. "See him on that cross!" my father cried in my ear. And I could. As I focused on Christ, called his name, and considered the magnitude of his sacrifice for me, the tears began to flow. I saw Him come down from the cross and begin walking toward me, just as my father had said He would. I called, "Jesus! Jesus! Jesus!" louder and faster until he was near to me, standing in front of me, taking me up in his rapturous embrace. I cried, smiled, and jumped about just as the other children had. What joy! Never mind that throughout the entire experience Jesus was a white man with sandy-blonde locks.

* * *

Among my siblings and me, Pep was the cool one, Keya was the pretty one, and I was the smart one. As we grew up, we learned to fit into our roles with amazing precision. Based on these roles, my brother and sister soon developed a base of fairly popular friends, girlfriends, and boyfriends. And I worked on my book collection. While my parents encouraged me in such pursuits, I longed to sit at the cool kids' table. Keya and Pep seemed to fit in so effortlessly, while I remained . . . well, bookish, to say the least. Few things are as accessible to Black Christian kids growing up in strict households as vernacular speech. If you could not look cool, at least you could talk cool, and what was cooler than rap music? We shared lyrics everywhere: on the school bus, in class, wrote them out on notepaper and hid them in our Trapper Keepers.[1] One day in fifth grade, a white student was summoned to the principal's office for sharing "explicit" lyrics. When the teacher intercepted them, the wide-eyed student exclaimed, "It's not mine!" "Well, whose is it?" the teacher shot back. Later, questions regarding rap's ownership, even when played out in our little country-town middle school, had racial undertones. Whose is it? Everyone knew rap belonged to Blacks. The two teachers I overheard gossiping about the incident were both white. They described rap music as a poison spreading through the school. Rap was bad. But to us, bad was cool. Everyone else had seen the lyrics by then, so I felt left out. Later that day at home as Keya and I sat on our parents' front porch after school, she pulled another folded, much-handled copy from her notebook. I voraciously read over her shoulder hoping to glean the epistemologies of cool. After all, what's cooler than "Ice Ice Baby"? So much for Blacks owning hip hop, much less rap music.

* * *

Perhaps seeing the influence of rap music, my parents offered us an alternative. We were allowed to purchase Hammer's new cassette single, "That's Why We Pray." When Kirk Franklin and the Family appeared on gospel music shelves in 1995, many staunch Christian family friends opined that his music "just went too far." But by Christmas, all the churches that we visited in my father's fellowship were singing "Jesus is the Reason for the Season" decked out in red and black outfits just like Franklin's own family. By the following year, Franklin was a staple in our household. The rapper Salt of Salt-n-Pepa and the whole Nu Nation crew bounced back and forth across our TV screen as Franklin proclaimed,

> For those of you that think gospel music has gone too far.
> You think we've gotten too radical with our message.
> Well I got news for you, you ain't heard nothin yet,
> and if you don't know now you know. Glory, Glory!!

By then, our family had moved to Rochester, New York. My grandmother, who had come up from South Carolina to visit us for the holidays, sat in my father's recliner with her legs crossed at the ankles, her cane slumped against one knee, shaking her head. "Humph-umph-ump," was all she said.

* * *

A family friend gifted me a number of CDs of a few new West Coast gospel rappers whose names I cannot remember now. By then I was fourteen. While my musical priorities were quite underdeveloped, I still knew: This. Was. Not. Hip hop. It lacked the driving lyrical flow I had heard from the Wu-Tang Clan, the narrative style of Tupac, or the dope lyricism of *Illamatic*. Christian hip hop was mad corny!

* * *

Christmas 1995. Overalls, flannel shirt, Timberlands, and a First Down bubble jacket. They felt much cooler on my fifteen-year-old body than they do laid out here in words on the page more than twenty years later. A string of female emcees had appeared over the course of the 1990s who had toyed with notions of gender normativity and had encouraged young Black girls from neighborhoods like mine to do the same. These otherwise masculine displays of sexuality were okay in my household, as they paralleled social norms regarding Christian modesty. Everything was covered. Somewhere in the middle of my teen years, I learned how to circumvent my strict Christian upbringing by selectively borrowing acceptable swatches of hip hop culture. Thank you Queen Latifah, MC Light, DaBrat, and TLC for giving us Black Christian girls a way into the culture.

* * *

> Debt to Lauryn Hill,
> Us dark skinned, nappy-headed girls
> felt and held your Ohh-oh-oh-ooooo-ohhhs[2]
> Those notes of hope
> No Monica, Brandy, or Bey (before Jay) you made night all right
> You made being conscious cool
> Talked of God and gods, earth and Earths
> And it was cool
> to hear someone I knew

In the music
Jill Scott, Macy Gray, Erykah Badu.
Them sistas carried me through
High school
Taught me it was cool to be conscious,
had me woke
while my Black Church slept.

* * *

It was an evening class in the first year of college that got me serious about spoken word. Bryon Bain taught the class, which was titled just that, "The Spoken Word." Very much influenced by the hip-hop bent of the class, my rhymes began to take on more of the culture by making use of a beat, internal rhyme structure, and a celebration of hip hop in my prose. That year, I saw Sarah Jones three times, twice at PS 121, and then on campus at New York University. I began performing at open mics on campus, at the Nuyorican, and, in my sophomore year, with Youth Speaks at another newly opened spot called the Bowery Poetry Club in 2002. By the time Jessica Care Moore performed "I'm a Hip Hop Cheerleader" at an NAACP student club event, I could confidently shout back "Hip hop! Hip hop!"

Spoken word and hip hop had become as integral to my Christian identity as being Black was.

* * *

From where I lived in 2001, the architecture looked like one of those 3D puzzles. The morning's own sharp edges made it feel as if every one of the buildings' dimensions were jutting out and moving in on me in jagged, domino-like succession. If you had cared to, you could have, from my apartment window—by pushing your face all the way against the glass and craning your neck—peered all the way down the crooked side alley that ran just off Water Street to see people jumping from the towers. I did not care to.

* * *

My roommate and I left our apartment at about 9:20 a.m. that day. We were waiting for the bus, while others milled about. No one had yet mentioned the possibility of a terrorist attack. When the first tower fell and began rolling down our street, we started running. We had never really liked each other, but that day I remember catching her hand as we ran. I remember us trying to pull each other along to safety. I remember looking back for a brief second to catch a view that haunted me for years afterward. Scraps from the building wafted through the air toward us like tiny bits of paper. But behind us, there were many more people being enveloped by the debris. The smoke grew like a monstrous beast, falling over itself as it bounded down the street.

Afterward, we walked for nearly an hour trying to get to friends in the Village. Once we got to Broome Street, we sat on the side of a curb to rest. I had never seen Lower Manhattan like this before. The streets were desolate.

When I'm scared and uncertain, I joke. "It's a good thing I wore my new Nikes. Didn't know we'd be in a fifty-yard dash today." We laughed. Then, she looked back and up from where we had just come and nodded for me to do the same.

"It's falling."

Two frightened Black girls, we watched the world change that day.

* * *

A friend from college came home with me that next spring break. She was a staunch conservative. I was staunchly in love with Black people. We watched the Iraqi invasion together with my parents. She bowed her head in prayer as the attack began. As a Christian, she was firmly in support of the war. I wondered how a Black woman like herself could separate her race from her faith. As a Black Christian, I was firmly against George W. Bush and his war. We had fought and healed over this issue before, though it remained an uneasy peace. I had been horrified by the anti-Muslim attacks and slurs that had become all too common in the City. I was confused when Bush had walked confidently to the podium back in September to declare war on terror. It felt too close to my own history, too close to the state-sponsored terror on Black men and women I was learning about in Robin Kelly's class that semester. Later in the semester, he encouraged us to participate in a walkout against the war. I joined the protest and heard young people my age deliver impassioned speeches in Washington Square Park. There were some, like my friend, who continued to believe their faith called them to support the Bush administration. But many more of us became increasingly radicalized after that. By the time Bobby Seale and then Sistah Souljah came to the campus, I was torn. Was my friend right? How do I reconcile my religion and my growing Black militancy?

* * *

"I'm leaving the Church." Those words had sat like four hard stones in my throat for some time. Yet I hadn't felt relieved in telling my parents. I had just felt their disappointment. I had finished seminary and was working on my PhD, while simultaneously serving as a youth pastor and chairing a host of church committees and Bible studies when needed. I felt drained. The church lacked relevance in my life. There was no socially conscious message coming from our pulpit or in our mission. Our senior bishop had recently called a meeting in which she condemned rap music, calling it "unintelligible" and "of the devil." She urged us to avoid Facebook and read the "Word" instead. I was drawing different lines between what was sacred and secular than my parents had. I felt myself being pressed into something I no longer was. So I left.

* * *

It's funny who you meet when you hang out on the margins. I began conducting interviews with gospel rappers when I moved to Buffalo, New York, as a way of studying a merger between the sacred and the secular (i.e., hip hop and religion). It was 2008, and most local rappers were using online tools to make connections and create and share music. Up until that point, most of the creative spaces I had explored in my research were connected to Black Protestant houses of worship. There were the hip hop open mic sessions that took place in one church's multipurpose room. There were the gospel rap performances sponsored by another local Black Church. Even the daily Christian hip hop radio broadcast I studied was part of another church's larger ministry. Online spaces, however, were not mediated by Black churches. Along with generational differences in internet usage, Black pastors and leaders were less likely than whites to go online; uneven technological access among racial groups meant local Black churches had little to no online presence. Those online spaces were where I was now able to examine eighteen- to thirty-five-year-old gospel rappers' religious interactions with each other and their personal attempts to articulate religious identity for themselves.

* * *

It was 2010, just before the formation of the American Academy of Religion's Critical Approaches to Hip Hop and Religion unit co-founded by Monica Miller and Chris Driscoll. Miller's (2013) book *Religion and Hip Hop* forced many of us young scholars to rethink such constrained binaries as sacred/secular. There was a growing similarity between those gospel rappers' stories and my own. All of us were in our early adulthood, and all of us felt like Black Church misfits. I watched as many of them began using the web to find a place of belonging and to get their work out there as artists. I logged on to the internet and then hung around on Myspace and Facebook doing what I soon learned was digital ethnography. Along the way, I began posting my own poetry performances on YouTube, developing a website, and staying connected with other digital Black Christians looking for a place to belong through social media.

* * *

Art. Performance. Hip hop. Christian. Black. Urban. Woman. Every part of me seemed at odds with other parts of my identity, so I wrote myself into the text. I wrote about my hip hop identity in poems and performed it in churches. I wrote about what it meant for me to be a Christian and Black and female, and I started performing in slam competitions.

And then there was Ntare.

* * *

I met Ntare at a poetry performance hosted by my employer. Later, I signed up to compete in a slam poetry event that Ntare was hosting. He had learned to make use of many facets of hip hop culture by advertising events, by attracting members of the culture, and by using DJs and even dancers in his performances. He was later instrumental in connecting me with many of the emcees I interviewed for my dissertation. We talked about everything: God. Performance. Poetry. He knew a wealth of hip hop history, and via YouTube, iTunes, and *MTV Soul* he schooled me on the aspects of the culture that my strict Christian upbringing hadn't afforded me. I knew all things Black Church. He knew all things hip hop. It was a marriage made in Black Christianity and hip hop. He, as did I, loved. My. Whole. Self.

* * *

Eight years later, I ended up joining one of the Black churches that I had studied, Elim Christian Fellowship. Eventually, I became ordained as one of the church elders. It might seem that I joined The Establishment, but this does not debunk everything I have laid out here about the new sociotemporal (fleeting or brief) worlds that digital Black Christians have configured for themselves. In fact, it adds weight to this book's thesis.

By the time I joined Elim Christian Fellowship, the church, much like me, had undergone a period of significant maturation. Perhaps letting go of its hip hop-inspired beginnings, it had become a more traditional, albeit still quite progressive Black church. Upon learning of my book project, the senior bishop began thinking critically about what this meant for a shrinking segment of his congregation—Black millennials. Together with another forward-thinking elder, we talked about how to reach this group and how to create space in the Black Church where they/I felt included. I shared my research with him. That space took the form of an offsite meeting in members' homes and coffee houses. Socially conscious and digitally driven conversations ensued.

As an ethnographer, I was not a distant bystander. I came to understand my role as both documenting and shaping the culture I was a part of. Throughout the process, I was changing, as was the world of the young adult Blacks I was studying. The world we were creating was built of a thousand profoundly felt experiences. Our use of digital media, hip hop, and Christianity necessitated a new way of being in the world. For me, this led me back to a Black church. For some others, the journey has meant leaving their Black Church context or Christianity altogether. We're okay with representing our whole selves in this way. After all, this rich diversity of Christian meaning and our approbation of it is intrinsic to being digital Black Christians.

* * *

Epistemology is everything to ethnography. *How* we know what we know about our research subjects is just as important as *what* we know about them. A number of social constructs inform both what we know as ethnographers and what we think we know.³ My own foray into the study of digital Black Christians has taught me as much. It is fitting then to include here with an exploration of the structures that informed my ethnographic approach.

In what follows, I use *autoethnography*—the "turning of the ethnographic gaze inward on oneself (auto) while maintaining the outward gaze of ethnography" (Denzin 1997, 227)—to explore my own subjectivity as a digital Black Christian from my initial engagement with hip hop and Black Christianity to my often uncomfortable position as a scholar-practitioner researching the religious lives of other digital Black Christians engaged in hip hop.⁴ As with the preceding narrative, I use this approach to both synthesize and reflect upon many of the ideas presented throughout this book's chapters and also to argue for such a methodological approach in the study of the religious lives of Black millennials, whom I call digital Black Christians. The digital mode of narration and self-revelation that characterizes much of digital Black Christians' online interactions must inform both how scholars document their lives and how digital Black researchers "come clean" about their own subjectivity (Dimitriadis 2001).

Through the book's narrative style, I seek to simulate the hypermediatization of digital Black Christianity through a dialogic approach to hip hop and Black Church traditions of flow, call and response, and whooping as a way of both performing and centering the rhetorical strategies that are at the heart of the way digital Black Christians make meaning. I end here, then, with just this sort of braggadocio and signifying through hip hop and Black preaching–inspired spoken word. Such an opening stays true to the culture and art form I have studied throughout.

* * *

> If they ask you who we are
> Tell them
> We are the product of Clinton's crime bill and gangsta rap
> Tupac and Biggie
> Lauryn Hill and Hillsong
> We saw nothing wrong with R. Kelly's "I Believe I Can Fly" in church

and a "little bump 'n' grind" in the parking lot
'Cause child
Hood
Life
was already selling us so many sweet lies
like bubble gum cigarettes
like blaming ice cream and cake for the bellyaches[5]
like counting to five ever kept you alive
like hands up meant don't shoot
like Amadou Diallo wasn't shot at 41 times
So we got smart and digitized they crimes
Martin,
Brown,
Garner,
Gray,
Boyd,
McDonald,
Castile,
Bland,
McClain,
Arbery,
Taylor,
Floyd
(remember the names)

But we were told our pain was our pain
That the terror of 9/11 was collective
and the terror on our communities was subjective
Please forgive me,
but I remember the names.
I am so full of memories
my memory is full
But trust me
all of my receipts are in order,
because all of my receipts are online
They have digitized my time(s)
My mind

These rhymes
This skin of mine
So call me crazy
(Crazy)
I'm just prone to stargazing
at Black computer screens
'cause I see reflections of me
if you know what I mean.
No?
Well,
Let me explain this physiology
Black is technology
We changing
We driving
Maintaining a steady following
Posting notes on my movements
Tracking movements to my movement
Digital Black is the new beautiful
You ain't know?
Oh you thought 'cause
they mobilized our hashtags
against us
Redlined the algorithms and
Mammified our memes
we'd forget
the thing we always knew?
That the Blacker the berry
the sweeter the juice.
But, oh, duplicity
'Cause the sweeter juice always seems to produce
Straaaaannnggee fruit

Do *you* know who I am?
Child, please!

I come in the name of the One
who created the world in seven days.

Give me 120 characters
I will set this world ablaze.
Our fingers are rockets writing machete-handed hashtags for days
But (Mom, Dad don't worry)
I'm still keeping the faith
Still believing in the Ancient of Days
in ways made out of no ways
And I ain't no ways tired
or
grown cold in my faith
Too busy building Holy Ghost fires for warmth
and hurling praises to the Son

But when I pray
I stay on one knee
knowing full well the backhanded deeds
that Christian nations have done.

From the same mouths
that promised us peace and ploughs
We reaped swords and violence
This nation (Shaytan, the Evil One) tried to kill the things I birthed
But baby, these babies will be allriiighht!
'Cause I will do justice in my lullabies tonight
Singing:
Come Tomorrow!
Come Tomorrow!
Come Tomorrow,
We will take the day.

Introduction

Performing: Black Christianity in the Digital

Hip hop, like religion, has always been a transmutative thing, and so it is little wonder that it is a deeply spiritual practice. It is a practice and culture of shapeshifters and changelings, its origins located in the epic flow of DJs, emcees, break dancers, and graffiti artists. Its labyrinthine networks stretch across time and space, making it even more difficult to define or nail down. Like religion, hip hop has moved from local to global, from analog to digital. Online hip hop and religion have gathered an ever more complex collection of actors, actions, and identities. Yet today the category of hip hop remains expansive enough to embrace and embody all these diverse identities and meanings.

Hip hop is female. Later in this book you will meet both Jackie Hill-Perry[1] (29, St. Louis, Missouri) and Aitina Fareed-Cooke (AI)[2] (33, Buffalo, New York) who will tell you that they were drawn to hip hop, in part, by Lauryn Hill. Hill was a dope lyricist, beautiful, spiritual, and brown, much like themselves.

Hip hop is Black. You will meet Jamaica West[3] (25, Columbus, Ohio) and Propaganda[4] (39, West Covina, California), who cannot remember a time when hip hop wasn't in their lives. It is as inseparable from their identity as the skin they inhabit.

Hip hop is life and it is death. Joseph Solomon[5] (33, Fort Hood, Texas) found renewed life through it. Rap music had always been the soundtrack to his life. Yet it was in college, while wrestling with the meaning of his faith, that the lyrics of Christian hip hop artists reached Solomon, articulating his very life. As a counterpoint, Beleaf[6] (34, San Diego, California) began to consider ending his own life, a thought sparked, in part, by the darkly suggestive lyrics of a rap song he played incessantly during an already dark period in his adolescence.

But hip hop is also art. Everything Daniel Steele[7] (34, Jersey City, New Jersey) hears, feels, and even smells accentuates this fact for him. Creating hip hop beats is Steele's way of speaking back to the world out of this same sensory experience. He is not alone. In high school, Natalie Lauren Sims[8] (34, Tulsa, Oklahoma) spent her lunch hours freestyling with friends to Ginuwine songs.

And hip hop is digital. As she moved into adulthood, Sims began using software and social media as a rapper, singer, and songwriter to articulate her identity as a Christian. And here the story grows more complex. From multiplatinum awards to collaborations with A-list hip hop artists, Sims, like Steele and each of the other digital Black Christians introduced here, found meaning in hip hop, and through digital media they have used hip hop to express their religious identities. Yet these are not isolated cases of minor Christian celebrity. As microcelebrities, their stories illustrate the networked religious experiences of millions of other young Black Christian adults who routinely follow them, interact with them, and build lives online and off that reflect their socio-temporal engagements.[9] *Digital Black Christians like these, through their webwork—the performative construction of racial and religious networks—have created a new space in and beyond the Black Church, one that is linguistic and socio-temporal (as in brief or fleeting communities) in design. In the process, they are changing physically located Black churches, modes of church activism, communication practices around evangelism and Christian identity, as well as the transmission and consumption of Black Church cultural practices in popular culture.* In short, they are rewiring The System. To make this case, I present two main arguments in this book. First, using the term *webwork* (meaning *networked racial-religious performativity*), I argue that any full understanding of the contemporary Black Church must offer a robust consideration of the role and impact of technology in the lives of young adult Blacks around identity, community, authority, and authenticity.[10] And second, digital developments among this group suggest that intimacy—spiritual, fraternal, and/or sexual closeness—guides religious life in the digital age perhaps more closely than we realize. This book explores young adult Black Christians' quest for such intimacy through *relationships, identity, visibility,* and *valuation.* Their experiences point more broadly to emerging patterns around intimacy-seeking and intimacy-building that currently inform American digital-religious life.

* * *

The darkened sanctuary is a cross between Friday night and Sunday morning. Tonight, a DJ with a penchant for blasting the latest Christian hip hop music has taken over the pulpit of Bethel Deliverance International Church in Philadelphia, Pennsylvania. Behind him, the stage is lined with four large sign boards, each with a picture of a young adult with duct tape over their mouths. Words like lust, addiction, and idolatry are scrawled on the tape in black ink. If the signs' symbolism is unclear, the event description on the Facebook invite page is not. It promises to offer live music and spoken word that discusses "issues common in the streets but seldomly addressed in pulpits." The event is the Xpressions Taboo Tour, hosted by Kingdom Promotions, known for bringing some of the most prominent Black Christian performers to venues across the United States.

Between interludes punctuated by hip hop songs, poets take the stage and offer their work. By now, many of the performers are legendary among Black Christian tweens, teens, and young adults. When Janette . . . ikz's (pronounced like *genetics*) headshot appears on the projection screen, the audience applauds wildly. The anticipation is just as palpable for a joint performance by Jamaica West and Joseph Solomon. Joseph Solomon is a YouTube personality and one of Christian spoken word's most recognized faces. Jamaica West is an aspiring singer/rapper, touring poet, and print model. Tonight they are performing their co-written poem titled "I'm So Black Christian." The title cannot tell us everything about this piece, however. This one is part young Black Christian manifesto, part scathing critique of white Christianity and the Black Church, part celebration of Black Christianity and Black culture, and part love letter to hip hop. Call it what you will, it is a beautifully complex and indefinable move toward wholeness, to being fully Black and fully Christian, as the final lines of the poem promise.

It is thus the perfect orientation to understanding what it means to be a digital Black Christian. And so, we begin here:

Jamaica and Solomon:

I'm so Black Christian
I am not every Black Christian
We feel estranged when our experiences are not the
same as other Black Christians
but we
are tapestries
threads of consciousness
that do not match
but intersect
paths
trying
to make sense
of our Savior in skin.

If Christ be fully man
fully God
I can be
fully Black
and fully His. (Solomon 2016)

"I'm So Black Christian" locates Black Christian identity in a space beyond Black Church practices, while still claiming a "Black Christian" identity. West and Solomon's description of young adult Black Christians as intersecting "threads of consciousness" points to a *networked* construction of self, a digitally created "me-centered" form of religion.[11] Mark S. Granovetter's (1977) seminal text on weak ties (connections with friends of friends) being more influential than strong ties (connections to family and close friends) has informed the internet-studies notion of "networks."[12] For religion, the "sacralization of self" mediated by social media allows for a continuum of weak ties—or threads of consciousness—that connect digital Black Christians (Aupers and Houtman 2010). In this book, I contend that these threads, networks, or ties are far more influential in the religious lives of digital Black Christians than has been acknowledged in the scholarly world. The digital Black Christians described in this book form networks through digitally created and shared intellectual productions (e.g., YouTube poems, videos, and talks, Instagram posts, memes, images, and other forms of discourse). Networks themselves often operate as a "third space" created in response to a certain dislocation or "betweenness" felt in digital Black Christians' current setting (Hoover and Echchaibi 2014). According to Joseph Solomon, "I'm So Black Christian" was born out of his frustration with both the white evangelical spaces he frequented at the time and the Black Church culture he had known since his childhood. In our interview, he describes this experience by saying,

> I found myself in-between those two worlds; this white seminary world, this white theological world and then, the Black experience. And for a long time, I felt like I was discrediting that Black experience and then eventually, I started having a reckoning where I started challenging both worlds. I had a critique for the Black Church, but I also had a critique for the [white] theology and culture that I was being taught [as] the only right way. (Solomon, interview by author, April 28, 2018)

Solomon is not alone. Respondents throughout this book refer to the Black Church both in defining their Christian beliefs in opposition to it and in celebrating their participation in it. Yet the digital Black Christians studied here define being a "Black Christian" as something entirely different than their oppositional or celebratory connection to the Black Church or being identified with white evangelicalism. Alfred Korzybski's ([1933] 1996, 58) dictum, "The map is not the territory," applies to digital Black Christians' conception of the "Black Church." As their religious affiliations continue to stretch across space and time, they create and participate in an increasingly fluid understanding of the territory of the "Black Church." Yet digital Black Christians call on its fictive mapping in locating and replicating its communal and liturgical practices (e.g., common phrasing, songs, and preaching) through their online discourse, more so than its institutional formations. The internet, and particularly the capacity of social media sites to allow users' self-curation, provides a space for them to work out this elastic racial-religious performance.

A post-performance video upload of "I'm So Black Christian" received nearly forty thousand views and numerous comments from like-minded digital Black Christians. Commenters related to the artists' description of themselves as part of a "hip hop generation" and feeling "kindred to Kendrick" (Lamar), a hip-hop artist known for his favorable (though layered) views of Christianity. This book focuses on the lives and words of a number of digital Black Christians, each of whom is an online personality with thousands of followers. Social media and hip hop are essential components of digital Black Christianity as lived by these figures. As the title of this book suggests, the story of digital Black Christians demonstrates the fluidity of Black spirituality and the problematic notion of a fixed understanding of the "Black Church."[13]

Given this adoption of aspects of Black Church traditions in the lives of digital Black Christians, this book takes a decentered approach to studying the institutional Black Church in digital Black Christians' lives. When attention is paid to digital Black Christians' more discursive practices, church membership becomes less important as an indicator of belief. Instead, the Black Church is understood here as a tradition that, as Stacey Floyd-Thomas et al. (2007, xxiv) describe it, "possesses distinctive characteristics and constitutive elements, including key questions, symbols, rituals, ideas, and beliefs that are always subject to adaptation, improvisation, reinterpretation, and even abandonment." In this way, this book joins the current body of literature in acknowledging the contrived nature of the term *the Black Church*.[14] Still, the term appears throughout the book in uppercase letters. This is meant to mark the way the legacy of the Black Church continues to reside in the discourse of digital Black Christians as a linguistic site for Black cultural expression. Through shares, tweets, and other forms of on- and offline discourse, digital Black Christians are able to disrupt, reconstruct, and—most centrally for those studied in this book—move beyond the institutional Black Church's locative map. This "flight to a new world," as the scholar of modern religions Kim Knott (2005) calls it, has been a patterned response to the notion of the Black Church, and has been taken up in the work of several scholars.[15] More recently, race and religion scholar Matthew Cressler's *Authentically Black and Truly Catholic* (2017) bears in mind the deep connection to Black spirituality that some religious adherents maintain despite others perceiving them to be beyond the bounds of the Protestant Black Church. Digital Black Christians operate in similar ways through their digital practices, calling on a certain imagined notion of the Black Church both to move beyond its borders and to embody an essential Black spirituality located in Black cultural practices (e.g., Black churches and hip hop). This is in keeping with the Black Church tradition even if it sometimes unsettles the Black Church polity.

In both the popular and the scholarly literature, digital Black Christians are often depicted as being at variance with or as leaving the Black Church. The story, however, is far more complex than that.[16] Through an in-depth examination of the lives of digital Black Christians, this book explores the multiple physical and digital forces that influence digital Black Christianity beyond Black churches. In particular, I discuss the multiple ways that digital Black Christians construct a religious identity and meaning through video-sharing and social media (e.g., YouTube, Instagram, Twitter) and, where relevant, how these interact with other forms of digital media (e.g., Final Cut Pro, streaming devices, etc.). The digital Black Christians selected for inclusion here are either friends or operate in the same professional and non-church religious networks as each other. Yet their "networked publics," as articulated by danah boyd (2008), include online followers that number in the thousands and they are regarded as thought leaders among digital Black Christians.[17] Being artists and online personalities, in some ways their experiences are unique. In other ways, given their publics, visibility, influence, and their interaction with other digital Black Christians, they are well situated to serve as representative examples of the practices of many other digital Black Christians.

A two-year ethnographic study of their digital and physical activities along with interviews over the same period provides the foundation for this book and its two main contentions:

1. *That there is a need for scholarship that reflects the lived practices of digital Black Christians.* It is essential that scholarship regarding indicators of belief among digital Black Christians advance beyond an examination of their ecclesial and Christian ritualized practices or lack thereof. That I trouble the notion of the Black Church from the outset is my first attempt in that direction.

2. *That digital technology and hip hop are key sites for the study of digital Black Christians.* The "embeddedness" of digital technology in individuals' lives, as noted by Daniel Miller and Don Slater (2001) in *The Internet: An Ethnographic Approach*, along with a hip-hop praxis in the religious lives of digital Black Christians, must serve as some of the primary sites

of inquiry when studying this group. An examination of the lived practices of digital Black Christians through an ethnography of their online activity offers an important approach to studying this digital embeddedness and hip hop praxis because, given their networked existence, it is only by sustained contact with digital Black Christians through ethnographic methods like participant observation and the content analysis of social media postings that we can ascertain the multilayered meaning of their lived practices.[18]

Studying the Lived Practices of Digital Black Christians

Research regarding digital Black Christians often reflects two divergent concerns. Research on digital Christians is often subsumed into data sets documenting mostly white millennials' shift away from organized religion. Conversely, research also highlights Black millennials' continued connection to Black churches. These statistics are misleading given their inattention to the diversity of religious belief and affiliations among digital Black Christians. In this book, the study of this group is influenced by earlier studies (unrelated to this project) that account for this diversity.

The mixed methods approach of the National Center for the Study of Youth and Religion has highlighted the diverse religious affiliations of young adults between the ages of eighteen and twenty-three (Cohen 2005). In *Souls in Transition: The Religious and Spiritual Lives of Emerging Adults* (2009), Christian Smith and Patricia Snell divide young adults into six groups that operate on a spectrum of belief, from committed traditionalists, selective adherents, and the spiritually open, to the religiously indifferent, religiously disconnected, and irreligious.[19] Smith and Snell's (2009) more expanded view of young adults' religious associations rings true for this book's ethnographic findings about digital Black Christians like Joseph Solomon and Jamaica West.[20] While the latter continue to identify as Black Christians, their poem demonstrates that what they mean by that is complex and layered.

My goal here is to explore the diverse and digitally mediated markers of Christian engagement that define digital Black Christians' lived practices.[21] Currently, most ethnographies of young Black Christians only document the committed traditionalists as they relate to churches (e.g., church attendance and weekly prayer times).[22] Even earlier landmark studies that incorporated young adult and youth groups still followed this approach (Lincoln and Mamiya 1990). I trouble the exclusivist tendencies inherent in studying Black Christian young adult culture in this way through a particular focus on the more discursive practices of digital Black Christian faith.

A rich ethnographic window into the religious lives of digital Black Christians exists. The field site is composed of shares, likes, posts, comments, and participant counts. For this reason, I contend that examining digital Black Christian beliefs and practices within the context of online media usage is the clearest route to understanding digital Black Christianity. This book thus offers an "internet-related" journey through the religious world of digital Black Christians. I examine the spectacular socio-temporal world found in hashtags like #CHHSexism (Christian hip hop sexism) and the online/offline Christian spoken word group Passion for Christ Movement (P4CM), alongside the patterned engagement with Christianity and Black churches found through exploring shares, likes, and comments among Black Christian creatives.[23] Through an exploration of a number of digital Black Christians' online practices, music creation, spoken word performances, video blogs, concert events, and conferences, this work charts the diverse and complex landscape of their religious life. Digital ethnography is central to the study of this world for an important reason.

Why Digital Ethnography? Seeing the Contradictions—Theirs and Ours

To gain a comprehensive understanding of the digital Black Christian community requires sitting with the troubling complexity of that community as much as digital ethnography allows, given its prolific use of online digital media tools in creating multilayered religious identities. I call this a troubling complexity because the beliefs and practices of the creatives in this book are often riddled with many of the same contradictions and problematic stances of digital Black Christians as a whole. For instance, in 2017, rapper, poet, and author Jackie Hill-Perry signed the Nashville Statement—a declaration against marriage equality and for a complementarian role for men and women—alongside conservative evangelicals in the women's purity movement. The following year, Hill-Perry rejected the Social Justice and the Gospel Statement, which takes a stance against current racial justice movements (among other issues). Both the Nashville Statement and the Social Justice and the Gospel Statement support conservative evangelical views. Hill-Perry remains a firm advocate of racial social justice, while nonetheless maintaining conservative Christian views on women's equality. Like Hill-Perry, the people being studied here see congruency in their contradictions. Their beliefs are guided by a biblical orientation. To be sure, such beliefs were formed in the context of religious institutions that, as noted earlier, have historically come with their own interests and thus baggage. For cultural scholars, digital Black Christians' embodied contradictions push up against how sex, sexuality, race, and intersectionality (to name only a few identity-centered discussions) are commonly theorized. In feminist thought, for instance, digital Black Christians like Hill-Perry defy present ideological currents regarding patriarchy, sexism, and sexual liberation with views that favor complementarianism and pre-marital abstinence. In feminist critiques of Hill-Perry's stance, however, rarely is the genealogy of feminist thought ever considered as perhaps being an ill-fitting paradigm for the study of Christian belief.[24] Cultural scholars have called "the delivered" "captives" of patriarchy. In allowing the lived practices of digital Black Christians to inform how they are studied, I ask, "Yes, but what were the terms of their emancipation?" What was *their* rubric for wholeness? And should it be their canon or the scholar's that informs how they are written about in the literature? Such inquiries pierce through to deeper issues of access and authority. In essence, do digital Black Christians get to bear witness to their own lived experiences and the inferences that are included in the scholarship? And how do we as scholars advance beyond deploying their contradictions in the othering of young Black Christians in the scholarship?[25]

The work of Hill-Perry and several others interviewed for this book raises several questions regarding how we deal with and at times deal *out* or exclude the presence of young Black Christians in the literature. And yet this book is not a declaration of decampment away from the rich and varied contributions on Black religion that have arisen from several Black feminist scholars and cultural theorists more broadly. Yet, by attending to digital Black Christians' troubling complexities, I wish to move toward what Angela Davis calls a "capacious [enough] feminism [and cultural studies more generally] that allows us to work at the heart of such contradictions" (SSEXBBOX 2017). My goal here is not to advocate for particular problematic religious views of digital Black Christians. To be sure, I make several critiques regarding the moves they make and the beliefs they espouse. Yet I also want to interrogate the way they are traditionally conceived of in scholarly work—that is, at the concluding point of their intellectual production (e.g., posting support for the Nashville Statement) with little insight or discussion of the genealogy of such beliefs as being rooted in their own biblical orientation and collective Christian understanding.

When I first began this study, I was struck by the anti-intellectual strain exhibited in more than a few interviews and in online content produced by digital Black Christians. Upon further analysis I have come to recognize this stance as a push-back against an intellectual community that often overlooks, diminishes, or dismisses this group's lived experience and its rootedness in a spiritual understanding. Scholars, myself included, must resist the urge to view these young Black Christians' ideological leanings and practices as anti-intellectual or unenlightened. We gain far more by considering their beliefs and practices as pointing to other ways of knowing. These understudied epistemologies inform the lived practices of digital Black Christians.[26] Theoretical conclusions aside, mine is a sustained reflection on the question: What would it look like if the approach to the study of young adult Black Christians encompassed and even welcomed the messy—that is, nuanced, unfinished, complex, problematic, and contradictory—evidence?

In *The Madonna of 115th Street: Faith and Community in Italian Harlem, 1880–1950* (2010), Robert Orsi discusses scholarly views of many of the practices of Italian Catholic immigrants. Scholars throughout the twentieth century viewed their practices, which included dragging women along the parish aisles as they licked the floor in devotion or pinning dollar bills onto the Madonna as offerings, as "magical, superstitious, cultic, and primitive" (xiv). Such scholarly descriptions served to "authorize and substantiate boundaries" between acceptable and unacceptable religion. What was "acceptable" derived from church-sanctioned practices alone. By contrast, in his book, Orsi uncouples the lived religious practices of Italians from the Catholic church in order to provide a study of religion "in the streets" (2010, 35). By uncoupling young Black Christians from the Black Church, in this book, I aim to present a fuller portrait of their spiritual lives "in the [digital] streets." My approach to hip hop ethnography elicits that "magical intersection" as Joan Morgan (2000, 62) puts it, "where . . . contrary voices meet." Brittany Cooper (2015) describes dissimilar beliefs as "percussive sounds" (see also Crunk Feminist Collective 2010). It is in such "noise" that meaning is located. This work lingers at the sites of contradiction, placing them in the context of digital Black Christians' biblical orientation. As others have articulated (Morgan 2000; Lomax 2018), this work "stays in the greys" so that Black Christian millennials' varied beliefs and practices can be clearly seen, perhaps better understood, and detailed in scholarly work with greater dimensionality and certainly vibrancy.

This also has bearing on ethnographic method, which for this book meant the use of grounded theory. This inductive approach allowed me to combine online posted interviews with those conducted by myself of most of the creatives studied here, and those of digital Black Christians posted online. It was, for example, by asking questions about Hill-Perry's contradictory views on racial and gender equality that I discovered the way digital Black Christians embody Blackness online and in public discourse as a way of gaining access to and acceptance in hip hop spaces. This I refer to as a *pretexting of the body*—the outward performance of normative values in order to offer a new value or way of being part of the Christian and hip hop communities and scenes. An example of this is found in popular Christian rapper Lecrae's 2017 interview on the Breakfast Club radio show (Breakfast Club Power 105.1 2017). Earlier interviews with popular artists Kendrick Lamar and Chance the Rapper—artists known for their explicitly Christian lyrics, but not as Christian rappers—largely focused on the rappers' artistic ability and their development (Samie 2012; LandOfHipHop 2015).

In Lecrae's interviews, in contrast, the questions sought to unpack his religious beliefs and practices. In their interviews, Chance and Kendrick are treated like artists who have become holy men; indeed, Kendrick fashions himself as a preacher in his interview. Interviewer Lenard McKelvey ("Charlemagne tha God") describes Chance as "spiritual," a "Black hippy," and as exhibiting a certain higher consciousness. Lecrae, however, he renders flatly as a "Christian" (Been Changed Magazine 2014).[27]

In his autobiography *Unashamed*, Lecrae described feeling "like a caged animal" in interviews like this one as a common Christian experience (Moore 2016c).[28] For his part, Lecrae solves this in the interview by embodying hip hop; he positions his own body in hip hop spaces and history by identifying with the life and lyrics of Tupac and calling himself "a product of hip hop" culture. Through his "digital performance of hip hop aesthetics," as Elonda Clay (2011, 8) calls it, Lecrae seeks to resolve the tensions around hip hop and Christianity often experienced by digital Black Christians in such a context.[29]

As both Lecrae and Hill-Perry's stories suggest, in the wider hip-hop arena, young adult Blacks who self-identify as Christians often experience disapproval from their young adult Black peers for their connections to white evangelical Christianity. Digital Black Christianity is often suspect to hip hop audiences, as represented in the Breakfast Club interview, because of its allegiances to white supremacy via white evangelicalism. Lecrae's posturing tells an important story reflected in the approaches of the digital Black Christians studied throughout this book: that digital Black Christians perform hip hop identity in order to play down their association with white Christianity more broadly and traditional Black Christianity in particular. Indeed, Black Christian rap *has* been culpable in extending white evangelicalism into Black Christian music in this second millennium. Religion professor Christena Cleveland specifically named Lecrae as white evangelicalism's "mascot" in a *Washington Post* article (Boorstein 2016). Hill-Perry, for her part, has been labeled a fraud and hypocrite for her stance on issues of gender and race; she once identified as a lesbian woman, before God—she believes—"called" her to "His Image" (of heterosexuality). Within Christian hip hop circles, claims that Lecrae is no longer a Christian have been voiced both explicitly and by Christian bloggers citing scriptures on hypocrisy and deception.[30] For different reasons, the same conclusions have been drawn regarding high-profile Black Christians like Hill-Perry and Lecrae. They are both seen as perpetrating a lie. Even we scholarly readers can fall prey to such biases in the study of young adult Black Christian practices, as the earlier example regarding feminists' scholarship on Hill-Perry suggests. In so doing, we miss some of the complexity and essence of young Blacks' Christian identity.

This book, however, welcomes and values what I call the honest lie. That is, there are beautiful ethnographic truths regarding the religious identity of digital Black Christians to be found in all of their contradictions, posing, frontin', and supposed lies. All of their performance is representative of much deeper meaning. If there are lies, then those lies contain truths. As such, I propose an approach that takes seriously who they say they are even if we as scholars do not believe them or like their beliefs. Through their posturing and performing, we learn the essential characteristics of digital Black Christian identity. And that online presence often reveals the shape of young Black Christian identity in physically located spaces as well.

Digital Black Christianity, as taken up here, attends to the work of digital religion studies scholars like Heidi Campbell, who views digital religion as "a bridge that connects and extends online religious practices and spaces into offline religious contexts, and vice versa" (Campbell 2012b, 4). According to Mia Lövheim, religious identity online often reflects one's religious identity in the material world in all of its rich performances (Lövheim 2012, 52).

I also write with a particular regard for how young Black bodies have received far less attention in digital religious studies. Several works have taken up religion in digital spaces, the use of ethnography in the study of digital religions, and the mediatization of religion (to name only a few concerns).[31] However, a white lens is usually employed, critical race/Black theory is absent, or racial homogeneity among research participants is assumed. Without question, when scholars of Black religion have written about Black digital-religious life, they have often turned to such theoretical frameworks. New methods for the study of the particularities of Black digital-religious life are needed. This volume offers the first such work on Black digital religion.

Embedded Digital Technology and Hip Hop as Central to the Study of Digital Black Christians

This book examines the doing and being of hip hop as it informs what being Christian means to these digital Black Christians. By studying how doing and being hip hop informs young Black Christian identity-making, I aim to demonstrate the fluidity of spiritual practices in what

I term *digital Black Christianity*—religious practices formed by Black Christians largely in their twenties and thirties, who are concerned with young adult Black culture, and who have embedded digital technology and hip hop in their religious practices. While at times still engaged with physically located Black churches, digital Black Christianity is constructed primarily in the socio-temporal world of online exchanges in which young Black Christians build a fluid set of beliefs and a certain worldview or religious orientation through a co-reliance on Black spiritual practices and several other ideological paths.[32] Such a "field site of events" includes various social media platforms, websites, podcasts, millennial conferences, and spoken word gatherings that together show a network of beliefs commonly held among these digital Black Christians, "a thread of consciousness," as West and Solomon term it in their poem (Solomon 2016).[33]

Digital Black Christianity here centers on obtaining and modeling *intimacy* (spiritual, fraternal, and/or sexual closeness) through identity, *relationships*, *visibility*, and *valuation*, as found in Chapter 1's discussion of the evolution of the identity of Lecrae and the digital Black Christian community. The book thus explores Christian *relationships*, as in Chapter 2 on digital discipleship, and gaining *visibility* as in Chapter 3's discussion of "making visible" female and nonbinary black bodies. Chapter 3 also returns to the topic of identity-building in examining the way creatives' prioritize Christian identity over Black/hip hop identity (*secondary Blackness*). Chapter 4 covers creatives' diverse approaches to online ministry and work, how they quantify their own self-worth (*valuation*), and the nature of woke economies. Chapter 5 brings into focus once again the physical Black Church and its relationship to all these intimacies with a look at the relationship between digital Black Christian geographies, pastors, and the creatives under study in this volume. Each chapter highlights one or two key creatives as a way of telling the story of religion, hip hop, and digital technology.

Additionally, as any internet researcher will tell you, a unique environment and design narrative influences creatives' activities on a given platform. I make a case for why and how digital Black Christians employ specific platforms, with an investigation of Instagram, YouTube, and Twitter. Three chapters speak to this reality. I discuss the Instagram environment in Chapter 2, the YouTube therapeutic space created through

Jackie Hill-Perry's poems in Chapter 3, and the Twitter workspace creatives seek to navigate in Chapter 4.

Through a sustained, close look into the online/offline exchanges of digital Black Christians through a triangulated approach to content analysis, participant observation, and direct interviews, which required sitting in community with young Black Christian hip hop folk, I developed a more holistic understanding of what it means to be Black, Christian, and young, which I pass on to you in the pages that follow. A few theoretical antecedents guide this proposition.

The first is from Daniel White Hodge's *Hip Hop's Hostile Gospel: A Post-Soul Theological Exploration* (2016), which embraces a "theomusicological" approach to the study of hip hop artists. Through what he calls theomusicology, Hodge demonstrates the value in pairing textual analysis with an investigation of the hip hop artist, album, or art within the cultural context, political climate, artists' upbringing and background, album cover and art, cultural art, religious landscape, and geographic location (2016, x). This approach favors critiques that argue against studying lyrics alone. Other critiques of past hip hop studies research have focused on the field's heavy reliance on lyrical analysis over other sound elements, such as melody or beats. As in my previous publications, I have sought to move against this trend. While I still follow creatives' lyrical content quite closely, I take up sound beyond beats and melody in other ways most cognizant of my guides' connections to both the Black Church and digital media. For instance, mediatized connections to death, wax sermon records, and Black homiletic traditions appear in Chapter 1, Chapter 3, and the Epilogue, respectively. This treatment of "preaching" sound evinces the long-standing intersections between youth, media, and the Black Church in novel and important ways.

With an eye toward placing digital religion studies and internet studies in conversation with studies of hip hop and religion, I note an overlap between Hodge's approach and seminal work conducted in digital ethnography. Daniel Miller and Don Slater's (2001) aforementioned work on the use of digital technology in Trinidad noted the embeddedness of digital tools in offline practices. Millennial internet use has grown to such widespread proportions that unlike in decades just prior to the second millennium there is no such thing as being "offline," which is why technological embeddedness is an appropriate context in which to discuss young adult Black Christian religious practices. I thus adopt Jenna Burrell's (2009, 190) notion of the field site as not only a physical location, but as networks or "chains, paths, threads, conjunctions, or juxtapositions of locations" (see also Marcus 1998, 90).[34] The fluidity of this approach seems particularly appropriate for studying the similarly fluid and ever-evolving function of digital Black Christianity for young adult Black Christians.

Digital Black Christianity is not to be confused with the many ways Black Christians of all ages participate in activities like meme-sharing, posting, blogging, or other forms of the digital curation of Christian-centric content. Nor does it include physical churches like the Potter's House in Dallas, Texas, which built and maintains an online presence through websites and social networking sites. The digital Black Christians who embody the practices studied here are not casual online spectators/users. Rather, unlike latent pastors to the digital pulpit, pre-pandemic, they began their ministries and/or maintain a devoted following through social media, consider themselves social media personalities, and are sustained economically largely through their social media activities. They evince a hip hop orientation and style of worship, and they access and disseminate Black spiritual practices and Christian teachings online at a rate significantly higher than Black Christian users of digital technology of any other generation. As such, they are uniquely situated to express the deeply entrenched role of technology and hip hop in their religious lives and in lives of the numerous other digital Black Christians who avidly follow them.

Hip hop is uniquely important for understanding religion among digital Black Christians, for a few key reasons. Despite its global rifts, hip hop remains the entry point for scholars for understanding young Black culture. For their part, digital Black Christians were a part of the first generation that did not know a time prior to hip hop. This reality has greatly shaped their cultural and religious practices. The digital Black Christians studied in this book embody spiritual practices that often embrace several elements of hip hop as indicated in their participation in hip hop–based

Christian spoken-word events, hip hop–style clothing, and hip hop–centered discourse. Jamaica West summed up this perspective by saying:

> Hip hop is very much at the core of who I am as an artist and who I am even as a Christian . . . I think a lot of people are afraid to say that because hip hop has been so demonized with the Illuminati and exposure tapes (from the Craig Lewis ministry)[35] on different artists. So . . . a lot of [Christians] were afraid to say I was raised on hip hop . . . For me . . . I'm not afraid to say that . . . There's no way that I can speak about who I am as an individual without mentioning hip hop . . . to do that is the silencing of God and [silencing] a blessing from God . . .

In a classic push-and-pull dilemma, Black churches' occasional disdain for hip hop and its sensibilities, coupled with digital Black Christians' view of hip hop as a site for religious expression, has colored their engagement with digital technology.

From its infancy, much of hip hop writing has exhibited a variety of embodied performances by making use of ethnographic elements, such as journalistic accounts, centering the lived experiences of the author within hip hop, and privileging subjective hip hop voices. Performance work in hip hop ethnography can be traced back to the foundational work of Greg Dimitriadis: *Friendship, Cliques, and Gangs: Young Black Men Coming of Age in Urban America* (2003) and *Performing Identity/Performing Culture: Hip Hop as Text, Pedagogy, and Lived Practice* (2009). Dimitriadis's work offered the first sustained ethnography on young Black male teens in hip hop. In his books, Dimitriadis introduces the reader to Tony and Rufus, situating himself as a mentor and eventual friend to the two young men. Dimitriadis's work provides an essential strategy for the examination of Black youth culture in hip hop. By owning his positionality, he is able to showcase the essential nature of hip hop praxis as rooted in performing identities.

Emery Petchauer (2009, 950–52) notes that such grounded approaches like ethnography, while embodying many of the characteristics of historical/textual works, has the additional benefit of providing methodological insights that can be duplicated in other researchers' work. There have since been a number of works that privilege participant observation and interviews over text-based analysis (Harrison

2009; M. Hill 2009; Ibrahim 2014; Madison 2005; Turner 2010). Yet only recently have analyses of digital technology, religion, and hip hop been undertaken through ethnography, mostly in my own research.

Elonda Clay (2015) offered an early ethnographic treatment (it is still one of the few) of technology's role in Black religion and hip hop practices, in her content analysis of Yezzianity, a religion based on Kanye West. Clay locates three characteristics of digital content creators: they create (1) to enhance authority, (2) to perform and maintain identities, and (3) to portray themselves authentically. Her concluding thoughts seek to stimulate a critical approach to the study of hip hop and religion online. I have already laid out a few possibilities for extending the conversation begun by Clay and Dimitriadis regarding performance. Bringing their work together, I call the spectacular and mundane activities studied here *webwork* (*networked racial-religious performativity*).

Performativity—how humans perform their own reality—speaks to the way digital Black Christians use race and religion to speak meaningfully regarding their own identity. Earlier, scholars originated the concept of racial-religious performativity that I expand on here. Patrick Johnson (2003, 7) coined the term racial performativity as an interdisciplinary approach to the analysis of the multiple "performance practices found within Black American culture." More recent works, like *Muslim Cool* by Su'ad Abdul Khabeer (2016), build on Johnson's terminology by using the term *racial-religious performativity* to discuss Black Muslims' appropriation of hip hop in identifying with Blackness in Chicago. Expanding Clay's (2015) three functions of religion and hip hop performativity, digital Black Christians' religious performativity/performance both creates spaces for resistance against white supremacy, and/or white Christianity or the Black Church (authenticity), for self-articulation (identity formation), and enables them to grasp power in online and non-church spaces (authority).[36] They are not alone in this quest, however. For hegemonic forces like media conglomerates, government institutions, and other capitalist, social, and political structures seek to maintain and reinforce their power and profit from their own and others' networked racial-religious performances. Digital Black Christians continue to respond to and resist such structural performances of injustice through a number of artistic projects that I explore in the following chapters.

So what I call *networked racial-religious performativity* or *webwork* pays special attention to the racial and religious dimensions of digital Black Christians' online practices. Networks denote the ways the online practices of digital Black Christians continue to create important ties that extend to their offline engagement. By *webwork*, I mean the professional and personal encounters (both online and offline) that connect digital Black Christians in meaningful, albeit typically brief (religious) relationships. Through such networks, we are able to understand more clearly the beliefs and practices that link all digital Black Christians.

Throughout this book, I use the terms *creative* or *guide* to refer to the digital Black Christians being studied. They are creatives in that they are content creators who move across platforms to construct multiple representations of themselves, well beyond the assigned categories and norms regarding what a young Black Christian "should" be. The term *creatives* also captures the autonomous and performative nature of their work. The term *guide* also appears throughout this book. It is meant to keep ever present in the reader's mind the emic approach I employ throughout. The central theories, arguments, and findings presented here I derived from the interviews, sermons, songs, and the hundreds of textual and digital artifacts created by my guides. While the next section discusses this methodological approach at length, here I note that I have given great care and attention to ensuring that I have used creatives' own words and their meanings, verified against other statements made by each creative, as a guide to the culture. As such, they became my guides in developing the major themes discussed in each section. This approach allows each of the guides to take us on a fascinating journey through their world.

More on Method / Doing the Ethnography of Black Digital Religion

Every writer assumes a number of choices in both their writing and research that an audience may later question or feel requires further probing. We scholars, whether portending the importance of our work or by way of the imposter syndrome, anticipate questions, and I, as a junior scholar, identifying as Black, female, and Christian, do this perhaps more than others. I understand both the importance of documenting communities that emerge around such identities, as well as the routinized way their voices even—and especially—in the academy are often overlooked. Throughout this process, maintaining the ethical treatment of participants that have been historically marginalized, not simply as a preliminary research matter, but one that must be continuously attended to, was paramount to me as a way of seeking a more just narrative for young Black Christians. To paraphrase Annette Markham (2006), ethics is method and method is ethics. I lay bare my decisions on securing participants and my method of study, but not in an attempt to validate my claims. This whole book comes with the assumption that the lived realities of Black folks are truth enough. Rather, there were many moves that I made writing this book that I think may be useful for providing a clear methodological guide for those conducting research in this area. I am considering here those in need of justice-centered ethnographic approaches to reading young Black bodies.[37] Such points follow.

JUSTICE-CENTERED DIGITAL ETHNOGRAPHY. In 2017 I accepted a faculty position at the University of Arizona in the Africana Studies department. It was a unique hire in that the job call specified research interests in hip hop, religion, and the digital humanities. I had little training in information studies, and the decision to accept the position was key in further shaping my digital humanities work. Bryan Carter had just assumed the post of director for the newly created Center for Digital Humanities, which I later joined as a fellow. Along with Carter and other data scientists, we began devising a digital method for the study of young adult Black Christians. Those early discussions were at times exciting and at other times quite frustrating as I struggled to articulate my vision not only of who the study should incorporate but how we were to study with care and justice the religious lives of young Black people. This period of learning assisted me in articulating the nature of my digital humanities work and how the ethnography of digital Black Christians ought to be conducted. For that experience I am truly indebted to Dr. Carter and my other colleagues who participated.

PANNING FOR PARTICIPANTS. The next section describes my initial physical meeting with many of the creatives who ultimately participated in this study. However, the research project began much earlier with my attempts at locating candidates. In a far more egalitarian fashion than the phrase "participant selection" perhaps conveys, like panning for golden specks along a sandy seafloor, creatives "emerged" as prized particles from the wider group of potential respondents. I threw quite a wide net, contacting anyone with a large online following in their twenties and thirties who self-identified as a Black Christian. I utilized contacts from an earlier study, as well as friends, family members, and my colleagues' own connections to creatives to secure interviews. In those early months I may have annoyed or bored many with my incessant discussions regarding young Black Christians and hip hop. But the approach did yield several new leads (though few actual study participants). After an event at the University of Arizona in Tucson where I mentioned my research in prepared remarks to the audience, one such contact emerged. An audience member, with whom I have since stayed in touch, mentioned that he could assist me in securing interviews with prominent artists. A few weeks later he followed through, helping me gain an audience with one creative I had reached out to several times before, without success.

As each subject agreed to participate, we arranged recorded phone conversations. The majority of the research was conducted between January 25, 2018, and January 25, 2020. During that time, I employed a "follow the thing" methodology as outlined in the work of Marla Frederick (2015), in order to locate subjects through their connections to material objects.[38] In this case, I was concerned with their connection to digital technology. I begin with places where technological objects like smartphones and computers were essential to young Black Christians' identity-building. This led me to informal settings like poetry events, tours, conferences, and into the digital itself, *"following things from site to site"* as Alessandro Caliandro (2018, 555) describes it, in locating other artifacts of the culture (i.e., artist merchandise, conference decals, etc.). For Black Christians who make their living through their artistic and intellectual production, the summer is an important time for securing conference bookings. I used these physical meeting sites to meet potential study participants and further immerse myself in the culture. Along with physical objects, I began examining the internet as an object itself. The notion of webwork discussed throughout this book was born out of this process of locating the connection between physical things, digital things, my human study participants, and other people online. I began incorporating actions as stand-alone participants in this web, as I noted that creatives at times responded to memes or algorithmic output in ways that were impactful to their faith and the faith of others without necessarily holding any human connection to such "things." In this way, I was able to draw connections between a few major digital "actors." I then reached out to them via email or direct message. I explained the nature of the study and highlighted the importance of their participation. Cue the crickets. This approach received limited success.

Most important to participants was my own connection to others who had already agreed to an interview. As Chapters 2 and 4 demonstrate, human relationships are key for digital Black Christians. They approached the decision to participate in this study out of those same sensibilities. Seeing me at the Legacy Conference in July 2018 and at the Toronto tour stop for the Poets in Autumn Tour in September 2018 seemed to relax potential participants and I was able to obtain informal interviews and learn more in general about creatives and their digital process after shows or backstage with artists. There were countless informal conversations that occurred against the blare of rock or rap music or at merch tables during intermission, and I am indebted to a number of individuals who shared their passion and knowledge of the culture in these encounters.

As creatives began agreeing to participate, I then employed snowballing techniques, closing interviews with one final question: "Is there anyone else you believe this study should include?" I received several leads and new contacts this way. In total ten creatives agreed to full-length interviews ranging from one to two hours. As agreed in our interviews, my study of their practices extended past the initial interview period of roughly January 2018 to November 2018. I notified them that I would like to also follow their social media activities, documenting posts, comments, and the like that were already viewable to others online. While notifying them of my desire to "follow" them was not a legal requirement, in keeping with the Association of Internet Researchers' (2019) ethical guidelines, I thought this approach preserved both their awareness of my activities and their agency in how they might be portrayed. Thankfully, they all graciously accepted. I continued to follow them across social media platforms for the next fourteen months.

As I wrote my analysis, initially eight participants emerged for inclusion in the book. Ultimately the number of study participants who are directly featured in chapters was narrowed to six, although the thoughts of the other two, and in some cases quotes from interviews with them, still occasionally appear. It became clear that some stories duplicated those of other interviewees, or offered a clearer timeline and/or represented more fully the multidimensionality of digital Black Christian life. However, beyond the six featured here, the other participants' words reinforced such narratives. While they may be mentioned only in passing, it should be noted that they contributed substantially to the key findings of this work. Nowhere is this truer than in the development of my method of study.

METHOD OF STUDY. I cannot overstate the tremendous difficulty I faced in those early months in settling on a methodological approach to doing ethnography. As I have already laid out in this introduction, there seemed to be varying or shifting meaning in the way young people, Black people, and Christians were approached in the literature. Adding to this difficulty was the dual focus of my research concerns on both hip hop and digital technology, which I believed from my early findings was intrinsic to the notion of who young Black Christians were and were becoming. As much as possible, I wanted their voices to guide my research and ultimately my findings. I settled on a grounded approach, as its deductive method allowed me to hit the pavement, collecting data and interviewing creatives. This is why I also call creatives "guides" throughout. I allowed what came out of our initial meetings and their own postings to guide the next steps in my research and the development of theories. For instance, Chapter 5's discussion of woke economies and secondary Blackness was a direct result of my initial interview with Beleaf Melanin. His views caused me to consider the emergence of similar ideas among some creatives and to note irregularities (and their implications) among others. Even the irregularities yielded other important findings regarding the overall group.[39] As I continued to collect data, I entered all interview transcripts into Dedoose, the web application for mixed methods research. I included the complete YouTube video transcripts, and the song and/or rap catalog of each artist. Through the use of the Twitter archiving program TAGS, I collected as many tweets from each of the study participants as I could uncover. While there was variation regarding what I was able to locate, for many, I retrieved posts and reposts dating back to their first live tweet. Initially I simply cut and pasted all of this data from a Microsoft spreadsheet into an online platform called Wordberry that enables word and phrase analysis. As the reader may imagine, the breadth of my textual corpus soon surpassed my personal computer's capacity to perform this function. Several crashes later, I more fully acquainted myself with Dedoose and begin arranging all text and recordings there through a tagging system.

That first year, I was a researcher learning on the fly, familiarizing myself with new software and machine learning programs in order to conduct my research. Such digital tagging was new to me and I soon learned the difficulties and pitfalls of tagging young adult Black bodies in particular. Suffice it to say, I found a home in the work of Sadiya Hartman, André Brock, Christina Sharpe, Jonathan Walton, and Hortense Spiller. An important article by Batya Friedman and Helen Nissanbaum titled "Bias in the Computer System" (1996), which appeared as part of the Critical Race and Digital Studies Syllabus, and another by Katie Rawson and Trevor Muñoz titled "Against Cleaning" (2016) rounded out my understanding of the topic. Through these works, I developed a healthy suspicion of any and all forms of defining and categorizing digital Black Christians in ways that might further silence, misrepresent, or misread their voices—and Black existence more generally—in the digital and in the scholarship. Jonathan Walton's work reminded me that I, too, had been one of those African American students he describes in *Watch This!* who "embrace the phenomenon as a guilty pleasure. Influenced by the social pressures and sense of shame imposed on students by the academic environment" (Walton 2009, xiv). A graduate student at the time, from a working-class, Pentecostal-Holiness community, I realized that in my desire to succeed in reading Black religion objectively I had often rendered my gendered-racial-religious identity silent. Despite what I felt to be true regarding young Black Christians, in those days I gave preference to biased accounts regarding the group. I later realized that scholarly bias against young Black Christians was yet another incarnation of anti-Black racism. Against such bias, my ability to *testify* as a young Black woman of faith presented a necessary autoethnographic intervention in the academy.

My autoethnographic approach to writing throughout this volume was culled from fieldnotes of my participant observations during the data-collection phase of my research. As discussed in Chapter 4, works like that of Christina Sharpe (2016) caused me to consider how all of my own work was being conducted "in the wake" of the history of Black trauma and survival. My guides in the process were also informed by and responding to histories of enslavement and quests for freedom. Yet I remained mindful that through the insertion of "I" there remained the risk of seeing only reflections of myself in the participants. Instead, through the process of looping, I identified statements or word reoccurrences and checked them against similar phrases and words mentioned in other interviews, lyrics, and online posts. As I obtained more information I looped whatever initial codes I saw in with new data emerging from online interviews and content created by guides like video blogs or poems. In this way I was constantly building my corpus, refining my codes, and affirming or disconfirming my initial readings of the group through their own intellectual production.[40] I continued to allow them to speak and verify what I thought I was seeing in the research.

While there were a number of web applications that aided me in this process, it was one Digital Humanities Institute that I had the pleasure of participating in during the summers of 2018 and 2019 at the CUNY Graduate Center that furthered my research approach and quite honestly allowed me the confidence to just "trust myself" as a young Black body studying other young Black bodies. Over lunch, Michelle McSweeny, a data researcher who works on natural language processing and machine learning, painstakingly assisted me in laying out an approach to machine learning using Jupyter Notebook that would ultimately allow me to "cleanly" list all data collected for the effective locating and tagging of essential concepts. Toward the end of this tedious process, she laid down her pen and said, "But you know, some things you're just going to have to give the eyeball test." I was appalled. I had come to the Institute to devise a method whereby the machine would examine my wide corpus and sift out the most important data. Since that Institute, however, this "eyeball" approach has become the most essential to me in "seeing" young Black Christians often rendered invisible by our mechanized processes. The work of Safiya Noble (2018) and the critical technocultural discourse analysis approach pioneered by André Brock (2012) have also been useful in this process.

While aided by web applications, this project ultimately used keywords from interviews to form its conceptual framework. In this way, five hundred hours of digital and physical participant observations, as well as data mining and text analysis of more than fifty thousand comments and/or exchanges (YouTube, Twitter, Instagram, and Periscope) between the six Black Christians and other young Black Christians were collected. A representative sample of Black Christian belief and practices emerged through the text analysis of comments from their mostly young Black Christian audiences. Following the foundational work of Anselm Strauss and Juliet Corbin (1998), the conditions, people, and actions that shaped digital Black Christians' webwork was identified.[41] I then developed a conditional matrix to identify overarching conditions/issues affecting digital Black Christians' actions. Recurring actions like "pushing me," "learning," "promoting," "finding," were extracted as direct quotes from my dataset or my own conceptual interpretations of respondents' use of particular words. In total, there were fifty-five codes created for the textual analysis of 488 data entries (transcriptions of song lyrics, interviews, video posts, Twitter posts, etc.). For consistency, I personally collected and determined all codes. Codes ranging from "evangelism" to "Blackness" elicited 758 applications and were ultimately filtered into four key areas of intimacy for digital Black Christians: relationships, identity, visibility, and valuation. I then secured the assistance of sociologist Emily Hemlock at the University of Arizona's School of Sociology to act as a peer reviewer. I am quite indebted to her for looking over my dataset and confirming and/or challenging my original findings. This approach, to quote qualitative researchers Yvonna S. Lincoln and Egon G. Guba (1985), kept me "honest; [it] asks hard questions about methods, meanings, and interpretations . . ."[42]

Through this process over a period of two years, the following guides were identified and studied for inclusion in this book. I begin with my first meeting with most of the creatives discussed in the following chapters.

The Creatives

> Every generation has its leaders, moments that articulate what God is doing.

> [The Legacy Conference] is one of those in our day. If you miss it, I think you're missing . . . what's happening in modern Christianity, especially in the urban context.
> —Lecrae Moore (*Rapzilla* 2010)

To the outsider, every bit of the Legacy Conference at Moody Bible Institute in downtown Chicago feels like a conversation overheard. Though the buzzwords and popular conference speakers require insider knowledge to understand, chances are that if you are a digital Black Christian you may easily feel at home here. Terms like "Reformed theology," "image-bearer," and "complementarianism" are commonplace. Just as frequently, names first popularized in digital Black circles like the Legacy Conference are announced from the dais to cheers or whispered by adoring fans excited to rub shoulders with their idols in the halls.

It's nearly half an hour before the opening session. I have chosen to stake out a booth angled between the cafeteria and the welcome desk near the front entrance. From here I can look out across the modest hall to the large courtyard and dormitories on Moody Bible Institute's campus. The Institute occupies the 900 block of North Wells Street near the heart of downtown Chicago. The early morning rumblings of this urban campus hint at its revivalist beginnings. This is, after all, the hallowed ground where notables like D. L. Moody, Mary Bethune Cookman, and Jerry B. Jenkins studied and preached. But old, (mostly) white male history is too distant for this crowd. The museum reserved to memorialize D. L. Moody's life and ministry sits just off the main hallway. Despite its accessibility, attendees rarely visit it. The legends of digital Black Christianity are of a more recent vintage.

It was 2005 when a little known rapper came to Chicago for a performance to promote his new album. The rapper had secured his plane ticket but did not have enough money for a hotel. Brian Dye, minister and Legacy co-founder, offered his home (Daniels 2015). Later, two-time Grammy winner Lecrae Moore describes his initial interactions with Dye in the rap song "Leaving a Legacy":

> He took us in his crib and let us meet his wife
> I was already saved, but that day changed my life
> He sat and told stories how that drama got real

> How they shot up in his crib, wife almost got killed
> Man, I sat there listening to him with tears in my eyes
> Every word that he spoke lit a fire deep inside
> If you ever take a trip to the Westside of the Chi
> Go and look that boy up, man his name Brian Dye

The Legacy conference soon became a hotspot for upcoming artists like Thi'sl, Flame, and several others. Well-known Reformed theologians like John Piper also tuned in to Legacy, helping to put the conference on the map. Each year, nearly two thousand mostly digital Black Christians beat a path to the conference to be a part of this invigorating atmosphere and to rub shoulders with well-known creatives. The following pages provide an on-site introduction to each creative, their network of friends, and fellow artists.

* * *

At the next table, I hear a twenty-something woman whisper excitedly to her friend, "There's Janette . . . ikz!" Janette Watson or Mysterious Janette . . . ikz (pronounced *genetics*) first became popular through her poetry performance at P4CM's annual Rhetoric event, the largest Christian spoken-word event in the nation. Each year, thousands of digital Black Christians descend on Los Angeles for a one-night performance. Yet, according to Andwele Williams, Rhetoric's marketing director, their largest audience is online. Janette's clip alone garnered 3.8 million views.

The twenty-something at the other table continues her excited whispering, "And that's her husband. They just had a baby. I watched their whole engagement and wedding online. It was beautiful." There's a hint of longing in her retelling of events. Later today, the couple's session on courtship and marriage attracts a standing-room-only crowd of mostly young Black women. After all, the story of Janette is the stuff of which Black Christian fairytales are made, a fact enhanced by careful staging and online documentation. The moments leading up to the wedding of Janette and Matt Watson—the pre-wedding preparation and the actual ceremony—required costuming, direction, and professional videography provided by P4CM, a mostly online Christian arts ministry. It was then packaged as a three-part YouTube series titled *Worth the Wait*. Viewers were encouraged to subscribe to the P4CM channel in order to watch the full series. The entire series reached a viewing audience of over 741,000.

The practice of digitally crafting and performing Christian beliefs through widely shared YouTube videos is not unique to Janette. Most of the well-known conference speakers here first developed a fan base through YouTube or other similar social media sites. Jackie Hill-Perry, a close friend of Janette's, first gained prominence with her performance of "My Life as a Stud" at the 2008 Rhetoric show. Since then, fans and followers have tuned in to watch pivotal moments in Jackie's life, like Preston Perry's poem proposal to Jackie Hill-Perry, also at Rhetoric in 2010. Like Janette and Matt, their subsequent "Journey to Courtship" and actual wedding were filmed by P4CM (Rhetoric) Executive Director T. Q. Senkungu and have garnered over one hundred thousand views. Through YouTube, Preston and Jackie were even able to appeal to followers to request contributions to defray the cost of their wedding.

Of the creatives studied in this book, Hill-Perry did not agree to an interview. She is perhaps the most extensively interviewed, followed, and documented of all the creatives, and composites of her practices and beliefs for inclusion here have nonetheless been culled from an extensive array of online materials. Her story of moving from lesbianism to a heterosexual identity has prompted a number of digital Black Christians both to protest and support her. Either way, fans and followers feel a particular investment in her digital activities.

If fans feel as if they know the prominent digital Black Christians featured at the Legacy conference, it is because in some ways they do. Nowadays, delineating between virtual or real social interactions is spurious, for the virtual is just as real as the physical in this context. Followers and fans have become intricately woven into the fabric of prominent digital Black Christians' daily lives in ways that allow meaningful dialogue and offline interaction. These creatives have both encouraged their followers' Christian faith and come to embody Christian identity for many digital Black Christians. As such, their followers have shared in a multitude of highs and lows in the lives of the creatives studied here.

In April 2017, when rapper and YouTube personality Beleaf shared news of the theft of his family car via his popular YouTube channel "Beleaf in Fatherhood," subscriber Chelsey Jones responded quickly, creating a GoFundMe site that drew thousands of dollars in donations. A few days later, Beleaf replied with thanks to his donors.

> WOW You guys Are incredible! I can't believe you guys have raised almost 10k in under a week! We are so blessed by your giving hearts! Still no sign of our car but a company called CLEK, Delivered and taught us how to install 3 brand new Car Seats! We are waiting for the detective to get back to us about the guy because they have an image of him. (C. Jones 2017)

One follower of Beleaf's YouTube channel decided to donate $50 because of his impact on her life. She wrote on his GoFundMe page,

> I believe in you Beleaf and watch daily. First it started because I needed some inspiration and now it has turned into something beautiful and has me very encouraged about the future for our people of color. Thank you for creating this and making me believe like you have. (C. Jones 2017)

On the second day of the Legacy conference, I decide to sit in on Beleaf's workshop. There I meet a young woman named Annie. She is a youth leader at her predominantly Black Church. Another woman, Megan, whom I met earlier at a lunchtime rap concert, joins the session late and quickly heads to an open seat next to Annie. Megan, a white woman, is a speech pathologist from Minnesota. She had never heard of Legacy prior to 2018. In the early spring of that year she became intrigued while viewing one of Joseph Solomon's YouTube videos. A longtime subscriber of Solomon's channel *chaseGodtv*, she watched one of his video posts in which he encouraged followers to attend Legacy. She is hoping to catch his performance before leaving. I ask her if she is also familiar with Beleaf. She has not heard of him. Annie chimes in to say that she has been following his show for some time. Pulling out her phone she quickly begins scrolling through her pictures to show images from Beleaf's show. With ease she rattles off the name of each member of his family. She goes on to mention fun facts about each one before catching herself in mid-sentence. "Why am I talking 'bout them like they're *my* family?" The three of us share a knowing laugh.

We all have an unusual familiarity with many of the featured artists. Their stories are well documented and closely followed by most in attendance. It dawns on me that social media sites have made us all ethnographers of sorts, cataloging tidbits of information about our favorite artists or developing helpful strategies for living our faith, learning skills for our own creative work, and interacting with creatives who may even become friends at some later point.

The night before, I had met Beleaf. We spoke only briefly. It was a somewhat awkward exchange, I thought afterwards, perhaps because our initial meeting was via Instagram. In fact, it was Beleaf who encouraged me to reach out via Instagram to other digital Black Christians for interviews. After several emails and phone interviews, it felt somewhat odd to offer an impersonal handshake and introduction. For many fans and followers of creatives, the intimacy of online encounters feels more personal even than a physical meeting. For them, digitally located social interactions are unbalancing the time-honored traditions of physical social interaction.

Yet, in the spirit of honoring traditions, I had started in with, "Hi, it's Erika, the researcher from the University of Arizona. A pleasure to meet you." All of us digital Black Christians are here meeting, mostly for the first time, a physical version of our online networks and relationships. It is a complex web of likes, shares, direct messages, conferences, and shows that have connected us. When I first interviewed Beleaf, he noticed that I had listed my Instagram profile location as Buffalo, and he asked if I know rapper Aitina Fareed-Cooke (AI). I told him I do. We have performed at some of the same venues as poets and our kids have played together.

The proximity to some of the most vocal among digital Black Christians can at times strengthen the ties first developed online. An instance of this occurred during Thursday evening's closing performance by Joseph Solomon. By looping songs as diverse as CeeLo's "Do You Remember" and his own self-written lyrics, Solomon tells a gripping story of his battle with depression, self-doubt, and living the Christian life. In earlier interviews and conversations, he offered the same transparency. He easily opens up about his wearying travel schedule and ministry obligations. His earlier work as a young male mentor for GRIP Outreach, another wing of Legacy's ministry in Chicago's South Side, also left him scarred and still struggling to process the violence he had witnessed. His weariness and raw emotion overflow in performance, seeming to grip

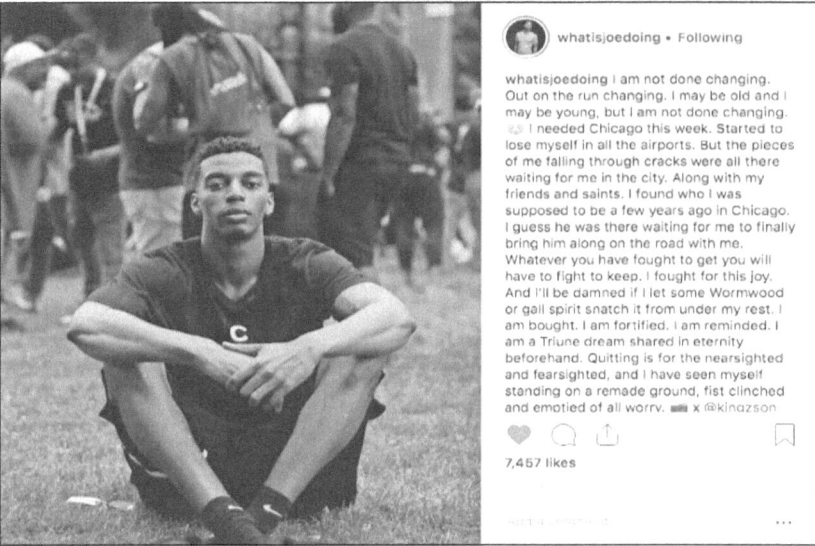

Figure 1.1. Joseph Solomon (@whatisjoedoing), Instagram post, July 22, 2018.

the audience, demanding that they stand and wave at some points and sit and listen attentively at others. Figure 1.1 shows his Instagram post on the closing day of the conference.

This kind of visceral connection affirms the online network established between many in the audience and the creatives discussed here. But gatherings like these not only strengthen the relationship between artists and audience; they also bring together the artists themselves, a collection of mostly digital Black Christians grappling to make some sense of their twenties and thirties. Like Solomon, the rapper, model, and spoken word poet Jamaica West's post the week of Legacy Fest evokes, in images of her playing and enjoying the company of friends, the value in reaffirming networks at non-church Christian events like this one. Their friends are, after all, now a collection of artists, pastors, poets, and singers spread all across the United States. The brief times they share are deeply meaningful.

Back in 2016, a poetry fellowship hosted in the home of Preston and Jackie Hill-Perry brought some of their friends together to read poems and scriptures, and to share fellowship. These times of fellowship bleed into other informal meetups at conferences and through shared performances. Later in the same year, the Xpressions Tour would bring together Joseph and Jamaica. Popular performers like Chris Webb, Ezekiel Azonwu, Preston and Jackie Hill-Perry, and Jannette have also toured together as part of the Poets in Autumn Tour. Such get-togethers and joint performances allow like-minded young Christian adults to build lasting connections or just to share their developing faith and religious knowledge.

Later I meet up with an Indiana-based artist and his wife at their merch table. A company called Blacksheep sells graphic tees. The couple, aged twenty-six and thirty-two, believe their work is about more than just selling t-shirts. "It's really amazing what God is doing with these t-shirts!" the artist tells me. He hands me a postcard that features three brown teenagers all outfitted in his graphic designs. The back reads,

> We are a faith-based lifestyle brand with a focus on encouraging others to embrace their own identity and uniqueness. Counter Culture. Stay Peculiar.

This notion of producing artifacts of the culture in order to remain countercultural is also shared by other performers, like twenty-six-year-old rapper NoBigDyl. NoBigDyl began as a road manager for Don Canon. He was later signed to a major secular label, Capitol Records, just behind Social Misfits. He is one of the first publicly Christian rappers to be signed to a major label. During his performance, he gives a shout-out to an audience member who is wearing a Tribe hat, a merchandise label produced by his company. "Whenever we see that logo, we know who you are. That you're a member of our tribe."

Ironically, NoBigDyl tells me later that he does not see himself as part of any special group, like the digital Black Christians that I am studying, nor has he given them much thought. The branding of Christianity in which he and other digital Black Christians routinely participate demonstrates a particular worldview of the culture, a unique outlook which other digital Black Christians support and promote, whether online or in person through clothing purchases. Like Christian iconography of the past, such markers point to the separateness of the group, that they are not just feckless youth or reckless Christians. They have joined a movement of digital Black Christians.

Months later at a Toronto tour stop for Poets in Autumn, featuring Joseph Solomon, Janette . . . ikz, Preston Perry, Ezekiel Anzouwa, and

Chris Webb, I browse a merch table full of 1990s throwback hoodies and tees that read "Living Holy." The reference to the hit TV show *Living Single* implicitly criticizes promiscuity while promoting abstinence among the mostly teen and twenty-something Black Christians in attendance. Creatives seek to capitalize on the fact that digital Black Christians and teens are ravenous consumers of 1990s hip hop culture. The Brooklyn-based *Living Single*, replete with rap icon Queen Latifah, Flavor magazine, and the opening homage to homegirls by Queen Latifah herself, represented hip hop's urban roots. Among creatives, there is a focus on embodying urban youth culture not by branding oneself but by rebranding the Christian faith. Christian youth culture has been roundly criticized for its overzealous attempts to evangelize the world by witnessing to unsaved friends or creating insular teen groups that ostracize other youth, viewed as unbelievers. Yet the creatives here embrace urban culture as Christian culture and as a way of making Black bodies visible. In unspoken ways, their attempts at rebranding the faith resonates with digital Black Christians who wish to situate Christian identity in the lived realities of Black people.

The 2017 debut image of Preston Perry's "Free Indeed" hoodie featured him in an all-Black hoodie pulled over his head. In an age in which the hooded sweatshirts of Black youth have become powerful symbols of Black male suffering and the unfair detainment and/or incarceration of Black male bodies, Perry's new line constructs a counter-narrative. The words "Free Indeed," taken from John 8:34–36 (KJV), "Whom the son sets free, is free indeed," appear to hang from the wearer's neck like shackles, a reminder of America's history of slavery. This image contrasts the bondage of sin with the liberty found in Christian faith. To be Black and free is a powerful assertion both now and in light of Africans' history in America. The promotion of such counter-narratives is a recurring theme among digital Black Christians.

* * *

The first plenary session of the day opens in the Torrey-Grey Auditorium. The venue, which seats well over five thousand, has hosted some of the most popular Christian leaders of the twentieth century. The doors swing open, seemingly to the beat of the hip hop music blaring from the stage. On most other days, the auditorium's pew-like seating and

Figure 1.2. Legacy Fest, opening day session with DJ Wade-O on the music, July 19, 2018. (Photo by author)

Figure 1.3. Legacy Fest, first night session, Joseph Solomon performing, July 19, 2018. (Photo by author)

pulpit-styled stage, organ pipes, and choir seating makes it feel every bit like the chapel for which it is often used. Today, however, the stage has been reconfigured into two distinct tiers. The band is still setting up on stage. Worship begins nonetheless, from another instrument of praise.

On the higher tier stands DJ Wade-O, one of Christian hip hop's most popular syndicated radio show hosts. On the curtain above his head are the letters "DF," an abbreviation for the conference theme, "Devoted to Fellowship." Below him a large neon sign with the words "Doxology" in bright letters extends the length of the upper platform. "Doxology," "Devotion," "Make Disciples," and "Fellowship" are words that appear throughout the session and are distributed on programs, banners, and decals. Their linguistic presence makes this moment alive in both its urgency and intimacy. If this is a chapel, hip hop sits metaphorically in the holiest of holies, high and lifted up. At the center of it all, the high priest of hip hop, DJ Wade-O, works with laser-like focus, continuously moving his fingers from headset to Apple keyboard, motioning his pleasure

Figure I.4. Rapper Da Truth performing, DJ Wade-O on the turntables, Legacy Rap Fest, July 21, 2018. (Photo by author)

or displeasure with the audio output (that *boom bap* that makes heads nod) to the sound person below. All along, he is bopping his head to the musical world he brings to life around us. From somewhere offstage, a fog machine, the smoky go-to for creating the look and feel of Christian coolness, is ignited. As the opaque substance fills the room, more teens and young adults file in, standing, singing, and bopping along to the music, creating an indescribable energy. It is a 2011 classic from Tedashii, a member of Lecrae's 116 Clique, titled "Dum Dum." The refrain repeats as attendees rap along,

> Eh, they don't know about us, they don't, they don't know about us
> They don't know about us, they, they, they don't know about us,
> They don't know about us, they don't, they don't
> They think we dum, dum diddy dum, dum
> But they gon' know, they gon' know about us, they gon' know about us.

Looking across the auditorium at the nearly two thousand digital Black Christians gathered here, this is a fitting anthem. Their world is beautiful, vibrant, and complex. The bricolage of digital Black Christian artifacts—pendants, hats, and t-shirts dotting its canvas—is mostly unknown beyond their numbers. One cannot help but be moved by these Christians' audacious project of self- and culture-making. It is an intoxicating atmosphere, ripe with a peculiar mix of gospel and hip hop adjurations. We are all here together, feeling and knowing what many organized churches and those beyond the faith either fail to remember or have not fully grasped. Some night a DJ really might save your life.

> And if it wasn't for the music I don't know what I'd do, yeah
> Last night a DJ saved my life
> Last night a DJ saved my life from a broken heart
> Last night a DJ saved my life
> Last night a DJ saved my life with a song (Indeep 1982)

We have been moved by hip hop music and culture in ways they (our churches, media, etc.) do not know about. Such epistemologies bind us together. I feel it now, here, deeply. A passionate sense of calling rises up in me. A biblical suggestion of Jeremiah, no? "It is like fire shut up in my bones. I can't keep it to myself."

> You gotta get up
> You gotta get off
> You gotta get down, girl.

I am bopping along and chanting too,

> They don't know about us, they don't, they don't
> They think we dum, dum diddy dum, dum
> But they gon' know, they gon' know about us, they gon' know about us (Indeep 1982)

Conclusion

This first work on the techno-religious world of young Black adults raises the possibility that loose online networks are creating strong religious ties that heal, deliver, support, and set free and they must receive as much consideration as the physical activities of the contemporary Black Church. I nonetheless welcome other scholars' critiques of what I have outlined here. Perhaps another work will find that I have gone too far in separating out digital practices from the lived realities of Black churchgoers of all ages. And this is fair. My hope is to underscore the richness and particularity of digital Black Christians religious practices that are often overlooked in more general assessments of all African American worshipers. Another critique of this work may argue to the contrary, saying that I have not gone far enough. The digital contours of young Black adults' religious practices have moved creatives to conferences, events, and organizations both physical and online that do not identify with the Black Church even where borrowing heavily from its liturgical practices. More data beyond the creatives documented in this ethnography may well make a case for that. My own future project goals include a national study of the digital-religious practices of all Black young adults. For now, however, this book balances these potential critiques by offering a portrait of what the Black Church is and is becoming through the digital activities of young Black adult Christians.

Recent events tell us of the importance of this book's discussion. At the beginning of the COVID-19 pandemic, young Black people were still reeling from a turbulent decade. It was filled with multiple instances of police brutality against mostly young Black men and women and the emergence of the Black Lives Matter movement. Added to this was the stark realization of health disparities as Black Americans grappled with soaring numbers among the infected in cities like Detroit. As the morbidity rate rose among young adults, Black Americans suffered most acutely. The brutal murder of George Floyd by police and the subsequent protests exacerbated these realities as the nation moved out of quarantine and into a summer already "sweltering with the heat of injustice," in the words of Dr. King. Digital Black Christians, as they had in Ferguson, in New Orleans, and earlier moments of injustice in the decade, used the moment in the digital to exercise their faith through protests, online prayer vigils, Zoom meetups, TikTok challenges, Instagram gatherings, rap battles, and a multitude of other video posts. Such events not only tell us what is at stake for young Black adults, but also reveal the capacity of digital Black Christians to use new media to speak out against injustice and define their own agendas.

The more we understand their religious relationships, identity, visibility-seeking, and measures of valuation, along with their unique expression through new media, the more we further our knowledge of this period in American history and the nature of religion among African Americans in particular and Americans more broadly. This book is a step in that direction.

1

Turns

The Story of Lecrae Devaughn Moore

At thirty-nine years old, Lecrae Devaughn Moore cannot be categorized as a millennial. Yet he is definitely a digital Black Christian. His tremendous impact on the culture and practices of young Black Christian hip-hoppers is discernible in his pervasive online presence, in popular digital magazines and websites like *Rapzilla* and *Trackstarz* that chronicle Christian hip hop, and in the success of his co-founded music label Reach Records, one of Christian music's most popular recording labels. As a signpost for other young Black Christians, the inability to define Lecrae as "a Black millennial" points to a glaring problem with the category itself. This issue is perhaps most apparent in popular digital discourse.

Try entering the phrases "Christian" and "Black Millennial" into an online search engine.[1] Most likely, the results will include blog posts and op-ed pieces discussing the continued exodus of millennials from the Black Church. Young Black Christians' disillusionment with the Black Church's antiquated liturgical practices, homophobia, or position on male dominance are some of the usual topics of discussion. Yet few of these discussions are rooted in empirical evidence, nor has much been offered to suggest where the next stop on the religious train might be for most Black millennials. The leaving/abandoning myth, as I call it, has constrained religious and scholarly readers' views of Black millennials to the sole context of the Black Church and totalized the focus to missionary-driven works at the intersections of hip hop studies and Christianity (e.g., How can we save young Black millennials?).[2] While several of the young adult Black Christians taken up in this work continue to strive toward revitalizing and even creating anew their notions of Christianity, much of the popular culture references about Black millennial faith and Black Church scholarly and institutional circles remain situated around the beleaguered sick beds of young Black adult Christianity.

Myths regarding Black millennials leaving and/or abandoning the Black Church imbricate assumptions about Black youth pathology.[3] Since the 1965 publication of the Moynihan Report, the notion of Black pathology it introduced has been met with severe rebuttals by a number of Black intellectuals.[4] These responses have nonetheless served to fulfill certain crisis-centered readings of young Black adult culture that continue to permeate Black Christian millennial research and the moral/religious panic with which Black churches have regarded young Black Christians. In recent years, a number of scholars have turned away from Black pathology–centered readings of Black youth and young adult culture.[5] Such approaches, beyond pathology or rescuing a generation, restore agency to young Black adults and allow us to examine the religious world as they conceive of it, not just as it has been reported on and then read back to them.[6]

This chapter seeks to locate and define, beyond assumptive notions of Black millennials leaving the Black Church, what it means to be a young adult, Black, and Christian. Through a techno-ethno-biography of Lecrae, we witness the birth of the word "millennial," why I use the term digital Black Christian instead, and the role of technology and hip hop in shaping the religious context of the creatives I am studying.[7] This book centers the role of digital technology in mediating young Black adult religious practices. Technological precursors in music foreshadowed such activity in Lecrae's own story. In studying the epochal moments in Lecrae's life, this chapter is as much a history of one prominent figure's influence on youth culture as it is a guidepost for understanding the origins of those I call digital Black Christians. Telling their story without Lecrae is nearly impossible. Lecrae is to digital Black Christians what hip hop is to Lecrae: inextricably linked. You cannot speak of one without the other. The evolution of Lecrae echoes the kind of deep racial identity work done by each of the creatives covered here. Given his prominence and friendship with many of these digital Black Christians, his movements, changes, and turns within Christian hip hop sent ripples throughout the community of creatives.

In considering Lecrae's personal and professional evolution, this chapter locates and defines digital Black Christians through epochal moments in the development of his techno-religious beliefs and practices. Making use of his autobiography, *Unashamed*, as well as his lyrics and online interviews, I consider four turns in his life:

1. The birth of Lecrae, 1979
2. The birth of the term *millennial*, 1987–91
3. The death of Tupac Shakur, 1996
4. The death of Trayvon Martin, 2012

1979

Lecrae Devaughn Moore was born on October 9, 1979. Straddling two decades comes with a mixture of beginnings and endings. Innovations in music and technology directly shaped his racial-religious development. The Sugar Hill Gang recorded "Rapper's Delight" the same year. Just a few months later, Michael Jackson released his first solo album, *Off the Wall*, with Quincy Jones on Epic Records. Jackson's mix of funk, soul, disco, and pop signaled a turn both in musical style and video production. His opening "Wooo!" on "Don't Stop 'til You Get Enough" can be understood as an expression of freedom, freedom both from Motown Records and from other racial and musical encumbrances. Jackson would say as much in an interview regarding his solo musical stylings: "What I do, I don't want it labeled 'white' or 'Black.' I want it labeled as music" (Spike Lee 2016). Much like Jackson, Sugarhill Gang member Michael "Wonder Mike" Wright intentionally sought to appeal to as wide a racial audience as possible. In an interview he says: "I wanted to appeal to everyone, I said: 'I'd like to say hello to the Black, to the white, the red and brown'" (Simpson 2017).

Yet, despite their attempts at universalizing Black sound, the visual imaging of Black artists worked to map Blackness onto technology in new ways. In the video version of "Don't Stop 'til You Get Enough," an innovation in video production called "chromo-key" allowed Jackson to be displayed in triplicate. By dancing and sliding back in awe as each version of himself replicated his movements, Jackson attempted to visualize through this medium what before had only been located in oral and physical forms of Black braggadocio. The translation of Black culture played well. A day following the birth of Lecrae, "Don't Stop 'til You Get Enough" reached number 4 on the Billboard chart.

The year 1979 was also a year of endings. In July 1979, Sony introduced its new personal cassette player, the Walkman. Its appearance, along with later innovations in handheld music devices, portended the death of radio. The Walkman, however, was only one of a number of newly developed ways of transporting sound. More popular, arguably, was the boombox. Jackson's hit music as well as that of rising hip hop stars could now be heard individually through earphones or plugged into much larger boomboxes. Popular for their sonic reach, the boombox's indispensability in urban Black youth culture would earn it the derisive moniker "ghetto blaster." The banning of boomboxes in public spaces signaled an attempt to circumscribe the movements of young Black bodies. Lecrae, however, like many of the other Black creatives you will meet in this chapter, early in his professional career framed such circumscriptions as personally felt engagements with poverty and fatherlessness rather than a commentary on the structures or histories that created and enforced the injustices he experienced. Even as his experiences were colored by race, he failed to rightly name them as such, at least until quite recently. Instead, Lecrae located some of his most impactful early childhood moments in his engagement with hip hop, vis à vis new forms of media.

1987–91

> The images were mesmerizing. One of the first music videos I saw was by Eazy-E and featured a kid who looked like I did.
> —Lecrae Moore (2016c, 17)

Lecrae, in this period, exemplifies the first generation of young Blacks to experience media-mediated forms of hip hop. Earlier hip-hoppers centered their narratives in physically located neighborhoods. For Lecrae, however, in the absence of his father, hip hop "rushed in like water to fill the cracks" through the new TV show *Yo! MTV Raps* (Moore 2016c, 17). Like Jackson's "short films" (as his music videos would later be called), *Yo! MTV Raps* provided a short, packaged narrative of young Black culture for global consumption. Hosted by Fab Freddy and Ed Lover, from its first air date in 1988 until 1995 the show centered on urban East Coast geographies as sites of Black artistic expression. Until then, rap music had remained largely driven by local neighborhoods, regional scenes, night clubs, and a few sporadic TV appearances like the Sugarhill Gang's 1981 performance of "Rapper's Delight" on the *Soul Train* music show. Rap music relied mostly on physically present DJs, emcees, and audiences for each performance. The music videos aired on *Yo! MTV Raps* shifted communal engagement from urban deejays, emcees, and audiences creating music together to media-mediated ways of experiencing Blackness through rap music.

For Lecrae, gathering to watch *Yo! MTV Raps* videos with older cousins spurred his own attempts at mirroring forms of Black culture exhibited onscreen. Lecrae's awe at seeing his own urban Black environ mediated by television was "mesmerizing." He writes, "The language, scenes, and sounds felt familiar, but embellished. It made my world seem glamorous and attractive rather than unfortunate. It was instantly relatable" (Moore 2016c, 17).

Seeing "language, scenes, and sounds [that] felt familiar" on TV informed his own performance of Blackness in physically present activities (Moore 2016c, 17). When Lecrae was unable to watch MTV, he sought out rap music by borrowing tapes, listening to former prison inmates freestyling at his mother's place of employment, and watching his cousins breakdancing in their front yard. For older hip-hoppers located on the East Coast, their rap origin story largely centered around parties and neighborhood projects.

Yet Lecrae represented both a chronological and spatial distance from 1970s East Coast rap. In fact, his late 1980s orientation to hip hop more closely resembles older digital Black Christians studied here, like Daniel Steele and Propaganda. For many urban Black youth outside of New York City in the 1980s, their orientation to rap music occurred simultaneously in physically located places and through television and cassettes. They saw the culture on TV and joined others in replicating it in their own communities, with regional variants. As such, perceptions regarding what was authentically Black and hip hop were partly driven by forces from outside their own Black community. The speed and immediacy with which television allowed this occurrence on the eve of the Telecommunications Act of 1996 foreshadowed the increased access to cable television and the rapidity of digital technology and its spread.

In the 1980s, however, televised engagement with hip hop remained a decelerated medium of the culture. Lecrae remained halted in his mediatized consumption of it by lack of access to cable in his own household. This forced him to move out into the world, seeking out physical sites within his own community in order to continue participating in the culture. In many ways, uneven access to broadband cable assisted rap music and hip hop in retaining a certain local flavor throughout the late 1980s. Viewers were forced to tune in to local stations with limited runs of hip hop showcases or, like Lecrae, go out into their neighborhoods.

It was in that context that Black youth culture was defined over and against the later term *millennial*. For his part, without ever using the word *millennial*, Lecrae provides a refutation of its terminology in his locating youth experiences (much as do the older creatives studied here) in the social and racialized experiences of 'hood life. Descriptions of its geographies rest in two worlds for him during his time living with his grandmother in San Diego, California, in 1990:

> So Southeast San Diego was, for me, a place where two worlds collided. There was Big Momma's world of Christian compassion, church services, and short-term mission trips to Tijuana. And then there was the world of guns, gangs, girls, drugs, and adventure. Had I been forced to pick between them, I would have chosen the streets every time. (Moore 2016c, 45)

For older digital Black Christians, their experiences may not have rested at such extreme poles, but they are likely to relate to the pull of both the Black Church and the streets. It is true that by the early 1990s, the crack epidemic, gun violence, and the AIDS crisis had severely colored the experience of most Black youth in America. Despite social, economic, and geographic differences, they were joined either in these common experiences or by the racialized way these events were depicted in the media.

Both their uses and their discussions of technology were often also locally focused on these realities. This phenomenon can be seen in Lecrae tuning into *Yo! MTV Raps* to view rappers telling stories of geographies that he knew, or in the use of the term *ghetto blasters* to denote technologies routinely used in this space. Hip hop technologies folded in on the communities they served. Tricia Rose (2008) has noted the way technologies like sound systems were constructed as they were largely driven by the limited electronic tools and resources available in Black urban neighborhoods. For Black hip-hoppers in the 1980s, their music imagined futures through electro-techno beats, as in "Planet Rock." Such works reflected the national mood in technology discourse by the final decades of the twentieth century. As the millennium approached, notions of what that future entailed filled the American lexicon and imagination thanks in large part to widely popular films in the *Star Trek* series appearing throughout the 1980s, to name only one form of envisioning future technologies. Yet the lyrics of Black rappers, even as they engaged with futuristic environs through beats and melodies, remained situated in the geographies of Black neighborhoods and experiences. The music did important work in the use of new synthesized technology to perform possible Black futures, spawning later innovations in Black music and culture. Yet they were always meant to be robustly imaginative, unlike the more concrete futures Neil Howe and William Strauss attempted to predict in their work in coining the term *millennial*.

In 1987, only a year prior to Lecrae's discovery of *Yo! MTV Raps*, coauthors William Strauss and Neil Howe were in the throes of a five-year project that would culminate in the 1991 publication of *Generations: The History of America's Future, 1584 to 2069*. The authors' approach to technology, and thus the term millennial, demonstrated a hopeful and Western-centric view. According to Neil Howe, "We thought that an upbeat name would be good because of the changing way they were being raised. They would be the first to graduate high school in the year 2000, so the name millennial instantly came to mind" (Raphelson 2014). Despite the book's hopeful gaze, it was mostly informed by a racially contrived view of the present. Strauss and Howe prophesized futures informed by racial realities of the day and their own racial bias. Describing representational millennials, they offer examples of white millennials, such as the first test-tube baby and five-year-old Jessica McClure being rescued from a well, while highlighting six-year-old Black child Dooney Washington's rescue from a crack house and "George Bush's Hispanic grandchildren" (Strauss and Howe 1991, 31). Race operated in these examples as an important signifier for white fears regarding drug addiction and immigration—both of which were hotly debated and often criminalized practices in public discourse at the time. Their use of the word *millennial* became less telling of the future than revealing of the severe racial and technological inequality in America at the time.

Yet there were other problems, beyond terminology. Strauss and Howe and similar market researchers based their generational theories on the US Census record's approach to determining age groups.[8] Given that the last published census occurred in 2020, one would then count back from a person's age twenty years to arrive at how the census brackets a generation. The vast quantity of research that relies on this method often requires overlooking a myriad of differences, such as gender, geographical location, and race to arrive at a common (and frankly rather minimalist) definition of a millennial.[9]

In *Generations* (1991) and in greater detail in *The Fourth Turning* (1997), Strauss and Howe noted as a pivotal turning point in generational history the death of John F. Kennedy in 1963. The question that must be asked, however, is: "Would this view be shared among all racial groups in America?" Black respondents might reply that the death of Martin Luther King was an equally if not more significant turning point for them in the sixties. Strauss and Howe also balance their generational theory between sacred and secular polls, arguing that each generational cohort continuously bounces between "secular crisis" and "spiritual awakening" (Strauss and Howe 1991, 35). For all the reasons and many more discussed in this chapter's introduction, such crisis-centered readings often largely work to misremember or exclude Black voices and racial/religious narratives considered marginal or transgressive. Such is the case with *Generations* (1991). Moreover, Strauss and Howe have been taken to task for the lack of quantitative research used to support their "turning points." Strauss and Howe claim that a generation will be guided by its artists, heroes, prophets, or nomads. Their analysis highlights central figures that have defined prior generations such as John Winthrop, Ulysses Grant, or Ronald Reagan. The authors argue that the influence of such figures is indicative of the spirit of a particular generation. However, the glaring omission of both women and people of color in defining a generation's turning points implies that either the impact of these groups was insignificant or that their histories did not occur. Absent from these authors' timeline of turning points are events like antebellum slavery, the abolitionist movement, the suffrage movement, and the civil rights movement. This should not be surprising, however, since Strauss and Howe are exhaustive in their omissions! Though they catalog global turning points since 1584, the transatlantic slave trade—a development that linked the economies of several bourgeoning nation-states and began the largest forced migration in world history—does not receive even a mention.

In 2000 the authors returned to the task of defining millennials with "hard" quantitative data. Yet Strauss and Howe's *Millennial Rising* (2000) also came up against fierce criticism. According to Joshua Jauregui et al. (2020, 62), Strauss and Howe based their findings on

> 202 teachers and 655 students from the class of 2000 . . . all the surveys were conducted in Fairfax County, Virginia, an affluent suburban area just outside Washington, DC . . . and are potentially biased as the surveys were administered by teachers and not necessarily anonymous, and the analysis included the removal of all "not sure/don't know" answers, which comprised 45% of the responses.

Some delineation between the sort of pop sociology conducted by Strauss and Howe and more deft scholarly studies must be noted here. As early as 1928, social scientist Karl Mannheim in *The Problem of Generations* proposed an approach to generational studies that continues to guide the scholarly methods of many (including Strauss and Howe). Mindful of such theories, projects like those conducted by the Cooperative Institutional Research Program have provided longitudinal studies of incoming college freshman since 1966 (Eagan et al. 2016). Yet Strauss and Howe's term remains in wide use in news articles, other surveys, and popular culture in defining young adults. Their overly simplistic generalizations have proven more attractive and easier to digest for popular audiences.

Add to this the fact that what we know about Black millennials is often severely skewed not only by a lack of statistical data, but also by where information has been collected and interpreted. The white norming that such data undergoes is significant. This raises important questions to be answered when studying young Black adults.

First, if those responsible for naming millennials and founding a pseudo-scientific theory around such naming—one that has had tremendous influence on cultural observers and media commentators—have omitted peoples of African descent, can we trust earlier work like Strauss and Howe's as valid in the study of young Black adults? So far, national studies, which claim to inform us about the beliefs and practices of all millennials, have actually proven either to misrepresent or to depict Blacks totally inaccurately.[10] We must therefore approach with suspicion general assessments that claim to speak for all groups while focusing on the history of a single group. In the case of Black millennials, we cannot trust Strauss and Howe nor other like-minded media researchers.[11] Given the trajectory of scholarship like theirs, it is important to keep in mind that the very name "millennial" was never meant to speak to or for young Black adults. Further, we must consider the implicit and explicit bias in most present data on millennials as shaping our understanding of Black millennials in general and young Black adults' religious identity more specifically. Moreover, we must also consider that among Black millennials, there is tremendous variation. And even where studies like those conducted by the Cooperative Institutional Research Program (Eagan et al. 2016) exist, they often are not designed to document the variants of religion or racial particularities of young Black adulthood.

The Black Youth Project provides the clearest way forward toward defining youth of color. Its work remains fluid regarding who is included in this group. To date, the Pew Research Center and the Black Youth Project have gathered the largest amount of data on African American youth. The latter has taken the next step, culling statistics from the US Department of Justice, Department of Labor, and other public and private agencies to present a more complete picture of Black millennials' beliefs and practices. Much of the statistical data presented here is taken from such sources.

This wider data set shows that what is more important than actual age is the common experience of members within this group. In October 2015, Jon Rogowski and Cathy J. Cohen, through the Black Youth Project, released a study regarding the experiences and political attitudes of young Black adults. That report describes its approach to defining a Black millennial by noting that,

> Generational lines are fluid. It is not obvious, for instance, that someone born in 1981 is uniquely "millennial," while someone born in 1980 has

had an entirely different set of life experiences. Thus, we focus generally on young people without drawing strong lines in the sand between who is and is not a millennial. This broader approach is of some necessity, as existing data do not always permit comparisons across established generational lines. However, in using a wealth of data that sometimes crosses slightly different age groups, a clear picture emerges, however the generational lines are drawn. (Cohen 2015, 1)

The Black Youth Project further argues for such an approach given the lack of specific data on young African American adults. It is through their comparisons of Black millennials with data on white millennials that they are able to draw a fuller picture regarding the beliefs of Black millennials. The term *digital Black Christians*, used throughout this book, thus identifies persons of African descent with common experiences with regard to religion and digital media technology. While this mostly encompasses those in their twenties and thirties, age is not the primary determinant. Instead of being a term that is centered on a particular (then) future date, *digital Black Christian* locates the group in their common experiences with digital technology.[12]

Lecrae's perspective is a far cry from Strauss and Howe's parade of white male figures used to define a generation. From Lecrae's own words in his autobiography paired with other interviews and lyrics, we see that the birth of hip hop, or, as the following section demonstrates, the death of Tupac Shakur, were equally if not more significant turning points in the lives of digital Black Christians.

1996

"Tupac was so special to me that when he was killed, I wept while watching his funeral procession on television. It was almost like my actual father had died" (Moore 2016c, 20).

As soon as these words appear, Lecrae attempts to qualify this statement in his autobiography. In describing his sadness and feelings of loss following the death of Tupac, he quickly adds,

> For those who grew up in a rural town with both parents or in a comfortable suburban community where your biggest concern is what time

Applebee's closes, my relationship to hip-hop might sound a little far-fetched or silly. But it makes perfect sense for those who were raised in the inner city during that time. (Moore 2016c, 20)

It is important to note that the absence of Lecrae's father forms the context for his perceptions regarding Tupac. His descriptions of Tupac are constantly made in contrast to his own father. Tupac provided advice, a calming force, and became a "surrogate father" through his lyrics. In the person of Tupac, Lecrae superimposes the notion of Black fatherlessness onto all young Blacks. In the 2012 rap song "Rise," Lecrae identifies himself among "a whole generation . . . raised by gangsters / Who probably never knew pops, we had 2Pac" (Moore 2012). His uses of Tupac are evident to readers as well, as one review by Christian writer and pastor Dr. Eric Mason demonstrates. In offering praise of Lecrae's autobiography, he writes, "I recommend this book for whomever is interested in seeing how God is authoring the journey of a fatherless generation in need of the navigator" (Moore 2016c, cover endorsement). The group that Strauss and Howe call millennials when engaging with hip hop are here rendered as the "fatherless generation." This is perhaps as telling of Lecrae's reading of Black youth culture as it is revealing of the white evangelical context in which digital Black Christians' narratives are often formed.

Lecrae's autobiography, *Unashamed*, is published through B&H Publishing Group, an imprint of Lifeway Christian Resources, the publishing division of the Southern Baptist Convention. The Convention is the world's largest Protestant denomination in the United States. Lecrae's autobiography was written with Jonathan Merritt, bestselling Christian author and son of past Convention president James Merritt. Lecrae surmises that the mostly white Convention audience may not relate to a fatherly description of Tupac. Yet he notes that such a perception of Tupac within urban communities was common at the time of his death. Lecrae is then writing both with and for white evangelicals. Without naming race, he implies racial differences by geography (rural/suburban, city) and affluence (leisure time/eating out) in determining one's view of an important historical moment.

Upon first reading, it would seem that Lecrae shies away from discussions of race, even as his experiences and the historical moments he emphasizes are highly contextualized by race. Yet there is something much more complex at work here. In the first fifty pages of his autobiography, mostly covering his life until his high school graduation, Lecrae uses the term Black as a racial identifier only twice. However, in the middle portion of the book, chronicling his later years in high school and college, in comparison to or in engaging with his white counterparts, the term *Black* suddenly appears quite frequently. Perhaps the words of Zora Neale Hurston (1928) apply to Lecrae's racial identity-making in *Unashamed*. "I feel most colored," she wrote, "when I am thrown against a sharp white background."[13]

Yet, as he discusses his experience of being fourteen at the time of Tupac's death, Blackness is present, though unspoken, for Lecrae in the context of the inner city, hip hop discussions of gangs, guns, drugs, and fatherlessness.[14] The implications of this sharply centers death—and, more particularly, mediatized forms of Black death—as an essential characteristic of young Black life. Death lurks in the shadows of his narrative from the beginning. The death of Tupac exposes its dark presence for those, Lecrae writes, "who were raised in the inner city during that time" (Moore 2016c, 20). Even in his attempted suicide as a teenager, he writes "I screamed in pure Tupac fashion: 'It's me against the world. I hate this life! I'm out!'" (Moore 2016c, 57).

Death surrounded his existence long before that moment, however. Lecrae discusses the violence caused to Black bodies by others and his own hands. The criminalized depictions of Black youth he witnessed on television and film were also influential for Lecrae. Two of his favorite movies, starring either hip hop artists or featuring hip hop soundtracks, are known for their grim portrayals of death and violence: *Boyz n the Hood* and *Menace II Society*. Lecrae foreshadows his later attempts at ending his own life in saying, "the implicit message from the [American] culture to kids like me was that the world wasn't made for me" (Moore 2016c, 21). Indeed, print and news media outlets by 1996 were responsible for reporting much more than the aftermath of Tupac's demise. As a precursor to the death of both Tupac Shakur and Christopher "Biggie" Smalls, news outlets instigated what later became known as the East Coast/West Coast hip hop beef.

For his part, Tupac centered much of his lyrics and discourse around death and dying. He greeted his twenty-first birthday with a mix of surprise and sadness. He shared his fears of an untimely death with numerous friends. In Lecrae's mind, Tupac as a figure who captured the ethos of young Black culture reveals the role of television first in exposing Lecrae to hip hop, and again in confirming the certainty of Black death.

The rise of digital technologies in the mid- to late 1990s, which personalized and commodified Black musical experience through CDs and widened access to cable television, further globalized hip hop and offered digital Black Christians, like Lecrae and those born in the first few years of the 1980s, a chance to capitalize on their knowledge of hip hop as physically present practitioners of its craft and skilled users of new technologies. A range of new digital media devices and software, like beat machines, Final Cut Pro, and Garage Band, gave older digital Black Christians the resources to impose new visions onto their world. Daniel Steele, producer for the popular Christian record label Humble Beast and some of Christian and non-Christian music's biggest stars, at thirty-five summed it up by describing himself as a millennial who "got the best of two worlds. I was there for analog, but I also use computers and am very into the digital. I feel like we're the guys that will take over the world." At thirty-nine, Propaganda, a rapper from the West Coast, tells me he still considers himself a millennial, though "I'm like an [older] OS [operating system] version," he says.

Like Lecrae, these older digital Black Christians see themselves as straddling technological time periods and have used this positionality to *re-mediatize* mediatized forms of Black culture.[15] Through their innovative use of digital tools, older digital Black Christians were imposing new visions on the world through their music. In discussing what a millennial is, they are saying something regarding their ability to see the necessity of translating, through embodied practices like beat making, one technological process (analog) into another (digital). As the attuned reader might suspect, I am here referring to Michel Foucault's (1988) notion of "technologies of self." While he identifies four major types of technology (production, sign systems, power, and self), he contends that these often function in relation to one another. Technologies of self allow the individual alone, or in conjunction with others, to affect their environs by transforming "their own bodies, souls, thought, or way of being in order" (4) to achieve happiness or wholeness. Not coincidently, Foucault locates historical examples of this transformation in the fourth- and fifth-century Christian spirituality of the Roman Empire. Digital Black Christians like Lecrae, Propaganda, and Steele tapped into this tradition by speaking about Black death and by resisting its certainty through their Christian practices. Yet, beyond Foucault's focus on Western practices, hip hop's African diasporic traditions map Blackness onto Christianity in their expression of technology of the self, as in Lecrae channeling Will Smith in attempting to transform his own life. The "ohm bop," which Amiri Baraka describes in the Africa-inspired Black American music of the spirituals and blues, coalesce once again in the art-making of Christian hip hop (L. Jones 1963).

Because of the trans-historical nature of media development, something must be said regarding how these multiple forms of media shifted context and meaning even as digital Blacks drew from its wealth of signs and symbols in constructing their own meaning through digital media technology. From earlier forms of broadcast like radio and television, each medium further sped up the processes by which audiences received information and offered greater options for interacting with its medium. Digital technology (e.g., software, digital images, digital video, video game, web pages, websites, and social media) altered the process by which audiences interacted with electronic media.

As a point of context, digital technology rapidly breaks down a string of binary codes in order to send information between devices, a process once achieved through electronic pulses (imagine a light bulb switching on and off). Like any technological innovation, then, digital technology follows a pattern. It makes use of older innovations in forming a more rapid, layered process for task completion. Data scholar Meredith Broussard (2018) demonstrates this process by cataloging the complex network of codes required to create a space between text when one simply hits the space bar. Beneath that single command is a structured process of information retrieval. Digital Black Christians who appeared in a pre-digital (analog) technology chain were able to go behind the curtain (or spacebar), so to speak, in order to digitize practices learned through their simultaneous investment in television and in physically located forms of hip hop. Rose's urban Black youth who used electronics to impose their sound on the world through the bodacious Black noise that filled their neighborhoods performed an earlier technology of the self. Through digital technologies like satellite TV, personal computers, and digital streaming, the hyper-focus on certain aspects of Black culture, like the struggles and death of Tupac, was globally consumed. While the world listened on, in the early millennium digital Black Christians used skills in digital art-making and social media to craft their own response. In this way, globalized narratives of Black death and Black fatherlessness proliferated even as digital Black Christians mined the past of Black media in constructing a bricolage of responses to such narratives.

Lyrical examples of re-mediatized responses to death and Black fatherlessness include digital Black Christians' copious references to 1990s sitcoms like *The Fresh Prince of Bel-Air* and the 1996 film premiere of *The Lion King* (examples are found in the songs "Fresh Prince" by Derek Minor, "The Lion King" by KB, featuring Natalie Lauren Sims, and "Sideways" by KB featuring Lecrae). This TV show and film have both been used by artists to represent Christian-centric readings of Africa, slavery, Black business ownership, and Black fatherlessness. In his ethnographic work *Performing Identity/Performing Culture,* Greg Dimitriadis (2009) notes that 1990s films like *Panther, Juice,* and *Boyz n the Hood* have been used similarly by young Black hip hop aficionados to create a relatable world of meaning. In describing his own feelings of abandonment, Lecrae discusses the significance of *The Fresh Prince* episode in which the character of Will Smith is abandoned by his father, played by Ben Vereen. He also, in trying to make life improvements, asks himself what characters like Will Smith or Theo of *The Cosby Show* would do.

In *The Lion King*, this theme of Black fatherlessness is followed through in the loss of Mufasa, played by James Earl Jones (who also plays an iconic role as the voice of Darth Vader, father of Luke Skywalker). Here, the father's death sends the son Simba on a quest for self. Young Simba's singing voice is played by Black actor Jason Weaver. Two years earlier, Weaver also played an adolescent Michael Jackson in the ABC mini-series *The Jacksons: An American Dream* (1992). Cast in the role of Simba's mother Sarabi is Jamaican actress Madge Sinclair. For digital Black Christians, *The Lion King* symbolized both the beauty and trauma of Black families. On a metalevel, the voicing of *The Lion King* provides a sound narrative to Black fatherlessness (Mufasa) and single Black motherhood (Sarabi). The racialized versions of Mufasa, Sarabi, and Simba further spoke to young viewers given the story's setting in Africa. The film moved digital Black Christians forward and backward in time, connecting them in mediated forms of Black cultural expression. It was some of these same voices that digital Black Christians and their parents remembered from earlier films like *Coming to America* (1988) in which Madge Sinclair (Queen Aoleon) and James Earl Jones (King Jaffe Joffer) play Eddie Murphy's (Prince Akeem) parents. The roles of Sinclair and Jones in the *Roots* miniseries in 1979 had already firmly entrenched them in African and African American cultural history.[16]

The simulacrum of earlier televised versions of Blackness in the millennium are central features of young Black digital expression. In the writing of Jean Baudrillard (1994b), the simulacrum appears as successive riffs on an earlier reality, until the original meaning is lost or exposed as nonexistent to begin with. However, simulacrum performs quite differently among digital Black Christians.[17] One example stretching from 1976 to the present evinces this. In 1976 Norman Lear's hit TV show *Good Times* featured one of its most emotional and highly viewed episodes. The father, James Evans, dies while away from his family in Mississippi. The mother, Florida Evans, breaks down at the episode's end, shouting, "Damn. Damn. Damn." This scene is revived in the 1990s sitcom *Martin*. Martin Lawrence, costumed as Mother Payne, provides a widely felt comedic moment. Hearing that her beloved pet bird has passed, she shouts the same lament: "Damn. Damn. Damn." Lawrence's performance plays to the raucous laughter of a mostly Black audience. Far from its original emotionally charged depiction of the loss of a Black father (the first ever televised instance of such a loss) today the expression lives on in the simulacra of memes.

The two panels of the meme move from the more specific instance of a Black father's death to a simple visual along with the caption "Damn. Damn. Damn." By the end of this chain of communication, the digital observer only sees or hears the expression in its comedic form. And yet it reads death back on to Black cultural expression in a subversively digital way. Baudrillard (1994a) writes that the present fact of the simulacrum disposes its original truth, exposing that the original was untrue from its beginning. Indeed, Evans's tears and pronouncement is in fact staged, a mediatized portrayal of Black loss and fatherlessness. However, through their own art-making, digital Black Christians are able to create simulacra that draw a line from the present to the past, infusing the mediatized Black past with meaning for contemporary Black Christians.

Digital Black Christians' reinscription of ideas and actions with meaning points to a particular orientation toward mid-1990s electronic technology in music videos and televised shows. In the rap song "Sidelines," Lecrae enshrines the meaning of TV shows like *Martin* for digital Black Christians. Through sound production, the track mimics the static-filled sound of television behind Lecrae's lyrical references to the show's characters Martin, Gina, and Bruh Man "from the fifth floor" in an attempt to riff on an even earlier history of Martin Luther King and affirm the divine selection and hard work of Lecrae and counter the jealous critics on the sidelines (Moore 2016b). Martin Luther King and Martin Lawrence thus act in a highly mediatized chain of Black historical narratives to affirm Lecrae's own Christian beliefs and practices. The track opens with a brief sample of James Brown's "Introduction to Star Time." Lecrae, in signifying on James Brown's earlier work, symbolically reminds haters of his star status and entreats them, as Brown's introduction would also, to "Let the brother rap." Lecrae's subversive speech act here parallels other digital "hush harbors"—digitally created Black discourse, in a reference to earlier furtive Black meeting places, as digital technology scholar André Brock (2012) has written about regarding Twitter and homiletician Melva Sampson (2020) has regarding Black preaching women.

However, there was considerable gender variance in how digital Black experiences were lived and understood during the mid-1990s and thereafter. Lecrae's view of the death of Tupac, the TV show *Fresh Prince*, and other, mostly male-driven narratives in hip hop films of the 1990s that were important in defining a generation, demonstrate a primarily masculine view of young Black hip hop culture, though a number of female emcees came of age just after Lecrae. While many Black males may have felt that they lost a father in 1996 with the death of Tupac, female digital Black Christians like Jackie Hill-Perry felt they had gained a sister two years later in Lauryn Hill.

Tupac, taken along with shows and movies like *The Fresh Prince of Bel-Air*, *The Lion King*, and *Martin*, embodied for many young Black males like Lecrae their own experiences of Black death and Black fatherlessness. Media's hyper-focus on these themes required a response by those on the frontlines. Advances and accessibility in digital technology in the first decade of the millennium allowed the crafting of such a response from young Black male emcees and a rising cadre of female artists as well.

2012

> See, we ain't never know Martin Luther the King
> Most of us probably couldn't tell you much about a dream
> We like Malcolm X, cause Spike made the movie
> And we saw him strapped up with the AKs and Uzis.
> —Lecrae Moore (2012)

In more recent albums and interviews, Lecrae revealed the influence of the Black Panthers and figures like Malcolm X on his early upbringing. As late as 2012, though, Lecrae's discourse on social justice and/or Black figures, as from his first album in 2006 onward, spoke only of Martin Luther King, a passing homage to Trayvon Martin in lyrics, and vague references to Frederick Douglass in interviews and social media posts.[18] Much like other iconic Black figures and movements discussed here, King's image and legacy has been the subject of a number of media reconfigurations. To the many white evangelicals who filled Lecrae's audiences at youth conferences and through organizations like the Southern Baptist Convention, King was often regarded as a Christian conservative do-gooder. In their imaginations, King offered little threat to their institutions given his death and Christian-inspired advocation of nonviolence; these factors enabled them to craft his legacy strategically. Lecrae's appropriation of King's message in lyrics and other interviews around "bridging the racial divide" provided white Christians with a welcomed and safe way of engaging with Christian hip hop. This is not to say that his audiences were totally white. In fact, Lecrae's early success was due in part to his appeal among young Black males in the Dallas Detention Center where he volunteered, through summer youth programs like Kids Across America, which offered his CDs to several hundred mostly urban Black youth in 2003, as well as at predominantly Black conferences like the Legacy Conference in Chicago and Impact in Atlanta.

Yet most of the programs and conferences mentioned were backed in large part by white Christian groups and remained, at their core, deeply conservative. When Lecrae debuted his first album *Real Talk* in 2004, he along with a growing cadre of other Black Christian artists like Canton Jones, Flame, and Propaganda were largely playing for audiences that consisted of avid young Black male fans. But, like funk, like soul, like rock 'n' roll before it, Christian hip hop's later acceptance in contemporary Christian music circles pushed the genre into white evangelical spaces. Lecrae soon began to espouse their message of Christian unity over racism. White evangelicals were experiencing a time of rapid change, as well. The same internet that exposed young white Christians to the music of Lecrae would be instrumental in galvanizing them around podcasts and online Christian teachers of Reformed theology. Reformed theology derived from earlier Calvinist thinking. Its adherents have described themselves as reformers of evangelicalism. For this reason, Lecrae's embrace of evangelicalism was not initially considered on par with the white Christianity of evangelicals like segregationist Jerry Falwell. Reformed theology, which swept through many once Baptist, once Methodist, or once other mid-century mainline Christian denominations, promised a new take on Christianity that moved against past the "isms" of traditional white evangelicalism. The Christian sect, too, was becoming trendier, urban, and "ethnic" as it embraced digital Black Christians like Lecrae through hip hop.

Later, however, Lecrae came to see that white audiences did not fully embrace his racial identity. Yet young Black Christian rappers found a home in such spaces initially because white churches were often more welcoming of rap music than Black churches. In fact, Black churches never fully embraced Lecrae, or Christian hip hop. This was partly because Black churches lacked the resources to support Christian artists in the same way white evangelical groups often could. In an interview, one prominent Black Christian DJ told me that even though many Black hip hop artists, himself included, want to serve predominantly Black churches, the reality is that white evangelicals "pay better over there." Not only were Black churches often unable to sustain the growth of Black youth culture through hip hop, but its politics of respectability created barriers to embarking on such a mission. Throughout the 1980s and 1990s, many Black churches often intentionally sought to distance themselves from hip hop in general due to the perceived harm perpetrated by its lyrics and its association with criminal Black youth culture.

Nationally, high-profile white conservative groups like Focus on the Family, the conservative-backed Parents Music Resource Center—the advocacy group responsible for the parental-advisory "Tipper sticker" (for Tipper Gore) on rock and rap albums—and Black Church figures such as Calvin Butts and Congresswoman C. Delores Tucker decried the ills of gangsta rap (on the heels of rock music) throughout the late 1980s and 1990s.[19] Lecrae's music, given its aggressive style—sans profanity and social commentary—offered an alternative. Couple this with the fact that when Lecrae did engage with the wider hip hop culture and the historical Black voices and movements abhorred in white evangelical circles, like Malcolm X and the Black Panthers, his lyrics were often focused on missionary efforts, and it becomes clear why Lecrae became one of Christian hip hop's most popular rappers by the first decade of the millennium.

Lecrae's first mention of Malcolm X appeared in his 2012 rap song titled "Rise." There, Lecrae describes the sentiments of "gangbangers" and "young dudes" who view Martin Luther King as absent from contemporary Black life—while finding consolation in the real presence of televised portrayals of other Black men: Malcolm X, Tupac, and Snoop Dogg. In contrasting Malcolm X and King, Lecrae demonstrates the impact of white Christian teachings on his own theology (Moore 2012). An analysis of Lecrae's interviews, autobiography, and lyrics reveals a marked polarity in his racial-religious identity during this period. Lecrae's story demonstrates the struggle of several digital Black Christians to reconcile their Blackness and Christianity. For Lecrae, to be a Christian required an allegiance to conservative Christianity and its portrayals of leaders like King and a distancing of himself from Blackness as identified in the message of Black nationalist and Black hip hop voices.

Beginning in 2012, however, Lecrae's views on race shifted. This new turn came, in part through his reading in the early 2000s of works by well-known evangelicals Andy Crouch, Charles Colson, and Nancy Pearcey. Charles Colson first received notoriety as one of the Watergate Seven. He was subsequently imprisoned for his role in the Watergate scandal. Following his seven-month incarceration, Colson was reborn as a Christian evangelical. Throughout the rest of his life he remained at the forefront of some of the major fights for Christian conservatism in America, alongside James Dobson, Jerry Falwell, and others. Christian apologist Nancy Pearcey has tackled issues ranging from homosexuality to bioethics. Pearcey gained notoriety beyond evangelical circles as one of the contributors to the intelligent-design school textbook *Of Pandas and People*, which became the center of controversy in the 2004 *Kitzmiller v. Dover Area School District* case. Both Colson and Pearcey's work posit a biblical worldview that fully engages with diverse cultures beyond Christianity.

While these thinkers moved Lecrae to embrace an audience beyond his mostly Christian fan base, given their white evangelical leanings it offered him little context for the development of a *Black* biblical worldview. It was media technology, once again, that facilitated Lecrae's engagement with Black death—for example, in the 2012 shooting death of Trayvon Martin. The Dade County police and, subsequently, news outlets reporting on Martin's gang affiliation and drug use used well-worn tropes of Black criminality to suggest Martin's culpability in his own demise. The acquittal of George Zimmerman the following year triggered the hashtag and movement Black Lives Matter. Lecrae, like several other young Black people, deeply felt the loss of Trayvon Martin and greatly sympathized with the Black Lives Matter movement. The significance of that time period for digital Blacks is recounted in their Twitter posts.[20] Jamaica West (@jamaicawest312) expressed her views in a retweet from @loveelizabethmae on July 30, 2018: "Trayvon Martin sparked a fire in my generation. His passing made us actually understand what history always told us. He will always be remembered. RIH baby boy."

Other than earlier childhood references to his grandmother, none of Lecrae's public writings, interviews, or lyrics seem to suggest that his Christian development prior to 2012 was solidly based in the Black community. While he was exposed to the writings and work of Black Panthers like Eldridge Cleaver and Angela Davis early in life, Lecrae said that "when I became a believer, I guess I was taught whether consciously or subconsciously to lay all that aside for Jesus" (*Truth's Table* 2019). This, coupled with his affirmation of mostly white conservative Christian ideals regarding racial unity, led many white evangelical supporters to believe that his views more fully aligned with their own. As such, white supporters placed considerable pressure on him to remain in solidarity with other white evangelicals calling for a disavowal of Black Lives Matter or at least insisting that "all lives matter" (*Truth's Table* 2019).²¹ In more recent interviews, Lecrae has revealed that this public perception of him was far from his personal reality. His publicly crafted persona suggested that he was an evangelical mascot, as described by Christena Cleveland in the *Washington Post* (Boorstein 2016). This shocked Lecrae.

> Wow, is that really how I'm perceived? When I saw that [Cleveland's article], it really made me do some internal soul searching and say, "Wow, I didn't realize that was the perception." I had to ask friends. I was in the dark. By placating people so often in certain circles, you're viewed as an advocate. If you hang out at the biker club so many times, people will say, "He's a biker." (Hanbury 2017)

Indeed, he moved in much more diverse circles racially, religiously, and economically than he was perceived as doing. In noting this complexity regarding his identity, we see how media-crafted images, like the *Washington Post* article, can create powerful but inaccurate narratives about a person's identity. Lecrae's attempts since 2016 to rebrand himself points to a technology of self that was endemic throughout his artistic development. In discussing the full discography of Lecrae on his popular Christian hip hop show, DJ Wade-O remarked that each album since his first in 2006 has offered a different sound both in terms of beats, lyrics, and Lecrae's own voice (*Trackstarz* 2017). The rapper's most recent incarnation appeared months before the release of his new album. Record labels' market-driven strategies to create intriguing stories around artists and newly released albums, in order to drive sales, are at least in part responsible for such image makeovers. Lecrae's very real spiritual transformation made for interesting and timely headlines throughout 2016, just ahead of the release of his album *Anomaly* and again in 2017 prior to and during the promotion of *All Things Work Together*. Even if partly manufactured, this performance of self via social media allowed Lecrae to quickly transform himself and his image around a new notion of young Black Christianity engaging with death, depression, and social justice.

Lecrae's shift in public discourse regarding white Christianity is evident in two talks given at Yale University, two years apart. The first appearance happened on April 28, 2016. Lecrae's message on hip hop's capacity to bridge the racial divide lies mainly in an examination of historical forms of systematic racism. His closing poem regarding attempts at social reform by the Crips (the African American street gang) and the federal government's intentional strategy of criminalizing and incarcerating young Black people offered a poignant commentary on white American racism. It revealed a Lecrae who had not yet been fully realized on any of his previous albums. Yet even here, his speech did not implicate white Christianity, nor did it support any form of protest. Like Grandmaster Flash and the Furious Five's rap song "The Message" from which he quoted, it simply narrated a historical problem and, in the Kingian mode, sought racial reconciliation through hip hop.

Two years later, in September of 2018 Lecrae was back in New Haven for a publicly posted Yale University Town Hall meeting. This time, Lecrae described the sort of identity bifurcation in his public Christian life and private racial experiences in the context of mental health, confessing that "in front of the world I was this level-headed, god-fearing man. I'm navigating everything just the way that I should. But behind the scenes I'm a ticking time bomb ignoring all of the trauma, ignoring all of the weight of these experiences, and this depression that is knocking at my front door" (YaleUniversity 2018). Through a performance of Christian transformation, Lecrae is reborn as a new, "more woke" version of himself. Beautiful in its duality, his identity is both authentic and performed. He describes how the weight of his experiences (witnessing death, molestation, a suicide attempt, etc.) found little room for articulation in the white context of his faith. The final trigger for Lecrae was the reality of Black death discussed in the work of many digital Black Christians and Lecrae's own decision to tackle it head on through self-transformation. Like hip hop, like Tupac's death, Lecrae's recounting of this moment is mediated by media technology and acted upon through media technology:

> During this time I remember watching a video of a young man probably about 15 years old in Chicago and he's waving a gun around . . . And I remember something being triggered [in me]. It moved me almost to tears. I learned about the facts of the murder rate in Chicago and I found myself sitting there emotionally, just devastated, and I couldn't understand why. Well, truthfully, I had a friend who was taken by gun violence at [the] age of

13 years old and that trauma was triggered. I didn't even realize it. I was the victim of witnessing the death of a teenager. And then I'm seeing this other teenager just flaunting and I didn't even connect those dots until later that year, I remember hearing about the death of Trayvon Martin. Now I was affected. (YaleUniversity 2018)

The death of Trayvon Martin triggered in him thoughts of other mediatized instances of young Black death, as well as physically located experiences with Black death in Lecrae's life. Yet initially Lecrae felt unsure of how to respond. The context of his faith left him ill-equipped to formulate a response. His uncertainty was also in some ways indicative of his racial age group's technological literacy. To be an older digital Black Christian like Lecrae means straddling a decade where Black death was reported on but much more rarely documented in real time by Black hands. Unlike earlier instances of violence against Blacks, like the Rodney King beating or the shooting deaths of Blacks like Tupac, hand-held recording devices and social media platforms offered ways to document and/or quickly respond to injustice. Like Tupac in the previous decade, the death of Trayvon Martin confirmed for many digital Black Christians not only the certainty of Black death, but also their ability to protest its root causes through media technology.

Figure 1.1. Lecrae, Twitter post.

For Lecrae, engaging with digital technology for social justice was directly informed by his faith. Being Christian online meant owning his Blackness in its multifarious manifestations and shedding many of his allegiances to white Christianity. This began in June of 2016 with a series of posts protesting the shooting death of Philando Castile, challenging #AllLivesMatter, and sharing images of Black sharecroppers.

Following his outspoken stance against racial injustice and the social commentary he added to his song lyrics, he saw a dip in invitations from respected white evangelicals, many of whom disavowed his work outright. In an interview on the *Truth's Table* (2019) podcast, Lecrae notes that whereas prior to his shift his audiences typically numbered three thousand, in some instances they now barely numbered three hundred. But Lecrae persisted. He continued tackling racial injustice on his albums and through social media and speaking engagements. The response to his stance, along with the death of his close friend DJ Official and earlier traumas like molestation, led to a severe depression as well as a reassessment of his connection to white evangelicalism.

Many viewed his subsequent album, *All Things Work Together* (*ATWT*), as unsuccessful, attributing its poor album sales to his political views (Sarachik 2017b). Natalie Lauren Sims, who once rapped under the stage name Suzy Rock, produced much of the *ATWT* album. In an interview with the *Trackstarz* website posted to YouTube on October 11, 2018, Sims said "it was hard" hearing criticism of the project because former fans focused on Lecrae's Twitter comments and not the actual project in expressing their dislike of the album (*Trackstarz* 2018). Judging the success or failure of *ATWT* reveals a few important realities for Lecrae and digital Black Christians like him. Racial play in digital spaces greatly influences religious and economic opportunities for digital Black Christians. Former white fans made no qualms about posting their decision not to support *ATWT* in response to Lecrae's politicized message. According to Sims, the dip in album sales from *Anomaly* to *ATWT* was likely attributable to both its poor marketing and the backlash of white Christian leaders and youth. Combined with this, however, was the fact that technology had also changed. The Neilson Soundscan system of judging album sales by fourteen thousand retail store points of purchase and radio played has changed with the rise in digital streaming and album releases through video sharing sites like YouTube. CD purchases overall have also declined (by 84 percent in 2017) as streaming use has climbed. Fellow rapper and Lecrae's friend Beleaf Melanin, who has appeared on a number of Reach Records' tracks and Lecrae's own songs, tweeted his support for Lecrae. Lecrae's response to his friend regarding the album being a "true success in so many ways" suggests a few measures of achievement (Sarachik 2017b).

While Lecrae made a name for himself in Christian circles, *ATWT*, and particularly his gold-selling track with Tori Kelly, pushed his work into larger markets and was the first album successively produced with the backing of the much larger label Columbia Records. Earlier in 2017, Family Christian bookstores, a major distributor for Christian authors and artists like Lecrae, closed all 240 of its stores. That *ATWT* did well despite this is a sign of the changing context for music distribution as well as Lecrae's ability to pivot successfully in such a Christian market climate. As he would later say, it also allowed him to "own his own narrative" (YaleUniversity 2018). His performance of self-revelation and indignation in lyrics and interviews has become a recurring part of his public talks and interviews. Yet his latest narrative has kept his audience engaged. While losing some fans, his raised digital profile opened him to wider audiences and suggested to other creatives a new blueprint for social justice-inspired promotion.[22] Clearly, Lecrae was becoming himself. In his interview with DJ Wade-O, he commented that "it feels good to finally be free" (Wade-O 2017). By this he meant that he was finally finding a way to be authentically Black *and* Christian, something that is also at the heart of racial identity work for other digital Black Christians.

More than of Lecrae's previous albums, *ATWT* represented the Black spiritual tradition. Lecrae sums this up by describing the sentiments of his friend, Tyree Boyd-Pates: "[On earlier albums] You have said some things that were poignant and provocative for Black people, but the phenotype of your music was not Black . . . sonically it wasn't resonating with our soul . . . It's like [the] 'I have a dream' speech over a rock record" (*Truth's Table* 2019). In *ATWT*, Lecrae moved deeply into Black culture and Black issues both to celebrate his racial identity and to serve notice to white evangelicalism that he would no longer be its "mascot."[23] Much like Joseph Solomon and Jamaica West's 2016 poem "I'm So Black

Christian," from this point forward Lecrae located his identity in Black cultural practices while challenging white representations of Jesus.

Conclusion: Intimacy through Identifying with a Community

Heidi Campbell (2010) outlines three major approaches to the study of digital religion: mediatization, mediation of religion, and the religious social shaping of technology. This techno-ethno-biography of Lecrae demonstrates a hybrid of at least two of these approaches. His experiences with both hip hop and religion were greatly mediated by media technology. Yet the medium, through a process of mediatization, itself came to inform the broader religious understanding of death. Through this dialogue on death, media acted as both conduit and conductor, locating a narrative of Black suffering readily identifiable for young Black Christians, while simultaneously informing their notion of the same. While the Black Church and its traditions hung in the backdrop of this narrative, an exploration of Lecrae's interviews, biography, lyrics, and social media postings reveals that through an evolving process, Lecrae accessed a broader network of actors and actions in forming his "Black Church." This loosely constructed community includes the creatives explored in the next chapters. They mirror Lecrae's patterns of intimacy-seeking. Like those engaged in the spirituals and blues traditions before them, digital Black Christians derive intimacy with one another through authentic and relatable communal meditations on Black suffering. Older digital Black Christians like Lecrae have led the way in telling a unique story of Black death and life in the digital age and in moving away from traditional Black churches, into more racially and religiously diverse spaces and alliances. Like Lecrae, they too accessed media in order to formulate religious meaning. Through Lecrae's music, postings, and physical friendship, many of them located their own stories and communicated the same to other young Black adults, thus widening their community. Mediatization allowed the closeness digital Black Christians needed in order to form intimate connections with one another, and to develop feelings of closeness to media itself. As we shall see in the following chapters, to be known through and by media has further unsettled the Black Church in the lives of digital Black Christians.

2

Race

The Story of Propaganda and Joseph

Of all things, a cat!
See, I hate cats!"
—Propaganda, "I Hate Cats," *Crooked*, 2017

"Know Where That Logo Came From?"

Joseph Solomon has just finished wrapping up his workshop on house churches and is fielding questions from a steady stream of attendees wanting to speak to him. He asks a young lady whether she knows where the logo on the t-shirt she is wearing comes from. She pauses, as if balancing two possible responses in her mind. She hesitantly shakes her head. Her knowledge of the logo's origins is only partial. She knows that it is from a song on Propaganda's latest album. But she assumes Solomon knows more than the average Prop fan at this year's Legacy Conference, an annual conference on urban ministry attended and led mostly by digital Black Christians.

Joseph encountered Propaganda's music long before he met the rapper. It was back in 2012 that he first heard, "I Ain't Got an Answer." "Ohhhh . . ." As he noted in a 2012 Instagram post, Solomon thought to himself, "soooo . . . I'm not the only one." He stayed up listening to Propaganda's album all night. By the time the two began touring together for the 2017 *Crooked* Tour, Solomon had come into his own as an artist. He did "poems, sang breakup songs, worshipped, and sang hymns with an audience enjoying craft beer and whiskey" (Solomon 2012). He says it was on that tour that he found hope, which he did not have before. Joseph no longer needed to find a "lane" to occupy as a Christian: he was crafting his own. His friend Propaganda enabled Solomon's move toward a Christian identity that did not fit into any one church's notion of acceptable Christian practices, or any one notion of them at all.

Several months later at the Legacy Conference, it is apparent that he is still very much affected by his time with Propaganda as he tells the young woman about the tour stop that inspired the t-shirt she is now wearing. It was Shay Scranton, a thirty-something punk metal musician and graphic designer for the Common Grounds Café in Waco, Texas, who created the image of a cat poised next to a lion, symbolic of Propaganda's track on the *Crooked* album titled "I Hate Cats" (see Figure 2.1). The performance piece describes Propaganda's actual dislike of cats and more importantly, racism. Propaganda says in the piece,

> Cats are related to lions
> You share taxonomy with tigers—tigers!
> Why are you so cupcake?
> Why does my daughter wanna bring you home?
> Of all things, a cat!
> See, I hate cats! (Propaganda 2017)

Upon seeing the image, Propaganda was immediately enthralled and asked the owner if he could take it home. Several t-shirt screens and merch tables later, it was one of the many fashionable tees, hoodies, and other Christian artifacts that attendees were wearing at the 2018 Legacy Conference in Chicago, Illinois, and at several similar conferences and performances. Propaganda and Joseph Solomon have created very different strategies for both dealing with and talking about race, strategies informed by their engagement with hip hop and digital technology. Like Lecrae, recent incidents of police brutality, high profile cases of racism, and personal experiences elicited their responses via their artistic work and social media.

Both of their stories tell of the unholy alliance between conservative white evangelicals and digital Black Christians and the quest for online intimacy in the digital age. Both digital Black Christians and white Reformed thinkers were looking for a place of belonging and found it through digital and other remote forms of discipleship. Both in interviews I conducted and in analysis of several online postings by and about the creatives under study, discussions on discipleship move past

Figure 2.1. Performance poster for Propaganda. A cat and a tiger. Designed by Shay Scranton. (Courtesy of Shay Scranton)

a simple decision to affiliate as a member of the faith or a particular church to a core concern with *relationships*.

Discipleship is a time of intense learning and cultivating the religious truths necessary for one's own spiritual development and ultimately for drawing others to the faith. Discipleship among creatives develops deeply spiritual bonds akin to those between parents and children or between siblings. Artists often talk about being brothers and sisters in Christ, or of having spiritual parents who discipled them. Such relationships are usually split along gender lines, creatives seeking and being most inspired by teachers, leaders, and peers of their own gender. The Christian archetype for discipleship is located in the relationship Jesus establishes with his twelve disciples. His command to "make disciples of all nations" ends with the promise of his eternal intimacy with his followers: "Lo, I am with you always, even unto the end of the world" (Matt 28: 20, KJV). Creatives act upon this assurance, believing that the real presence of Christ exists in the multiple physical and digital sites they use in seeking discipleship and in making disciples. For Solomon, this has occurred through multiple instances in his late teens and early adulthood through both physically and digitally located interactions. Thus, for him, discipleship occurred through the sermons of his childhood pastor Nathan Holcomb and through his youth pastor, but also, during his early twenties, through the online sermons of white Reformed thinkers, and more recently through the music of Propaganda and through spending time with him on tour.

In response first to Jesus's and then the Legacy Conference's command to "make disciples," Solomon has impacted countless other digital Black Christians who log on to his YouTube channel for spiritual wisdom and guidance on Christian living. It is not uncommon for physical instances of discipleship to multiply into online forms of discipleship. For Lecrae, discipleship took the form of countless hours spent with seminary friends (including later popular rapper Ambassador), hours in which they hashed out their positions on topics covered in courses at Dallas Theological Seminary.[1] Lecrae later said, "They were investing their expensive education into me. And so, I felt like I got a seminary education just by being discipled by these guys" (DeWitt 2013). In turn, now YouTube comments on Lecrae's rap videos routinely consist of fans who describe being "discipled through [his] music." Each creative offers a story of informal training in Christian living through times of intense intimate relationship-building with other mature Christians. Access to online technology early in the millennium led to increased engagement with a network of Christians beyond creatives' local communities.

Such forms of *digital discipleship* extended to white Reformed thinkers. For while connections to white Christianity existed before the existence of social media, through such avenues as white-led seminaries like the Dallas Theological Seminary, the Reformed Theological Seminary, and the Southern Baptist Seminary, as well as through the proliferation of podcasts, websites, and online opportunities for immediately connecting to white Reformed thinkers, creatives had unfettered access to white Reformed evangelicals.[2]

Beyond its community of believers, evangelicalism, both as a set of theological beliefs and as a community of shared cultural practices, is at best described as the religious arm of the conservative party. At worst, its appellation is frequently used in media reports as a catch-all to describe Christians of all shades who take a literal view of the scriptures. Many long-time critics of white evangelicals have welcomed the current "reckoning" in white evangelical circles due to scandals and wider movements' influence on religious circles. However, young white adults and some African Americans in preceding generations have chosen to affiliate with this tradition, both as religious participants and as leaders. It's essential to examine why some digital Black Christians gravitated to such circles, despite widespread cultural criticism of its ideologies as being antithetical to Blackness and/or as overtly racist.

During the late nineteenth- and early twentieth-century expansion of liberal Protestantism, many believers viewed innovations like radio and then, later, televisions as the source of the moral and social decay of their period. Yet not all Christians felt this way about new media technology. In fact, white evangelicals and African Americans Christians alike saw an opportunity for the amplification of their message through these mediums. For their part, white evangelicals understood the utility of radio and then television for reaching the masses, many of whom did not identify with the higher-brow Christianity of liberal Protestantism. Evangelists like Billy Sunday, Billy Graham, Charles Fuller, and Aimee Semple McPherson deployed radio and television in the expansion of a new brand of American Christianity.

Much less has been written regarding the same use of broadcast technology by Black American male preachers, however. Popular ministers like the Rev. James M. Gates produced hundreds of sermons on wax records. Lerone Martin (2014) contends that not only did these works serve as a tool of entertainment for upwardly mobile Blacks in the first decades of the twentieth century, but that it was through such media technologies that modern Black American Christianity developed. The comparable trajectory of media use among white evangelicals and Black Christians continued in the age of televangelism. White preachers like James Dobson and Pat Robertson became popular alongside Black preachers like Creflo Dollar and Bishop T. D. Jakes—with one important caveat. While the airwaves served as their principal modus operandi, Black televangelists, like Black religious men of earlier eras, approached these technologies on an uneven footing with their white counterparts. Jonathan L. Walton (2009) notes that while televangelists like James Robertson were able to garner prominence strictly through financing a broadcast channel, African American televangelists also required a physical church location whose expansive membership could propel its pastor into the spotlight. I would add to this assessment that Black televangelists also benefited greatly from their associations either through seminary training at institutions like Oral Roberts University or through broadcast sponsorship by white evangelical leaders. For Jakes, this would come through his association with popular Black televangelist Carlton Pearson. Pearson acted as a "religio-cultural point person," as Tamura Lomax (2018) describes him, in linking small-time preachers like Jakes with white TV moguls like Oral Roberts.[3] Now with *religio-digital* point persons, in the first decades of the new millennium, this trend continues as digital Black Christians and young white evangelicals gathered in the shared space of seminaries and through new media and hip hop.

The story of Joseph Solomon shows how many creatives first established relationships with white evangelical groups, in part because of their increased internet usage in the early millennium. However, creatives' digital connections to white evangelicalism remain fluid and also often fraught largely due to white evangelicals' acts of *racial erasure*, by which I mean digital and physical ways of denying racial difference and/or racism through appeals to shared theological beliefs. Sherrow Pinder (2015, 9) more directly describes this as "racism without seeing race." In chronicling the movements of race and racism in Reformed spaces, it is useful to engage with John Fiske's (1996) term *exnomination*, the way white power structures maintain their supremacy by un-naming whiteness and thus universalizing it. Fiske describes this process as "the means by which whiteness avoids being named and thus keeps itself out of the field of interrogation and therefore off the agenda for change" (42). Derived from earlier works by Roland Barthes and, even earlier, Ferdinand de Saussure's sign/signifier theory, *exnomination* indicates how myths are created. Certain groups and ideas need not be defined given their apparent naturality and innocence. Instead, all others must be defined against them, whether as in Barthes's assessment of the French bourgeoise, or Fiske's discussion of whiteness. Exnomination also occurs in the techno-religious behaviors of contemporary white American evangelicals. Through social media, however, creatives can articulate their own racial-religious views and combat such attempts at erasure through what I call *troubling Blackness*—well-crafted inquiries, like Propaganda's "I Hate Cats" piece, meant to challenge the presence of racism in sacred physical and digital spaces. Troubling Blackness is creatives' attempt at forcing white evangelicals to deal with the "fact of [their] Blackness" as they reshape injurious theological beliefs and practices.[4]

In our interview, Propaganda—Jason Emmanuel Petty is his given name—states that he deliberately uses such narrative styles, or what he calls being "descriptive rather than prescriptive," in order to "shape thought."[5] This he does under the ever-watchful eyes of an "invisible audience" of thousands of other digital Black Christians. These creatives enjoy quite an intimacy with online followers as they step into their bedrooms, bank accounts, and relationships to offer spiritual, sexual, and economic proscriptions for Christian living. For both white evangelicals and digital Black Christians there is much at stake in social media discourse. This reality is revealed in an analysis of Propaganda's lyrical content on race and a recent Instagram exchange between Propaganda, Hill-Perry, and other white and young Black adult Christians.

Joseph Solomon @chaseGodtv

When poet, singer, songwriter, and YouTube personality Joseph Solomon first logged on to the internet back in 2001 it was mostly part of an attempt to grow in his faith. He was raised in a church of fifteen hundred worshipers called Christian House of Prayer in the military community of Fort Hood, Texas. "It's a non-denominational church with very Pentecostal/full gospel roots . . . theologically you could definitely see their roots in Pentecostal and full gospel."⁶ He had always received encouragement from his parents and youth pastor. At 6′ 7″, his athletic frame might belie his past involvement in competitive sports. Throughout much of his childhood and for a time in college, Joseph played basketball. Yet from early on, it was his potential for ministry that many people remarked on. As Solomon recounts, "I never really set out to be a preacher. I just thought I was doing YouTube videos." It was his steady tutelage from older members in his Black Church that first whet his appetite for greater knowledge of his faith. This is evident in our interview when he discusses the impact of his grandmother. "She would always say, 'Yeah, you're going to be a preacher one day.'" In one poem performed at the Legacy Conference on July 20, 2018, titled "A Shadow of a Doubt," his voice is reduced to a near whisper as he recounts her passing.

> Last year my grandmother laid in a hospital bed
> like a bus stop
> waiting for God to come pick her up.
> I
> had never seen such pain and such
> confidence living in the same eyes.
> Then she told me, "I don't know what I'm gonna
> do, but I know who I belong to"
> and I was so happy for her
> and something inside of
> me wished that somehow before she passed
> away she could pass down her confidence
> in God to me
> like an old family picture. (Solomon 2018)

For many of my guides in their early adulthood, multiethnic or white evangelical churches often filled a familial void left by the Black Church they grew up with. The influential role of the Black Church in the early religious development of many individuals studied often came in the form of grandmothers, mothers, and other mostly matriarchal figures. For such persons, the transition from Black churches to multiethnic or white evangelical churches is directly linked to internet usage (coupled with a major life transition like moving out on one's own or going to college), which in some ways mimics these strong family connections. For Joseph Solomon, this digital discipleship came in the form of a number of podcast and online videos in his early twenties.

From conjectures regarding the end of race to suggestions of America's entry into a post-racial society following the election of President Barack Obama to the prominent police shootings of unarmed Blacks like Sean Bell, by all accounts Joseph entered his adult years in a time of intense racial and political ambivalence.[7] His first opportunity to participate in the electoral process occurred in the 2004 electoral contest between George W. Bush and John Kerry. Regardless of who he may have voted for, it was evangelicalism that emerged as the clear winner of the election. The reelection of George W. Bush further strengthened the role of conservative evangelicals in political and social life. The 2008 election of Barack Obama represented a historic moment for many Black churches across the nation that was not lost on Joseph Solomon and his own Black Church community. Yet while issues of race and racism remained present and communities like his own were aware of its historical import, its subtler influence on their religious lives went uninterrogated.

In the 1990s, Solomon was exposed to Christian hip hop through conservative-leaning artists like DC Talk, a rap trio composed of one Black and two white male rappers. While the group centered race in their discussions, it was often within a framework of reconciliation. In 1997 the group created the ERACE Foundation (Eliminating Racism and Creating Equality), which sought to promote ideas like integration and interracial unity. Much like the organization's name, DC Talk's music aims to diminish racial difference around Christian unity, as in the song "Colored People." Such efforts are early examples of racial erasure to which digital Black Christians like Joseph Solomon were exposed. John Fiske's (1996) term *exnomination* is apropos here given the way such racial discourse largely failed to interrogate the role of whites and white supremacy in the maintenance of racism. Yet by the turn of the millennium, Solomon had moved far from these earlier rap interests. By then, DC Talk no longer resonated as authentically hip hop for digital Black Christians who had come of age listening to artists like Nas, DMX, Tupac, and Biggie. Ironically, Solomon's new interest in Cross

Movement Records artists like Ambassador and Da Truth would lead him back to conservative evangelical circles, only this time a Reformed brand of white evangelicalism.

The rise of Cross Movement Records (CMR) in the mid-to-late 1990s bolstered the impact of Reformed theology among young Black Christians. The label was founded in 1993 in Philadelphia, Pennsylvania by a Black Christian hip hop group called Cross Movement. CMR had a significant influence on Lecrae's early musical style, producing his first album and enabling him to join Cross Movement. Lecrae's success as a rap artist, first on the CMR label and then through his own Reach Records, gave both Christian hip hop and Reformed theology an even larger platform. From its inception, CMR was known for both theologically sound and lyrically impressive rap albums. They were responsible for ushering in a brand of Black Christian rap that was overtly biblical, urban, and increasingly popular among Black teens. They proudly wore the title "the Christian Wu-Tang Clan." Branding themselves as the Christian wing of hip hop culture, CM's mission was to become "missionaries to the culture" of hip hop.

Cross Movement's first album, titled *Heaven's Mentality,* appeared in 1997. Each track featured aggressive lyrics that challenged, if not all-out dissed, popular secular lyricists. Such so-called "diss" records in hip hop have a long history, dating back, perhaps most popularly, to the "Roxanne, Roxanne" tapes. But for a Christian hip hop group to take on this tradition made many digital Black Christians immersed in hip hop culture take notice. While "Heaven's Mentality" appeared in 1997, it was created at the height of the East Coast/West Coast feud that culminated in the deaths of Tupac Shakur and Biggie Smalls. In a 2016 interview with *Rapzilla* reporter Brady Goodwin Jr., Cross Movement member Phanatik described the moment in detail.

> If you don't understand what was happening in Northeast hip-hop in 1990, 5, 6 and 7 you will not get "Heaven's Mentality" . . . you heard us come out talking about "lowercase God" to "bow down to the capital" . . . [we] talk[ed] about "who's the man," you know what I mean? "Whose world is this? The world's the Lord's." . . . that's what I'm saying at the end of the joint. But that's responding to Nas's [lyrics], "Whose world is this? The world is yours." I said, "The world's the Lord's." *Heaven's Mentality*

was a response album to all the disses that secular hip hop had been giving to Jesus Christ and Christians. I think it was Nas or Black Thought who said "I'll resurrect the blond haired blue eyed and crucify him again." Nas said, "When it's my time to go I'll wait for God with the four four [.44 caliber hand gun]." "When I was twelve I went to jail for snuffing out Jesus," you know [what] I mean? Those are all the remarks that were coming at Jesus back in the mid-90s. And then dudes on the streets were really running with that! So when we did *Heaven's Mentality*, as Christian as it sounded . . . it was not to Christians. It was to northeastern inner-city cults: Five Percenters, Hebrew Israelites, the Malachi Yorkians . . . it was to them. And when the Christians heard it; we did it at the first Rap Fest here in New York, when we did "Who's the Man" cars stopped in the middle of the street. People [were] hanging out their windows like "What the hell?" Because in that context, in that arena, in that region of the country that was saying something! (*Rapzilla* 2016)

Playing some of CMR's earlier records reveals why their music was attractive to digital Black Christians seeking a lexicon for their hip hop Black Christian experiences. Its use of hip hop aesthetics (beefing, battling) situated it as a distinctly Black practice. Digital Black Christians were able to locate Blackness through its rich linguistic performance.[8] In that deeply spiritual practice rooted in gospel, spirituals, funk, blues, and several other musical traditions of the African diaspora, digital Black Christians sought and found that *nommo*, feeling, or impulse found in Black cultural expression.

Several intellectuals since Amiri Baraka's articulation of a "blues aesthetic" (L. Jones 1963) have expanded upon what specifically Black culture entails—that is, authenticity and identity.[9] Imani Perry (2004) argues for a hip hop aesthetic. In discussing realism in *Prophets of the Hood: Politics and Poetics in Hip Hop*, she writes, "realism in hip hop is an artistic format inextricably linked to the material conditions of Black American urban communities" (88).[10] With great innovation and skill, hip hop artists construct epistemologies that, according to Perry, cannot simply be understood as a result of socioeconomic barriers. I have written elsewhere, in conjunction with Travis Harris, about the continuation of African spiritual traditions at the intersection of modern Black Christianity and hip hop (Gault and Harris 2019). Despite the now global contours of rap, particularly for those I study in this volume, hip hop must then be understood as rooted first and foremost in these Black practices. Digital Black Christians gravitated to the hip hop work of CMR as a way of being authentically Black and Christian.

Linguistic strategies such as battling also aligned Black Christian hip-hoppers with Western traditions in apologetics.[11] Listening to rappers like Ambassador, dubbed the "CHH Nas" (the Nas of Christian hip hop) by fans, could at times feel like sitting in on a systematic theology class. Yet Ambassador's lyrical approach was highly congruent with many of the lessons offered by the Five Percenters, Nation of Islam, and other religious groups that proliferated in Philadelphia at the time of CMR's development.

In the late 1990s, the northeastern development of Christian rap music fell firmly in the conscious rap category, often offering the same cerebral approach to lyricism as the Five Percenter and Nation of Islam rappers they were surrounded by. Gospel rapper Shai Linne became known for his "lyrical theology" and drew comparisons to Mos Def and Talieb Kweli, both influenced by Black American offshoots of Islam (Kweli 2012).[12] While rap was seen as play, a site for acting out whites' fetishes regarding Blackness, serious and rigorous intellectual and spiritual work was also taking place for Black artists. It is no coincidence that many of CMR's founding members attended seminary or later established church plants (new churches). Songs by other Reformed rappers on CMR's label, like Flame (now with Clear Sight Records) were described with arcane labels like "modalistic monarchianism" and lyrics by the 116 Clique discussed recondite topics like "theopneustos." The aesthetics of hip hop and Reformed theology were strongly aligned for Christian rappers like Ambassador. His first album, in 1999, now considered a Christian hip hop classic, is titled *Christology: In Layman's Terms*. He followed it up with *Thesis* in 2005.

As Ambassador had for Lecrae through their many conversations while the former attended Dallas Theological Seminary, so too the CMR artist's theological moorings provided a culturally relevant musical form of discipling for Joseph Solomon. In the first decade of the millennium, the music of CMR rappers like Ambassador and Da Truth helped him to grapple with a notion of the Christian faith that seemed to move beyond his earlier knowledge. Despite being deeply affected by his home church, he had begun to feel as though he required more theologically. Solomon logged on to the internet to search for more of this theologically deep music and Christian videos. Along with hip hop, he found the work of the emerging Passion for Christ Movement (P4CM) artists around 2008. Jackie Hill-Perry was the first Christian spoken word artist he encountered. Hill-Perry's video "My Life as a Stud" played a dramatic role in his decision to start doing poetry. Spoken word artists Janette . . . ikz and Ezekiel Azonwu further inspired him. Rap music and online spoken word videos soon combined with his growing interests in a number of podcasts and readings by white Reformed thinkers like John Piper and books by John Calvin and George Whitefield.

While evangelicalism in modern America holds many separate streams, the digital Black Christians studied here were, for the most part, attracted to the Young, Restless, and Reformed Movement (as it has been called) among white evangelicals. Churches like Bethlehem Baptist Church (John Piper), Capitol Hill Baptist Church (Mark Dever), Mars Hill (Mark Driscoll, now of Trinity Church), and the Village Church (Matt Chandler) represent some of the most well-known organizations among young Reformed Christians for their attachments to the movement's leading pastors. Reformed rappers Shai Linne and Trip Lee served as interns at Capitol Hill Baptist Church before beginning their own parachurches. Yet this brand of evangelicalism would far surpass the reach of these brick and mortar churches in its online formations. As noted by Reformed writer Collin Hansen (2019), in the early millennium "Blogs gathered together and encouraged young pastors and theologians leaving mainline and pragmatic churches for Reformed theology." At the time, the trend in white evangelicalism bent toward charismatic preaching or ministry as business models, and the rise of seeker-friendly churches pushed doctrinally minded adherents to the margins. The mostly twenty-something white males who experienced resistance from pastors and older members in their local churches for reading Reformed works by R. C. Sproul or John Piper took to the internet through blogs, video sharing, and websites to share their newfound understanding with like-minded Christians. In fact, by 2012 when Joseph Solomon began his own YouTube channel, *chaseGodtv*, he had joined a number of other popular vloggers like Mark Chandler in Reformed spaces. Young, white, and mostly male, this group desired a return to a theologically serious approach to the faith. They either became a part of a growing exodus from mainline churches or they fought to change their churches from within after returning from conferences like Together for God (T4G) or Passion.

Two white males, Collin Hansen and Mark Dever, loom large in digital historicizing (articulating an online community's backstory in order to offer meaning and prominence to the group's cause) on the "resurgence" of Reformed theology. Collin Hansen not only wrote the book *Young, Restless, and Reformed: A Journalist's Journey with the New Calvinists* (2008), but was a past council member of one of Reformed theology's most powerful organizations, the Gospel Coalition. Mark Dever founded the popular Reformed website *9Marks*. His article titled "Where'd All These Calvinists Come From?" (2014) remains popular reading for understanding the resurgence of Calvinism in the first decade of the twenty-first century. In the first version of Dever's article, he answers the question of new Calvinists' origins by highlighting Reformed thinkers and controversies throughout the twentieth century. Yet he failed to highlight one central reason for the resurgence: "Reformed rap," as he calls it. This description and his earlier dismissal of rap music's significance in Reformed theology points to the kind of racial erasure prevalent in Reformed circles. The distinctly Black identity of rap and hip hop music, which attracted digital Black Christians to its sound, is supplanted by Dever's description of it as a tool of the wider Reformed movement and rappers as "conservative evangelicals." Lecrae, however, paints a far different picture of Black Christian rappers' impact on the movement in calling their music through albums like *Rebel* the "soundtrack to the [Reformed] movement" (Wade-O 2017).

In a 2014 lecture that is a further revision of his article, Dever identifies "Reformed rap" as being at the forefront of the rise in Reformed theology in "urban centers" in the last twenty years. Dever views the early engagement between white evangelicals and young Black rappers as attributable to theological education and to their rejection by the Black Church. He observes that due to the

> unprecedented growth of Reformed theology in urban centers . . . [Rappers] tried to work in traditional African-American churches but were doing so uncomfortably so they came together. They called themselves Cross

Movement . . . these artists were merely conservative evangelicals . . . Back in Seminary, Deuce (Ambassador) had learned a conservative evangelical reformed soteriology . . . [though] it hadn't been called that. That's simply what he had been taught through scripture. So, these artists were merely conservative evangelicals. But what did hip hop culture focus on? In a worldly sense? Glory. So when they turned that same culture to focus on Christianity, what are they going to end up focusing on? The glory of God. So that became a prominent theme in their work. Since then others followed in their path . . . scores of others, profoundly affected younger Americans of all ethnicities, urban, and suburban, in the US and beyond. (Dever 2014)

For Dever this phenomenon of Black rappers in the Reformed tradition demonstrates the sovereignty of God. His focus on the glory of God suggests God's sovereign work in attracting rappers and fans to Reformed theology—by which is meant more precisely God's divine ability to draw human beings to himself through the use of Black cultural expression.

This consideration of glory connects with a core theological belief in Reformed circles—that of the supreme authority of God, often associated with the TULIP acronym which stands for Total Depravity, Unconditional Election, Limited Atonement, Irresistible Grace, and the Perseverance of the Saints. The divine is described as a king whose will humans are obliged to follow. Older Calvinist theological controversies that centered on election are central here. Can a human choose salvation (i.e., God) or did God before time choose who would be saved/elected? Reformed theologians, or New Calvinists as they are sometimes called, argue the latter—that a sovereign God chooses whom he wishes. Thus, the Christian believer finds ultimate fulfillment in living the life God has already selected for them. There is an apparent flaw in this theology, however. By the time of the resurgence of Reformed theology, God had apparently chosen mostly white male evangelicals. As a marker of exnomination, the naturality of this goes uncontested in Dever's narrative. Instead, according to Dever, young Black rappers are thus cast as catalysts in the resurgence, but also in need of enlightenment—which comes in the form of mostly white-led seminaries. When the Black Church refuses to accept these young Black rappers, it is the mostly white evangelical seminaries that assist them in becoming missionaries of Reformed theology. Dever's assessment centralizes the tension between young Black rappers and Black churches, while assuming the benevolence and understanding of white males and their institutions.

Yet perhaps because reporting and analysis of the movement has often come from within its ranks (e.g., Hansen and Devers), two key aspects of its development have been overlooked: (1) The role of the internet, and (2) shifts rather than growth in the "new Calvinist resurgence."

The Reformed Movement: The Role of the Internet

Many digital Black Christians have attended one of the popular new seminaries for Reformed thinking, like Southern Baptist Seminary or Reformed Theological Seminary. Online, they have simultaneously connected with white Reformed teachers of the same ilk. This was the case for Joseph Solomon. In 2010, he read the work of author and theologian Tim Keller and describes how he became "overwhelmed by the grace of God and heard the Gospel." He soon enrolled in the mostly white-led Reformed Theological Seminary. Many of the Reformed thinkers to whom he gravitated differed from the passionate homiletic style of the Black Church in which he had grown up. Solomon liked the precision and depth with which they broke down theological truths. As he drew closer to other digital forms of Christian teaching along with Reformed rap music and spoken word, for a time they distanced him from his Black Church roots. He recounts,

> [the] podcasts and books exposed me to a part of the Christian faith I had never considered before and those things were really making a big difference in my life. . . . I found myself listening to almost exclusively white preachers and found myself in white churches. Where the theology was . . . a lot more extensive than the theology of the church I was raised in . . . I grew up in a more charismatic Black Church and found myself in these white evangelical circles . . . (Solomon, interview by the author, April 26, 2018)

Little did Solomon know that his drift into white evangelical teachers and teachings via digital media tools was part of a larger trend in

American Christianity in the first two decades of the twenty-first century. A 2012 national study conducted by the Public Religion Research Institute revealed that while overall numbers of African Americans engaging with technology in search of religious experience were lower than for white Americans, there was a significant numerical uptick for Christian respondents identifying as evangelical (Jones and Cox 2012). In general, prior to the COVID-19 pandemic, few Protestant Americans relied on technology when engaging with their local faith communities. While they might have access to and regularly make use of social media platforms like Twitter or Facebook, they rarely made use of these tools to watch or download sermons, join a spiritual group, or follow a religious teacher.

Yet one in five white evangelical Protestants did report using social networking sites to share information regarding their church attendance, to download sermons, or to listen to a podcast. This online participation was driven by heightened on-site technology use at their houses of worship. White evangelicals were more likely than other racial or Christian groups to make use of television or multimedia devices in their church services and to connect with members of their churches through a Facebook page or other website. This increased interaction is directly linked to the large number of white evangelical content creators on social media and other online platforms who have strategically used digital media tools to reach their vast network.

When Solomon begin his quest to deepen his faith online, it was nearly impossible not to encounter works by white evangelicals in order to do this. Couple this reality with another finding of the Public Religion Research Institute study, that younger Americans (18–34) are more likely than any other age group to use social media during worship services to connect with religious leaders or like Solomon to download a podcast (twice as likely), and Solomon's story becomes representative of the unique way white evangelicals and many digital Black Christians began to connect with one another in the first two decades of the twenty-first century. As Joseph notes, "A lot of Black Christians my age and younger were relating to that . . . finding this [Reformed] theology . . . in the Internet Age . . . the age of podcast and YouTube videos." Like Solomon, this often led such Christians to reevaluate the Black Church and the

Black culture from which they came. This had much to do with both the theology and the theological circles of which digital Black Christians became a part.

There, Joseph found the kind of theological depth he felt he was missing at his home church. However, it was also there that he was made starkly aware of his Blackness, thanks to its absence in course material, people's reluctance to deal with racial injustice, and even in local white church members' suggestion that he date the only other Black woman in their congregation. Reformed theology, as preached and lived in Reformed circles, required racial erasure, a denial of the distinct differences that are central to how racial groups construct theology.

In this setting, Blackness operates not as an essential marker of identity, but rather as a means to achieving true (sovereign) identity. The outcome of this theological trajectory is often (Black) self-rejection/white acceptance or a view of race as a missionary tool. This occurred on a personal level for Joseph Solomon as he continued to delve into the core theological teachings of many white evangelical preachers. He says,

> for a while I found myself at odds with the Black Church. I felt like this new theology I was learning, [that] I didn't learn when I was growing up and I felt cheated in some ways. . . . [it] had me disparaging the Black Church and the Black experience I had grown up with. I was taking in a lot of theology, not realizing I was taking in a lot of white culture."

The "white culture" that Solomon was taking in was raised to the level of divine truth in leaders' insistence that their (white evangelical leaders') views on race be considered in line with the sovereign will of God. In essence, this white culture was saying that God wills racial (meaning Black) erasure. Reformed Christians may have had many gripes with the mainline Protestant churches that bore them, many within its ranks coming to see themselves as church liberals. However, as the next decade of the twenty-first century approached, it became ever clearer that on the issue of race they proved to have much in common with their progenitors.

The Reformed Movement: Shifts Rather than Growth in the "New Calvinist Resurgence"

While Collin Hansen's (2019) article touting a Reformed "resurgence" received the attention of major news outlets like the *New York Times*, time has told a different story. The Barna Group (2010) reported that Reformed churches have actually grown at a very slow rate over the decade that Hansen indicated. This is in keeping with the modest numbers of Reformed churches (31 percent) among evangelicals in previous decades. However, Barna Group president David Kinnaman concludes that while little evidence was found of a "resurgence" in other American churches described by Hansen, the study's findings, having only documented responses from pastors, do not account for affiliations to certain theological views held by individual adherents nor "new methods Reformed leaders are using to market their views to their peers and to the public" (Barna Group 2010). The "new methods" unaccounted for in most studies prior to this volume include the emerging digital-religious practices of young white and Black Christians.

Solomon: Responding to Racial Erasure

Like Dever's initial article, a documentary film on the history of Reformed theology that was popular in Reformed circles would initially omit the role of young Black rappers in its resurgence. When Joseph Solomon first viewed the trailer for the film, he was angered by this act of racial erasure. He had come of age listening to many of the rappers responsible for the Reformed rap albums that John Dever mentions. His YouTube channel, with over 256,000 subscribers, had ignited his artistic career as a spoken word artist and singer. He now traveled and performed with many of the artists that had exposed him to Reformed theology through their online work and music. Solomon had recently arrived back from touring with Trip Lee, one of Reach Records' recording artists. The artists were all Black. Yet when Solomon looked out into the audience of sold-out shows in Houston, Atlanta, and Denver, it was mostly white teens looking back at him. "The biggest shows are always with a bunch of white teens," he told me. "White teens connect with Christian hip hop like crazy."

Gospel rap had become the soundtrack to the Reformed resurgence, yet it served as a footnote in the minds of many within Reformed circles. Solomon couldn't let this slide. He took to social media criticizing the film for its omission. "Christian hip hop was never really recognized in the resurgence of Calvinistic or Reformed thinking. . . . See, there's not really a place for us here. Only [for] white males. That definitely played a part in me considering my allegiance in Reformed circles." He was not alone in his growing awareness of and his attempts to combat forms of racial erasure he experienced in Reformed circles. An artist known as Propaganda was right there with him.

Propaganda @prophiphop

> If you would allow me a second to deal with some in-house issues here
> Hey Pastor you know it's hard for me when you quote Puritans
> Oh, the precious Puritans
> Have you not noticed our facial expressions?
> One of bewilderment, and heartbreak, like "Not you too, Pastor"
> You know they were chaplains on slave ships, right?
> Would you quote Columbus to Cherokees?
> Would you quote Cortez to Aztecs, even if they theology was good?
> It just sings of blind privilege, wouldn't you agree?
> Your precious Puritans
> —Propaganda, "Precious Puritans"

"I received a lot of criticism for my stance on 'Precious Puritans.' I received a lot of push back. I think it was more a testament to . . . culture's sacred cows," Propaganda coolly tells me in our interview. The 39-year-old, self-described "O.S. millennial" is of slender build. Long, unkempt dreads and a scruffy beard frame his face, a kind and disarming smile often breaking his oak-colored skin. You will find him in a plaid shirt, jeans, and Chuck Taylors most days of the week. His appearance, much like the rest of his life, is antithetical to all that most people associate with white evangelicalism. Former battle rapper, slam poet, art school teacher, and youth pastor at a multiethnic church in LA, Propaganda's background is diverse, to say the least. The son of a Black Panther (his father), he describes his paternal family as full of either "preachers or criminals." The geography of his earliest religious experiences weaves a diverse web through Los Angeles. In elementary school, he spent countless hours in church listening to uncles and other family members preaching funerals from the pulpits of their churches located in South Central, Compton, or downtown LA. During his childhood, his family moved to a predominantly Mexican neighborhood, known for its high crime rate and gang activity. As one of the few African Americans, Propaganda remembers regularly being taunted and feeling like an outsider. However, while there his family joined a church that reflected the surrounding community. He describes his church experience as "a bunch of families, and those families like legit [sic] really shaped a lot of the way I think." Later, while he was in his preteens his family moved to a white suburb of LA. There, too, he received teasing from his peers because of his race. In that context, he says he made friends of diverse backgrounds while also developing "the African sort of heritage of the Christian faith and [I] pull a lot from that." His early understanding of discipleship was directly shaped by the Latinx community in which he lived and worshiped. How he understood discipleship changed for him once he reached adulthood and became more fully immersed in hip hop.

While earning his degree in illustration and intercultural studies, he also became a student of hip hop and slam poetry. He gained a name for himself across LA as a skilled battle rapper and poet, and he had become a disciple of hip hop. When asked to describe the meaning of hip hop in his life, he remarks,

> Man, it's sort of indescribable. Like it's as much a part of what I am and who I am as my ethnicity . . . this is the culture that I am. You know when I say that, I say that much differently than like someone else, in the sense that like, I mean I grew up climbing on the side of freeways writing my name on the walls. Eight years old watching the big kids at Venice Beach sort of spin on their heads, like whatever that was, being caught up into that world. The lens [through] which I could see the world and how to express it, just something [about] this resonated deep in me . . . Like most people say hip hop, they mean rap . . . [It's] so much bigger than

rap . . . I'm talking the culture. I'm talking police brutality marches. I'm talking you know, like I said, I'm talking Deep Scribble Jam competitions. I'm talking record store digging. I'm talking fat beats, you know, hip hop shops. There was a time in my life [that] like four days a week I was at some sort of . . . underground something, whether it was Poetry Lounge, Mike and Dim Lights, Foundation, Elements, Good Life, Project Blow. These were weekly events in Los Angeles whether they were open mics, open dance floors, dope DJs, sound lessons, sound bombing. Like every night, four nights a week. I was participating in hip hop.

His discipleship, in this regard, was different from that of Joseph Solomon. It was through his intimate and sustained encounter with hip hop, and through learning several of its crafts, that he was drawn into its more spiritual practices. Yet he says he didn't find Christian hip hop—Christian hip hop found him. When he joined a group called the Tunnel Rats in 2003, a further process of discipleship occurred. He first met members of Tunnel Rats while traveling and performing with rappers who were not explicitly Christian. He describes them as believers who "just happened to be in the hip hop scene." The Tunnel Rats were founded in 1993. A bi-racial collective out of Los Angeles, they were known for their battle rap style and braggadocious lyrics. Many of its members, like the earlier group Gospel Gangstas, were former gang members and had witnessed the hard realities of violence and the drug culture of East LA neighborhoods. Tunnel Rats bought every bit of this grit to their onstage performance. For this, they received heavy criticism and were barred from several churches. LA did not have a Christian rap scene as far as Propaganda knew. Tunnel Rats introduced him to a new audience and the possibility of being a Christian rapper. He emerged from that collective as a veteran emcee able to speak as a conscious Christian in his lyrics and also possessing a distinct battle-rap presence in his lyrical flow and sound. He soon encountered the music and movement of CMR artists. Conversations with Lecrae and other members caused him to think deeply about Reformed theology. He joined a Reformed church and for a time identified with much of its theology.

Though he describes himself as very much influenced by Reformed thinking, Propaganda has shifted lyrically since 2012. In earlier lyrics, his racial discussions often centered on transcending race. By the time of the

2012 release of his album *Excellent*, his tone had changed. He began targeting white evangelicals. Tracks like "Precious Puritan" are evidence of this.

According to Prop, the point of this searing 4' 15" track was to critique notions of Christian inerrancy—all Christians are "crooked sticks," he feels. The driving quotation of this rap is from Protestantism's initiator, Martin Luther, who famously said that "God can draw a straight line with a crooked stick." The fact that his theological thrust derives from the same stream of thought as Puritanism was lost on white evangelical preachers who rushed to disapprove of Propaganda's new song through online blogs and prominent Christian digital journals like *Christianity Today*. One of his most ardent critics is pastor, rapper, and senior fellow at the conservative think tank Council on Biblical Manhood and Womanhood, Owen Strachan. Strachan (2012) warned readers of the "danger" in Propaganda's lyrics. "I wonder if Propaganda isn't inclining us to distrust the Puritans. He states his case against them so forcefully, and without any historical nuance, that I wonder if listeners will be inclined to dislike and even hate them." The prohibitory and cautioning tone with which many white evangelicals discussed "Precious Puritans" soon after its release proved Propaganda's point: certain historical white heroes are apparently beyond critique; so too are the systems of injustice they created and in which they participated. One can feel the "Evangelly-fish" (as Propaganda calls them) squirming in the pews as he takes them to task later in the same song.

> How come the things the Holy Spirit showed them
> In the Valley of Vision
> Didn't compel them to knock on they neighbor's door
> And say "you can't own people!"
> Your precious puritans were not perfect
> You romanticize them as if they were inerrant
> As if the skeletons in they closet was pardoned due to they hard work and tobacco growth
> As if abolitionists were not racists and just pro-union
> As if God only spoke to white boys with epic beards. (Propaganda 2012)

One of Strachan's (2012) other critiques of the song is that, as exemplified in the above passage, Propaganda discusses Puritans as a homogenous group, both as contemporaries and throughout history. But Propaganda did this intentionally. By collapsing sixteenth-century Puritanism with nineteenth-century white abolitionist activities, Propaganda demonstrates the commonality of whiteness as a power structure throughout American history. Propaganda is not alone in his assessment. Around the same time as the release of his album *Excellent*, several creatives began using their platforms to unpack the historical parallels and antecedents to modern white supremacy located in Reformed circles.

It was 2012, and there were several reasons it seemed that white America needed to be reminded of its connection to past racism. In February of that year, the tragic shooting death of Trayvon Martin took place. By April, the indictment of George Zimmerman and subsequent details of the case filled social media chatter. The shift in digital Black Christian thought and artistic work studied here can be traced to these events. It was not that they had not known of racism's existence. But a deepening awareness of its presence in the white evangelical circles in which they operated became painfully clear in the immediate aftermath of Martin's death. With each successive murder and court case—Eric Garner, Michael Brown, Freddie Gray, Sandra Bland—creatives took note of both the continued defense of police and the deafening silence from the pulpits of their favorite white evangelical pastors. Propaganda says, "These were things, where being a person of color, sitting in these Reformed churches, that's what we all thought about. We just never said nothing."

Since then, however, through his music and self-created avenues, like a podcast titled *Red Couch*, produced jointly with his wife, he speaks out on social injustice within the church and around the world. His 2010 marriage to Mexican-born Alma Zaragoza-Petty, a PhD and professor at Vanguard University, deeply affected his views on race, ethnicity, and migration. A recent episode of their podcast discusses everything from "'hood politics" to recent news on the White House. It cannot be thought of as a Reformed theology discussion but certainly is another method that Reformed Blacks use to honor their multiple ways of being Black Christians. They create such a space, beyond white evangelical churches, through their use of digital technology.

Propaganda also continues to disciple youth as a youth pastor. The dual function of rappers like Propaganda as both preachers and performance artists puts them in a unique position. Many other digital Black Christians like Shai Linne and Trip Lee, following their training at predominantly white evangelical institutions, later became pastors, and used rap music in the same sermonic capacity as Black preachers who employed whooping before them. Yet, thanks in part to digital media, they are not beholden to the established Black Church structure in the same way. A May 2013 cover feature in *Christianity Today*, titled "Hip-Hop Theologians and Preachers: The Artists Most Shaping the Movement," featured Propaganda flanked by fellow friends and Christian hip hop artists Trip Lee and Lecrae (Strachan 2013). The movement to which the article referred was the Young, Restless, and Reformed Movement. According to Lerone Martin (2014, 8), religious ideologies have mostly remained the same; it is the technological and financial scale of ministries that has changed. Like earlier generations, creatives both benefited from and were directly influenced by the white evangelical power structure. While evangelicals' capital gains continue to entice many artists, a number of digital Black Christians are using digital tools like Instagram to create intimate space for discipleship and racial dialogue. This has afforded digital Black Christians greater resources to advance their ministries and networks (both digital and physical) apart from either white or Black churches. Their specific brand of Christianity is viewable in informal digital settings. Such webwork builds important new networks among the group.

Troubling Blackness: Propaganda and Hill-Perry on Instagram

To discuss race, and Blackness in particular, the creatives studied here have employed a diverse set of tools to navigate difficult religious terrain. One digital event that moves to physical locations and other online spaces will offer an illustration of how digital Black Christians deploy Blackness across multiple platforms in response to white evangelical racism as a way to *trouble Blackness*. Troubling Blackness describes how digital Black Christians question white evangelicalism, with care and attention to the financial, social, and theological linkages they hold to it. Their assertions are often marked by careful inquisitions and methodical and at times dispassionate analysis of systemic oppression.

Such analysis is not easy, because race is an ever-moving thing or, as Stuart Hall calls it, "a floating signifier." Hall argues that race is

> never . . . finally or trans-historically fixed. That is, it is always, or there is always, a certain sliding of meaning, always a margin not yet encapsulated in language and meaning, always something about race left unsaid, always someone a constitutive outsider, whose very existence the identity of race depends on, and which is absolutely destined to return from its expelled and objected position outside the signifying field to trouble the dreams of those who are comfortable inside. (Hall and Jhally 1996)

Because of its agency "presence, will, and movement—the ability to move freely as a being," Beth Coleman (2009, 177) rightly describes race as a technology. In this vein, I describe the following racial scenario as an event in keeping with works like "A Performative Digital Ethnography" by Wendy Hsu (2016) and Johanna Drucker's "Performative Materiality and the Theoretical Approaches to Interface" (2013). According to Drucker (2013), performative materiality "suggests that what something is has to be understood in terms of what it does." Hsu extends this point to argue for a kind of digital ethnography that is concerned with the verb of objects or digital artifacts. Here the object is text or, more specifically, textual and verbal discussions of Blackness as they move across physical and digital platforms. In examining these discussions as events, we see what Blackness does in order to understand what it is to the digital Black Christians who deploy it to reconstruct notions of self and Black Christianity. In loosely binding ways, these events operate together in the lives of creatives to provide a network that extends beyond white evangelicalism as well as the Black Church.

July 12, 2018

It is a beautiful early-fall day in downtown Indiana. All along South Capitol Avenue, a steady stream of women can be seen making their way to the Indiana Convention Center. As soon as you enter the doors, the excitement is palpable. Thousands of women have arrived from across the globe to take part in the True Woman Conference.

It was back in 2008 when conference founder and well-known Christian book author Nancy Wolgemuth (née DeMoss) and a group of friends, three of Reformed theology's most prominent contemporary voices, gathered in Wolgemuth's home to discuss the dangerous path America was heading down. In several guest spots, interviews, and televised discussions, the three women have recounted those early talks. Their portrayal of those events, however, fails to fully capture the deep anguish many in their ranks were feeling. A litany of doom-laden pronouncements awaited America for having elected Barack Obama. The Obama presidency served as an important catalyst in the three women's drive to restore "true womanhood." The push for abortion and same-sex marriage posed a direct threat to their heteronormative views. The groundswell of support Wolgemuth and her passionate band of female friends received from women across the evangelical world was a call to action against American liberalism, as she later observed. Race, as a floating, though tangible, signifier, was part of this process.

Wolgemuth describes a late-night conversation with planning partners Holly Eleft and Mary Kassian. While lamenting the rise of the allegedly evil movement called feminism, Wolgemuth asked, "Who is directing the hearts of women in America?" "Oprah!" they replied in unison (Revive Our Hearts 2018). Oprah Winfrey represented the ideologies of the feminist movement that they sought to combat. Eleven years before the inception of the True Woman Conference, Wolgemuth had read *The Feminist Mistake* by Mary Kassian. Once she had read Kassian's take on the historical development of feminism, Wolgemuth says she began to ask, "If a handful of women have succeeded by their writings and influence in destroying and brainwashing an entire generation with their godless philosophies, what could God do with a handful of women who were determined to 'reclaim surrendered ground'?" (Revive Our Hearts 2018). The question was galvanizing.

The founding members of the True Woman Conference threw a gauntlet down at the entire feminist movement. As an easily accessible cultural reference, Oprah served as a symbolic adversary representing the feminist movement in their minds.[13] Yet with Oprah, gender came bound up with Blackness. By de-emphasizing Oprah's race, the founding members simply further underscored the universality of "true" (i.e., white) womanhood while never explicitly expressing that whiteness remained its measure of authenticity. The textual and spatial goals of true womanhood are not only reminiscent of the Victorian era's own cult of womanhood. The goals are a wholesale return to many of its objectives.[14] Its manifesto, laden with biblical support for its positions, aspires to glorify God through dedication to family, motherhood, and the promotion of traditional gender roles in the home and in church life.[15]

Theologies of complementarianism—the belief in complementary but distinct roles for men and women—are comparable to the esteemed virtues of middle-and upper class white women of the nineteenth century. Much like the time of intense economic and social upheaval within which such ideals initially found currency, the presidency of Barack Obama presented another such moment in American history. As with its nineteenth-century historical model, it is a theology that holds up white femininity as a goal. By attending or watching any of the live-streamed events of the conference, despite the significant sprinkling of women of color, one quickly becomes aware that this is a mostly a white women's event.

After popular blogger Betsy Gomez announces, to enthusiastic applause, that there are five hundred Hispanic women in attendance, Danna Gresh, her co-host and founder of Pure Freedom Ministries, jokingly adds, "You can tell who they [Hispanic women] are. They're the loud, spicy ones." Gomez seems to pause, but only for a second before the show moves on without incident. Such casual instances of stereotyping fail to raise an eyebrow in a space where most of the musicians are white, the selection of songs are by overwhelmingly white artists, and the speakers and attendees are mostly white as well. In this atmosphere, the power of white evangelical women is not to be underestimated.

Its inaugural meeting in 2008 was attended by three thousand women. In its tenth year, the 2018 True Woman Conference boasts seven thousand women from all fifty US states and from thirty-three countries. One indication of how deep its roots run in the evangelical world can be seen in the fact that Moody Publishers, of the same Moody Bible Institute that hosts the Legacy Conference, serves as its main publishing sponsor. In published interviews and online postings of her teachings, Wolgemuth appears to be a meek and unassuming woman, but her presence at the conference is firm and commanding.

She is, after all, a powerful force able to ignite the professional ambitions of several up-and-coming young women in these circles. She makes no qualms about the fact that she "hand-picks, carefully selecting who needs to be on that stage" at the True Woman Conference (Revive Our Hearts 2018).

Later in the day, Jackie Hill-Perry, rapper, poet, and self-professed former lesbian is setting up for her talk at the True Woman conference. If the Legacy Conference is a metropolis for Black urban Christians, True Woman is its alternative for mostly young to middle-aged white female evangelicals. Jackie's message of leaving behind lesbianism is particularly attractive to this audience. It adds a new wrinkle to the well-worn abstinence-only trope. She can speak to single women regarding an issue of sexuality that is rarely discussed in depth.

Though Wolgemuth has known Hill-Perry for some time, 2018 is the first year that she has invited her to participate as one of the keynote speakers. For a rising star in the evangelical world, this is a monumental moment for Hill-Perry, and she wants to share it with her followers on Instagram. She posts a photo of herself alone behind the lectern. A single, almost celestial light envelops Hill-Perry as she looks out onto thousands of empty seats soon to be filled by women anxious to have their lives changed by her message. On July 20, 2018, she writes to her Instagram followers:

> Pride wants us to point people to ourselves. But what are we going to do when they end up coming to us, for authentic freedom, and all we have to offer them is our measly best? We might be good at what we do, but that's not enough for the world. The world needs something more. The world needs Who it was created for. The world needs Someone eternal to give it life. We can't do that. We can talk about life. But we can't give it.

Jackie Hill-Perry espouses many of the views regarding complementarianism, biblical womanhood, traditional gender roles, and personal rights supported by the True Woman organization and other individual Reformed evangelicals. From Jackie Hill-Perry's conference message to her Instagram post, she links her online and physical followers to the True Woman Conference manifesto in her particular usage of terms like "authentic freedom," her allusion to the world's need to know "Who it was created for," the belief in God's ultimate glorification, and the admonition against pride or "selfish insistence," as the manifesto states. This "co-construction" of online and offline behavior reflects a congruency in young adult religious practices across multiple platforms, as well as the way loose networks of belief are developed among digital Black Christians.[16]

The "self-insistence of personal rights," which Hill-Perry mentions, alludes to recent claims by groups and movements like those highlighted earlier (the feminist movement, the gay movement, the Black Lives Matter movement) that advocate for social justice. Yet race, among other social categories, does not appear in her post, only the apparently universalized tenets of the True Woman manifesto. Hill-Perry's digital performance of the ideologies of the True Woman movement offers a glimpse into the fluid practice of Blackness. Her following response to a commentor to her post, then, is unanticipated given her advocacy of True Woman beliefs. As such, it reflects the multidimensionality of digital Black Christian beliefs, even in white evangelical spaces.

In most of her postings, Hill-Perry rarely replies to comments, perhaps because of the sheer volume of feedback she receives from followers. The aforementioned comment alone received 10,147 likes. Usually she reserves her responses for friends, those who inquire about merchandise, engagements, or other artistic projects, or those who challenge her beliefs. A reply in the latter category appears further down in the comments section.

Much of the cataloging of the lives and beliefs of digital Black Christians about which I am writing in this volume details their relationships to other digital Black Christians, to older African American Christians, and to white evangelicalism. It is interesting then to examine such creatives' encounters with white Christian millennials regarding Christian belief. Jim Mann,[17] a thirty-three-year-old white male Christian, replies to Hill-Perry's post on the same date, July 20, 2018, by saying:

> I'm glad you haven't jumped on the #sjw train. I love your ministry. God has blessed you with amazing talents. And your new album is 🔥

The term *social justice warrior* (#sjw) has become something of an epithet in white evangelical spaces after having already been popular in the American vernacular. It was the 2014 Gamergate controversy that popularized it in several online communities. Following a blog post by Eron Gjoni (2013) disparaging his former girlfriend Zoe Quinn, Quinn and other women in the virtual game world were subjected to death threats, doxing, and other threats of sexual harm. Many of these threats used the hashtag #sjw when referring to Quinn and female gamers (Jason 2015). Jim Mann's reference to the term regarding another woman in an online space is thus at once unfortunate and quite revealing.

His comment is unlike earlier attempts meant to frighten and silence the voices of women. Yet he does use it to draw parameters around acceptable religious belief and practice for women. He also further describes Hill-Perry, if she does in fact identify with other "social justice warriors," as "left leaning, race obsessed . . . worldly." In this, Mann represents several other dogmas routinely evidenced in conservative millennial conversations. On March 21, 2018, a few months prior to Mann's post, popular YouTuber Allie Beth Stuckey, who goes by the Twitter handle @conservemillennial, posted "Bible Matters: SJW Christianity." Describing the rising tide of "social justice Christianity" as a plague that is "sweeping the nation," Stuckey warns against those who preach inclusion, ordination of women, and a host of other "liberal" sins. Like Mann's response to Jackie's post, she argues that such people are not really Christians. It is important to note that, without saying it explicitly, in Stuckey and Mann's views, rallying for social justice causes calls into question certain groups' right to belong in the Christian community. Women and people of color in particular endure racial and gendered erasure in this context, as they are usually the group most likely to have this epithet lodged against them. Jackie's allegiance to conservative evangelical spaces is thus a delicate balancing act.

In April of 2018, Jackie was on hand with a large number of conservative evangelical leaders in Nashville, Tennessee to sign the Nashville Document, which affirmed traditional gender and marriage roles. The document was drafted by the Council on Biblical Manhood and Womanhood during the annual convention of the Southern Baptist Convention. As noted earlier, her signature was one of the few representing digital Black Christians. Many of her peers criticized her participation in its signing given its wording, which, much like Stuckey's comments, seemed to suggest that those who affirm gays and lesbians are not Christian. It is actions like these that may have led Mann to consider Jackie a part of his and Stuckey's camp. However, like other creatives studied here, Jackie Hill-Perry does not fit neatly into the category of evangelical stooge, as her response to Mann demonstrates. Jackie Hill-Perry recognized the subtle implications of his response to her post and replied in kind on July 20, 2018:

> *Jackiehillperry:* @jimmann1985 oh, you mean the train that says that all people are worthy of dignity? And that racism, oppression, and systemic injustice is not only present in the world and in the church? And how it needs to be addressed and uprooted not only by the preaching of the gospel but by applying the gospel practically and specifically? If so, it's a train that I'm not ashamed to ride on my friend. ♥

As a social media platform, Instagram mostly attracts users wanting to share images of themselves via photo-filtering, or following other users and viewing posted stories in a highly controlled environment. Its hyper-self-centered model often encourages both narcissism and surveillance by users (Buffardi and Campbell 2008), who are likely to be young, female, and engaged in photo-based activities that allow for appearance-related comparisons (Pew Research Center 2015a).[18] Jackie has, in the past, engaged her followers in kindly joshing, particularly regarding facial appearance. Thus, in early July 2018, Jackie posted an image of her freshly arched eyebrows. Her followers, mostly women of color, responded with a number of affirmations that continued when they met in person.

Just before meeting Hill-Perry at the Legacy Conference in Chicago, I joined a Q&A for one of the plenary sessions she led.

At this event, the room is full of mostly digital Black Christian women. Just in front of me sits a woman with closely shaven hair and a baseball cap. Block letters of the words "Hood Preacher" form an arch at the back of her baseball cap. I arrive late. She turns and smiles as I try, rather unsuccessfully, to move quietly into the seat behind her. On the stage sit four women charged with discussing women in leadership—a weighty topic, given the resistance that so many of the women on the small platform and the audience have faced in their churches. The panelists spend most of their time sharing their own stories, wisdom, and laughter with the audience. The audience forms a chorus of "hmmms," "yasses," and other knowing gestures and expressions that Black women share when in safe spaces. Rituals of affirmation occur in similar ways to those noted in social media exchanges.

Toward the end of the Q&A, a Black woman in her mid-twenties comes forward to ask Hill-Perry a question. True to her online persona, Jackie begins by first complimenting her eyebrows. Thanking her, the young woman remarks that she saw Jackie's post about her brows and wanted to make sure that her own eyebrows "were on point!" Black women often use Instagram, in the same way as other body-centered appropriations of hip hop (i.e., dancing to "Baby Got Back"), to push back against the way their bodies and Blackness are often reduced to objects online (Brock 2012). Affirmations like "Eyebrows on fleek" or "Come thru legs!" have commonly been used to celebrate the Black body. As hashtags, these are commonly paired with #Blackgirlmagic or #melaninpoppin. Those who post to sites like the Facebook forum Unfit Christian Congregation, consisting mostly of digital Black women, periodically participate in "thirst traps"—pictures of their body parts posted for the admiration and often sexually suggestive compliments of other forum members.

In André Brock's (2012) groundbreaking work on Black Twitter "From the Blackhand Side: Twitter as a Cultural Conversation," he describes a phenomenon in which white commenters on Black Twitter—the colloquial name for Twitter as used by Black people—were more likely to view Black Twitter users' practices "as a game and a waste of resources," while Blacks were more inclined to view Black Twitter "as the mediated articulation of a Black subculture" (545). While Black Twitter has continued to evolve in the presence of a racially diverse audience, Black users recognize its value for replicating physically located practices in Black discourses of signifying, practices that "focus on invention, delivery, ritual and audience participation" (545). Given the religious dimensions of this volume, I suggest that additional emphasis on ritual is warranted. The ritualized nature of Black female affirmation is a recognition of the "divine-in-her." Amid Hill-Perry's biblical commentary is the consistent conjuring of Black self-love, which draws both spirit and body (of Black women in particular) into the intimacy of her discipleship. Because his whiteness does not afford him this nuanced understanding of the space in which he has entered, Mann and Hill-Perry are approaching Instagram (to which the aforementioned insights about Black Twitter also apply) from two distinct vantage points.

The preceding exchange between Hill-Perry and Mann can be considered a carefully staged sequence of events or racial acts against the communal space of affirmation initially engendered by her post. Jackie is aware of who is watching, both her circle of affirming followers and those who seek to reduce her to the object of her Blackness. In response, through several precise moves, she has engineered the context for Jim Mann's comments and carefully worded her own response to his comments. Consider again the selection, timing, filtering, and associated wording of the photo. As an Instagram event, it is clear Hill-Perry had not intended to make this about race or gender. Yet both become the object of the event, and so too the fact that she is reduced to her appearance—a common occurrence given the nature of Instagram surveillance. "The fact of Blackness," as Frantz Fanon (1967) called it, is unavoidable in the social context and is always inscribed with the intention of setting apart and alienating. Mann's comments force Hill-Perry to deal with Blackness and its oppressive intersectionality. Her decision to raise questions that are in themselves answers that Mann did not ask takes the discourse in the direction of her choosing and thus gives greater clarity about who Jackie is and what she believes. It is by troubling Mann's notion of Blackness, and by questioning what actions and comments are appropriate online and in the physical world, that Hill-Perry reclaims the right of Black female bodies to exist and be heard and seen in white church spaces.

Troubling Blackness in this way is not without its challenges, however. In this context, it invites further dialogue with white evangelicals. There, race becomes like putty in the hands of a child. Like the "floating signifier" Hall describes (Hall and Jhally 1996), race is constantly pulled, pushed, and forced to expand and contract as it conforms to the fluid online exchange. Mann's next reply to Jackie settles on comparing her to Propaganda:

> *Jimmann1985:* @*jackiehillperry* I'm all for what you just said, but there's a difference in how you approach it, versus someone like @*prophiphop* and his wife on their social media. I think that there's a balance and some people in Christian circles have become imbalanced on this subject. You have a song on your new album that addresses some of the issues mentioned above, but for some reason it didn't come off in poor taste and your whole [*Crescendo*] album wasn't dedicated to harping on

it. That's what I meant. My point was mainly that I appreciate your ministry. My wife is at #truewomen2018 conference and got to see you speak at the conference. ☺

One could argue that here Mann chooses to point to Propaganda as an example, given his comparative prominence and similar artistry of rapping to Jackie or given that they are both signed to Humble Beast Records. However, when Propaganda decides to join the conversation later on, Mann's decision to use white power emojis in response to Propaganda's Black fist emoji clearly reveals the centrality of race in Mann's analysis. Propaganda employs his emoji [as have other white respondents to the same post] as an expression of solidarity with Hill-Perry and others defending Propaganda. Yet Mann perceives the very appearance of a Black hand, the fact of Blackness, as un-Christian:

Jimmann1985: @prophiphop and if it's wrong for one race to promote their "power", the(n) it shouldn't be ok to promote any particular race's "power" "✊🏿" . . . shouldn't we strive to be consistent?

Race, according to Mann here, is about the acquisition of power. He believes Propaganda is attempting to put Blackness above whiteness. He will achieve this gargantuan task with a single Black fist emoji. Yet Mann's racial speech acts cannot be dismissed as a misinterpretation of online visual cues, for in reality they are an example of webwork or a performance of white evangelical belief. Racial erasure online, as in physically located white evangelical circles, presupposes that Blackness and the struggle for the rights of Black people is an affront to Christian belief because it is an affront to whiteness. Yet the exnomination of whiteness, its assumed normalcy and predominance, directly guides Mann's approach here without any recognition of it on his part. When we wrestle apart the pieces of Mann's grievances with "social justice warriors," we find that at the center of his speech acts are a desire to preserve whiteness and white supremacy by policing Blackness. As a social media platform structured to allow hyper-surveillance, Instagram is uniquely designed to allow such activity.

While it ultimately backfires on him, Mann is not unique in his attempt to pit one Black Christian millennial [Hill-Perry] against another

[Propaganda] as a way of critiquing Black practices. Rather, he highlights an experience of many of the creatives studied here. Many discuss examples in which the actions of other Black Christians are used to instruct or admonish them regarding appropriate beliefs and behavior. In other examples, creatives become exemplars for other digital Black Christians of what they should do or believe in order to "fit in" in white evangelical spaces. All prominent digital Black Christians who operate in mostly white spaces know this reality. Yet Mann's presence in an Instagram context mostly centered on the affirmation of Black bodies like this one offers creatives a chance to fire back and, if only briefly, to offer a counter-narrative of what it means to be Christian as a young Black adult. Propaganda weighs in on Jackie's post once again to say,

> Prophiphop: @jimman1985 it's only wrong if you think power is a zero sum game Prophiphop @jimman1985 and to reduce an entire swath of your brothers and sisters in the faith to a hashtag intended to shame and mock them, ala "sjw" seems to me like you're guilty of the same worldliness you're protesting.

Troubling Blackness, as Jackie does and Propaganda does even more directly, pushes back against attempts at racial erasure and argues for the irreducibility of Black life. Propaganda moves past the hierarchical definition of racial power and the digital categorizations of race and religion. This allows Blackness a space in discourse to be present as a "fact." Yet, unlike earlier assessments of race where it must be "set apart and alienated," race is an intrinsic feature of the online event. It is as if Propaganda's words from "Precious Puritans" come back to us as "Pastor, you see my Black skin." And so too does Mann. And it is troubling.

Conclusion: Intimacy through Relationships

Joseph Solomon confronted racial erasure by critiquing white male histories of Reformed theology. Propaganda undertook the same racial justice work in his creation and performance of rap songs like "Precious Puritans," his co-led podcast, and through his support of other digital Black Christians like Joseph Solomon and responses to white evangelicals, as in the case of Jackie Hill-Perry's Instagram post. Through digital activism, both Solomon and Propaganda gathered and influenced a developing network of digital Black Christians. Solomon and Propaganda's forms of digital discipling mirrored their own trek into the Christian faith—Solomon through Reformed theologians' online postings, gospel rap, and later through Propaganda's music. Propaganda was initially discipled through Latinx churches and hip hop communities. Whether through a physical or an online presence, both artists' stories describe the desire and construction of intimate relationships as central to their Christian growth. Most present work on intimacy and closeness using the PAIR (Personal Assessment of Intimacy in Relationship) model to describe the emotional, social, sexual, intellectual, and recreational paths humans take in building relationships. As this model is derived from social psychology and mostly relates to couples therapy, it fails to fully account for the kinds of relationships desired and developed by Solomon, Propaganda, and other digital Black Christians, given their digital-spiritual aims. The desire in such cases remains to encounter the divine in community with other digital Black Christians. Digital discipleship afforded them a unique opportunity to develop acute feelings of closeness (as with Solomon forming a vital friendship with Propaganda after first being moved by the work of other Christian rappers online), reciprocal forms of self-disclosure (as with Hill-Perry's affirmation of Black women), and supportive actions (as with Propaganda coming to her defense on Instagram) that build intimacy in relationships. Such digital-religious relationships displace traditional models of relationship-building once associated with the PAIR model. On the one hand, this can be thought of as a challenge to Black Church authority. Yet in considering the Black Church as a tradition, such authority has never received full adherence. Some have always existed on the margins of the Black Church. As such, the story of digital Black Christians, rightly so, moves beyond its parameters in defining new religious meaning. Their affiliation within Reformed circles is telling of this fact.

Yet even this is a story of nuance. The voices of advocates of Reformed theology have greatly expanded, particularly in the digital age, providing digital Black Christians with strong relationships with other older Blacks within its ranks. Digital Black Christians can point to a number of well-known Black pastors (all male) and thinkers who came to prominence in recent years and have powerful voices in Reformed circles. Men like

Tony Carter and Thabiti Anyabwile make a poignant case for why African Americans should accept Reformed theology. Like Solomon earlier in his journey, their arguments are at times tinged with disapproval of the practices of the Black Church. Their attacks, for example, on the anti-intellectualism of African American churches appear in subtle phrasing regarding the lack of a systematic theology in African American churches or regarding the Black Church's reliance on fervor over sound doctrine. This is no wonder, however, given that the leaders listed have been tutored in white seminaries that have a strong focus on Reformed theologies. These critiques of Black culture and Black theologies that center Black bodies and Black stories continue to permeate even Black Reformed circles. Other groups, such as the Reformed African American Network (RAAN) and podcasts like *Pass the Mic* and *Truth's Table*, led in part by digital Black Christians, draw other digital Black Christians in search of a racially just message in Reformed theology.[19] This has been the answer for many digital Black Christians affected by the lack of diversity, or worse, intentional racism in Reformed circles. Like Solomon and Propaganda, they are creating digital safe spaces that provide intimacy through relationships with other Black believers.

3

Body

The Story of Jackie

. . . I'm struggling with a couple of things right now. Ya'll don't want me to tell you the truth. You want me to stand up here and act like because I got this mic in my hand that I'm just so sold out for Jesus that don't nothing bother me . . . and I don't never get frustrated. I don't never just want to fall and have some sex . . . But the devil is a liar. Come on here somebody! Every day of my life I'm struggling to kill the flesh!
—Juanita Bynum, "No More Sheets," sermon, 1997

"God, I am really struggling. I wanna go back so bad. Lord, help me" . . . Temptation was slapping me around like a weightless doll in the hands of an imaginative child . . . The struggle with homosexuality was a battle of faith. To give in to temptation would be to give in to unbelief. To decide that the body mattered more than God, or that the pleasure of sin would sustain all that I am better than He. It was incredible how real and tangible and persistent they could be, but their power was an illusion.
—Jackie Hill-Perry, *Gay Girl, Good God*, 2018

Introduction: The Struggle Is Real

The Black Christian female body is deeply troubled, *ipso facto*. At least, that is the takeaway the religious discourse of both Juanita Bynum and Jackie Hill-Perry leaves us with, more than twenty years apart. However, by turning their struggles over sexuality against their own Black female bodies, both accounts fail to name the historical structures (e.g., the Black Church, societal racism, sexism, or homophobia) that shaped their trauma. Western Christianity has historically rendered the female body fractured both in its theologies regarding female's innate dissemblance and imbalance and in its Cartesian mind(soul)/body dualism. The Black female body in America bears the further historical weight of quotidian sexual attacks in antebellum slavery. During the Victorian era, belief in the impurity of the laboring Black female body aligned with notions of white women's purity. Unlike its more ethereal goals for the white female body, the cult of true womanhood divided the spirit from the body, reducing the physical attributes of Black women to a mammified shell of themselves. According to Patricia Hill Collins ([1991] 2008, 267), quoting Barbara Christian, she was "funky" and "sensuous" (Christian 1985, 2) but rendered harmless in her asexuality, in her complete devotion to white families. The Black female body has endured, despite Black Baptist tropes of respectability and Pentecostal doctrines of sanctification. The corollary of a few centuries spent with this injurious reading of Black Christian bodies is found in Bynum's struggle to "kill her flesh" and in Jackie's reduction of its bodily matter to a necessary sacrifice in an exchange for divine conciliation.

Religion scholars like Tamura Lomax (2018), Monique Moultrie, and Marla Frederick have noted the role of media in mediating Black women's view of their bodies. In *Passionate and Pious: Religious Media and Black Women's Sexuality* (2017), Moultrie argues that much of the talk regarding Black televangelists often centers on their prosperity theology. Texts like *Watch This! The Ethics and Aesthetics of Black Televangelism* (2009) by Jonathan Walton offered important readings of Black televangelists, though mostly through a discussion of male preachers. Yet what Moultrie calls "faith based sexual ministries," like the ministry of Juanita Bynum, have been equally important in informing Black women's beliefs. In ways distinct from her male counterparts, Bynum combines a word of faith or prosperity theology with her own sexual narrative. In *Colored Television: American Religion Gone Global*, Marla Frederick (2015, 99–102) describes Juanita Bynum's form of self-disclosure as a market-driven presentation of the "real" in a hyper-mediatized context. Indeed, following her meteoric rise to televangelist popularity in 1997, Bynum continued to parlay her real experiences with bodily trauma, sex, and sexuality into solicitations for donations for the construction of a threshing floor in her home, books on singlehood and marriage, and even selling her weekly personal diary to website subscribers. Her troubled body continued to be a lucrative product in the Christian marketplace.

While Hill-Perry exhibits many characteristics of Bynum's trope of sexual redemption and self-disclosure, she moves away from its market-driven aspirations, away too from the visual and rhetorical presentation of Black Church–styled televangelists like Bynum, whose story of self-disclosure in many ways still required the sanction of the Black Church. Though raised in a similar Baptist and neo-Pentecostal context as Bynum, Hill-Perry summarily critiques Black churches and Black people for their acceptance of prosperity-centered theologies in poems like "Jig-a-boo" and rap songs like "Dead Preacher" from her freshman album *Art of Joy*. In so doing she attempts to unfetter herself from the traditional Black Church, offering an example of digital Black Christianity at work—loosely constructed online and non-church religious practices of digital Black Christians that seek to pivot away from the Black Church.[1]

For digital Black Christians, Bynum operates as the media precursor to Hill-Perry's own digital testimony of sexual healing. Yet Jackie, in a way largely absent from Bynum's popular 1997 "No More Sheets" testimony, speaks openly regarding her same-sex attractions. Bynum did not discuss her own same-sex relationship publicly until 2012, and then described it as an aberration following her divorce from Bishop Thomas Weeks. We owe this shift in sexual discourse among Black Christian women, in part, to the move from electronic and broadcast television and video recording to digital media—social and video media sharing sites like YouTube. As in my earlier discussion of mediatization in the religious development of Lecrae, the medium here also directly informs the message.

Bynum's talk of masturbation, sex work, and sexual desire read as authentic to Black female audiences in the late 1990s given the proliferation of candid discussions of sex elsewhere on television. Digital media technology allowed unfettered access to the "real." As such, by the 2008 arrival of Hill-Perry's spoken word piece "My Life as a Stud," venturing into "the raw" as a marker of the real became necessary in authenticating one's story in the Christian marketplace. Spoken word, largely rooted in Black performance practices, has been leveraged by female creatives like Jackie Hill-Perry online to speak openly about a range of body-centered topics. Through the life and ministry of Jackie Hill-Perry, this chapter explores how creatives take on or "wear" hip hop in physically located and online spaces as a way of working out bodily dissonance. At the root of their styles of dress, a certain sexual intimacy undergirded both Bynum's and Hill-Perry's attempts to make the Black female body visible.

The chapter offers a descriptive analysis of embodied styles of dress, from Juanita Bynum's "wearing purity" to Jackie's "wearing hip hop." It answers the question, "How is the digital Black Christian female body materially presented and read by female creatives?" To answer it, I use two examples of *secondary Blackness*—the prioritizing of other identities over race, as exhibited in Hill-Perry's spoken word performances of "My Life as a Stud" and "Jig-a-boo" on YouTube videos, triangulating them with her rap lyrics and her autobiography *Gay Girl, Good God*.

Pretexting Defined

Pretexting can be defined as temporarily affecting—"putting on" or performing—a hip hop identity for a specific purpose, whether authentically or inauthentically. In short, pretexting at its best and worst is complicated and messy. Bodily strategies of pretexting allow female creatives like Jackie Hill-Perry a socially acceptable way of employing multiple percussive strategies to realize their spiritual liberation. The way ideas and practices like abstinence, transitioning from gay to straight, attempts at modest dress, or cross-gender play are taken up in Black Christian women's online postings of artistic work represents a particular performance that challenges the value claims both of hip hop culture and of white Christian and Black Christian spaces. In the case of Hill-Perry, this cross-gender play is demonstrated in hip hop styles of dress or in the goals and use of language in spoken word performances.

The etymological root of the word *pretext* lie in the Latin word *praetexere*, meaning to take on a disguise or outward display, from *prae*, before, and *texere,* to weave. The body is then weaving its form and function into something else before one's very eyes. When used here as a verb, as in "the body is weaving (pretexting)," *pretexting* denotes the body's shifting and active nature. For instance, one of my guides, who grew up in the Black Church and remains rooted in its traditions, remarked on participating in freestyle rap ciphers and dance battles in Leimert Plaza Park in Los Angeles. Her decision to shift or weave her body into hip hop movements and rhetoric in order to translate her faith to others in the hip hop space is an example of pretexting. The term *pretexting*, as derived from its etymological root, appeared in the late twentieth century to describe the practice of disguising one's online identity in order to obtain access to privileged data. Given the frequent criminalization of young Black bodies and their attempts to assume normative identities in order to extract privileged data, this term holds related value for digital Black Christians. This includes my guides' creative approaches to increasing online audiences, negotiating white evangelical spaces, and either ascending or repudiating Black Church polity in order to gain access to information that repositions them in a historically unequal power dynamic (i.e., white evangelical churches, the Black Church, etc.).

Creatives like Hill-Perry make Cartesian notions of the dualism of body and spirit—"killing the flesh"—a central act for achieving liberation. Yet, in holding fast to such theologies, this approach also becomes a way of normalizing practices and people at the margins of Black Christian life, youth and women, granting young Black women access to act in nonnormative ways. The testimonial style of spoken word effectively situates Black women's sexual experiences and styles of dress in conventional Christian liturgy. By fitting into traditional tropes of respectability, it becomes permissible to stand out on taboo topics regarding their bodies. In short, pretexting can best be described as free-*ish*, in that liberation is never fully achieved in a paradigm guided by concealment, disguise, or a theology that separates the body and spirit (often privileging the latter while persecuting the former). As a liberatory strategy, it largely enables personal freedoms (acceptance of sexual past/desire, hip hop dress/gender cross-play) in the body and corporate freedom for the spirit (e.g., heaven, salvation).

It must be noted, then, that pretexting is not sex-positive and largely not LGBTQIA-affirming. It does not often acknowledge the intersectional nature of Black women's oppression. It privileges racism over sexism, yet places both behind Christian identity (secondary Blackness). Pretexting of the body is a sometimes deeply troubling way of reading Black women's intersectional experiences. Yet it is an essential orientation in Black women's body work (efforts to materialize one's experiences through movements and actions) that has received less attention as a deeply meaningful path to self-liberation for some young Black Christian women. To be sure, such pretexting captures a complex situation in which the outcomes are not always clear, healthy, or morally acceptable to a diverse reading audience. As womanist ethicist Monique Moultrie notes, "subversives often participate in the very same oppressive structures" that they hope to counter (Moultrie 2017, 7). This has meant that creatives at times can be equally harmful and helpful to other digital Black Christians.

Understandably, this leaves the reader uncertain concerning where and who the "villains" are in this text. As an ethnography, this volume makes clear: there are no villains, only creatives whose beliefs and actions are complicated by their multiple allegiances and identities. This does not always sit well with audiences, I know. When I presented earlier versions of this chapter's findings at conferences and invited talks, commenters expressed disdain for Hill-Perry's views, even questioning my own prudence in choosing to consider her work. The complexity of Hill-Perry exemplifies the layered nature of body work taken up by Black female creatives and how essential it is for scholarly observers to sit with all that is beautifully and wonderfully complicated about these bodies in order to arrive at some small understanding of digital Black Christians. Through pretexting Hill-Perry conceals her attempts at repositioning and making visible LGBTQIA bodies in more affirming ways in Black Church and digital spaces. Yet, even as Hill-Perry centers and celebrates specifically Black women and queer folk in her work, at other times she reaffirms white racist readings of the same Black bodies. Yet this is much larger than just the personal choices of Jackie Hill-Perry. Examining her process of pretexting demonstrates the way social media technology and the national and Black Church moral panic have both structured and caused embodied dissonance in the movements and practices of digital Black Christian females.

A Brief Introduction to the Digital Black Christian Female Body

Jackie Hill-Perry was born in St. Louis, Missouri, in 1989. During her early life she attended a Missionary Baptist church with her aunt. At nineteen she began her own Christian journey as part of a Black Apostolic Pentecostal church. Both Baptist and Pentecostal traditions have greatly influenced her style of public speaking, poetry, and rap performances. And like many other digital Black Christians, Jackie remembers the growing influence of pop/gospel artists like Kirk Franklin and John P. Kee. She carries with her a love of the Black Church worship traditions that she experienced throughout the 1990s and early millennium. Yet there were other influences, those of a much larger white evangelical temper that developed throughout the 1990s and which also influenced adolescent Black Christians like Hill-Perry.

Jackie Hill-Perry came of age after the 1993 creation of the True Love Waits (TLW) campaign. Begun by the Southern Baptist Convention, its goal of encouraging teens and young adults to sign a pledge of abstinence until marriage attracted scores of mostly white Christian youth. The TLW campaign was sponsored by Lifeway Resources, the publication wing of the Southern Baptist Convention and one of North America's largest booksellers; it would later publish the autobiographies of both Lecrae and Hill-Perry herself. With the 2018 publication of her *Gay Girl, Good God*, Hill-Perry joined a long-standing tradition of marketing purity to young Christians.

Throughout the 1990s, Black Christians' material consumption of religious books, clothing and other expressions of the faith introduced them to, among several others, the brand and message of the TLW campaign. White evangelical groups like TLW often focused their efforts on television, criticizing its hypersexual and anti-Christian viewing material. One such example appeared in the same year of Jackie's birth. In 1989, the first episode of *The Simpsons* was met with much opprobrium from Christian groups. In an attempt to curry the support of religious broadcasters, then-President George H. W. Bush also criticized the show's content. In his 1992 State of the Union Address, Bush called for a society reflective of *The Waltons* instead of *The Simpsons* (Bowler 2001,

2). Bush's overtures to Christian nostalgia for a bygone era played well to evangelicals. Their hope was to impact the rapidly changing television offerings of the 1990s. In October of the same year, Bush vetoed the 1992 Cable Act for its supposed potential overregulation of the telecommunications industry. Quite ironically, the Senate's later override of Bush's veto effectively opened more diverse channels and an accessible route for broadcasters of Christian content (Associated Press 1989). In the 1990s, new regulatory laws similar to the 1992 Cable Act directly benefited evangelists and conservative Christian groups like TLW as they sought to promote their own message. Through their on-air presence, they positioned themselves as an alternative to the secular beliefs that filled the airwaves. These realities were reflected in the stories of many digital Black Christians, including my own.

As a pre-teen, I vividly remember browsing our local Lifeway bookstore one afternoon with my father. I loved surfing the children's section for comic books like *McGee and Me*. In my teens, the Tim LaHaye and Jerry B. Jenkins *Left Behind* series captured my fascination with the urgency of its end-times message. But at twelve, I was growing too old for McGee, and LaHaye's series was yet to be discovered. Instead, I found a Bible that promised to provide teens with everything needed to navigate the perils of secular society. Through anecdotal commentary appearing episodically throughout the Bible, issues like teen pregnancy, abortion, and relationships were covered in great detail. In its own words, the TLW Bible sought to provide "a compelling alternative to the bland, barren promises of happiness that this world sells twenty-four hours a day on fifty different channels" (Broadman & Holman 1996). In critiquing television, TLW positioned itself as the better Christian alternative. While I was curious about this book, which seemed to speak to teens, like many Black Christians my own world operated on a completely different channel.

I did not know yet of the national political climate swirling around young Black bodies like mine. The incarceration rate among mostly young African Americans was growing to epic proportions, beginning with policies like the Anti-Drug Abuse Act of 1986. Clinton's 1994 Violent Crime Control and Law Enforcement Act increased measures to both police and incarcerate Black bodies. Its provisions, which later became the rallying cry for anti-drug and policing activists, among others, included a three-strikes mandatory life sentence for repeat offenders, the hiring of one hundred thousand new police officers, and $14 billion in preventive programs which were often punitive instead of rehabilitative (Eisen and Chettiar 2016). Such provisions made way for local law enforcement tactics geared toward halting the free movement of Black bodies in their own communities through heavy surveillance. Since the 1970s, incarcerated African Americans had experienced first-hand the muscular growth of the prison industrial complex. Its reach extended into the mostly rural white farming communities far from inmates' own neighborhoods. Maintaining ties with families remained difficult given distance and the economic challenges travel presented for families struggling to make ends meet. This physical displacement created geographies of hopelessness as Black families fought to remain connected or deal with the severe sense of dislocation from little to no physical contact with loved ones. Black bodies of the 1990s carried such migratory patterns in their language and in the style of hip hop dress.

Talk of family members going or being sent "upstate" had long offered positional epistemologies, ways of situating loved ones, despite their absence in family photos, at birthday parties, and graduations. Hip hop fashions often associated with gang and prison culture, like Dickies work uniforms, baggy jeans, and overalls, were popularized by hip hop groups like NWA. and Tupac. From which of these sites, gang or prison culture, such style choices originated is debatable, yet the links between perceived Black criminality and Black incarceration rates married the two in the minds of young Blacks seeking to associate with urban youth fashion. Beyond its ephemeral goals of keeping up with fashion trends, Black youth responded to the politics of the Black body by attempting to wear the truth of Black experience on their person. Within predominantly Black urban spaces such style choices ensured that Black youth both remained connected to those sent upstate and inscribed their own neighborhoods with meaning, since imprisoned Black bodies walked free in their narrative wardrobes.

The irreparable harm caused by Clinton's crime bill was matched only by his administration's objective to "end welfare as we know it" (Deparle 1994). The move from the federal assistance program Aid to Families with Dependent Children to the Temporary Assistance for Needy Families program was a hotly debated topic among liberals and conservatives, centered largely on Black bodies. The stiff mandates on working and time limits for receiving government aid reflected the stigmatized view of mostly single Black mothers. While the numbers of recipients of government aid, historically and presently, have largely remained white, since the 1970s, media reporting and political discourse centered Black women as the face of poverty and thus government aid. Their depiction as lazy, overly sexual bodies given their inability to find consistent work and their multiple children was sometimes stated explicitly as in then-presidential candidate Ronald Reagan's memorable description of the "welfare queen" Linda Taylor (Demby 2013). At other times, in liberal corridors it played out in their political maneuvering in order to enact policies like the Personal Responsibility and Work Opportunity Reconciliation Act of 1996.

By the end of the century, the Act's provisions, if only in part, provided something many impoverished Blacks had wanted: security and dignity through work. Through its federal childcare subsidies, the expansion of Medicaid, and the earned income tax credit, the government was now obligated to "make work pay" (Haskins 2008). Yet, for all of its good, the Act's passage and subsequent enactment of Temporary Assistance for Needy Families also confirmed many of the stereotypes regarding Black female bodies. They were sites of social deviance that required policing and tutelage. Without the paternalistic guidance of the state, and left to their own devices, the Black female body remained unruly.

Rap music and hip hop videos seemed to convey this point through songs like "Rump Shaker" (1992) and "Pop That Coochie" (1991). Throughout the 1990s, male fantasies of breasts and backsides that refused to rest but jiggled and moved in synchronous rhythm were the hallmark of the genre. Even female artists like Bytches With Problems, Salt-n-Pepa, Lil' Kim, and Foxy Brown left cultural critics and scholars mixed in their assessments of their hypersexual portrayals of the Black female body. While the sexual agency exhibited by Lil' Kim in songs like "How Many Licks" was praised by bell hooks (1997), Mark Anthony Neal (2014) argues that it plays to long-held notions of Black women's sexual powerlessness.

Amid hypersexual portrayals of young Black bodies, some digital Black Christians gravitated to more approving, though still culturally relevant artists like Lauryn Hill. Like the Bell Biv DeVoe song "Poison" for young Black men in 1990, Hill's 1998 "Doo Wop (That Thing)" cautioned its young audience to "watch out" for a melee of social snares like teen pregnancy, domestic violence, and excessive material consumption. In the video, two images of Hill played side by side. Appearing in split screen as a 1950s doo-wop singer, Hill's stylish bob and platform boots were pictured alongside similarly modestly dressed Black men of the era outfitted in suits. This frame played against the more dressed-down, modern Hill, with locs and a thigh-high skirt. Equally noticeable for young Black Christian audiences were Hill's overt references to faith. Hill coolly admonished fans against bodily acts that were in violation of their beliefs, "Talking out your neck, sayin' you're a Christian / A Muslim, sleeping with the gin / Now that was the sin that did Jezebel in." For female digital Black Christians, in particular, the stark beauty of Hill's dark body offered an important media presentation of their own skin. Hill-Perry mentions the effect of the bodily presentation of Lauryn Hill in her 2014 rap song "Ode to Lauryn." Speaking of the video for "Doo Wop," she raps,

> Saturday morning, I see you on the TV singing in the split screen
> 50s theme with a picture
> It's a sister with a crown that isn't made of gold
> But skin like mine, that's when my mind froze like the summer's gone
> That color wasn't popular, changed me in the winter. (Hill-Perry 2014b)

As they had for Lecrae, hip hop music videos provided Hill-Perry with a new way of reading her own Black Christian body. The "50s theme" visual suggestion presented by "Doo Wop" played with other mid-twentieth-century portrayals of Black life popular in Black film at the time. It is interesting to note, then, that at the same time that the Southern Baptist Convention through the TLW campaign was calling for purity in broadcasting, the hip hop imagery most appealing to young Black Christians like Hill-Perry enforced the same by centering notions of a historical Black modesty located in doo wop music. To what extent these twin goals were noticeably linked in young Black Christian minds is unknown. Yet it does demonstrate the multilayered nature of the way digital Black Christians have used media in interpreting the meaning of their Black bodies.

Along with the messages regarding their bodies gained from music videos, the digital Black Christians studied here, like Jackie Hill-Perry, were largely raised in Black Christian spaces that often espoused conservative doctrines on sex and sexuality. For its part, the Black Church sought to respond to more sexualized hip hop imagery, as well as the national political climate around Black bodies, with a number of censures of the body. Particular attention was paid to the Black female body. Michael Eric Dyson (2008, 245) describes this sort of "erotic repression" as responsible for the "unmadeup faces, in long dresses that hide flesh, and the desexualized carriage of bodies (notice the burden is largely on the women) in the most theologically rigid of orthodox black churches." The fetishizing of Black bodies that seemed to fulfill the sexual imaginings of men in rap videos or that required the paternalistic support of the state through 1990s welfare policies were sanctified by a politics of respectability in Black churches. Evelyn Higginbotham (1994, 202) has noted the way the Black Church offered an oppositional space against white racism and yet remained largely beholden to the wider white American social structure. The women's movement among Black Baptists of the early twentieth century, for example, "reflected and reinforced the hegemonic values of white America" (187).

Extending this legacy of Black churches into the latter half of the twentieth century were conferences like the 1997 "Woman, Thou Art Loosed" gathering headed by Bishop T. D. Jakes, where Bynum first drew national attention with her "No More Sheets" sermon. "No More Sheets" was, as mentioned before, Bynum's attempt to play to the "real." This approach proved highly effective. Her performance of authenticity was conveyed through her style of dress, but also in the rhetorical imagery of the "real" presented in her language. Toward the end of her popular "No More Sheets" message delivered in July 1997, she says, "I ain't nothing but an everyday homegirl. Ain't nothing special about me. Know what I'm saying . . . I'm real. What you see is what I am." Such statements, and their reliance on common Black rhetorical strategies, effectively located her in the everyday geographies and wardrobe of the average young Black woman—homegirls. As she describes other such features of her spatial existence in the "projects" she delivers to her audience, through language, the possibility for purity in Black women's bodies. Yet even as she sought to bear "the 'hood" in her language, Bynum's material presentation told a different story.

Bynum offered a performance of respectability in the material presentation of her body. She appeared on that first national stage at the Woman, Thou Art Loosed conference with short, cropped hair and modest makeup. Outfitted in a pink-colored two-piece suit with an almost floor-length skirt, she was accessorized only with pearls and a scarf tied around her neck, seemingly meant to cover the last remaining suggestion of a feminine anatomy. It was through this grand performance of Black erotic repression that Bynum preached and prophesized her way into the bedrooms of Black Christian women. Hosted by Bishop T. D. Jakes, the Woman, Thou Art Loosed conference deeply reflected an African American Christian tradition in its homiletic and liturgical practices. Yet it mirrored much of the Christian dogma of the TLW Campaign and the word-of-faith theology all rolled into one: essentially, the notion that one was awarded for sexual abstinence with both material and marital bliss.

Yet, much to the chagrin of conservative Black Church folk, Bynum spoke openly regarding the body, particularly the brokenness of the female body. A Black woman in the Black Church had never been offered such a highly visible platform in which to discuss her sexual journey. New media technologies that allowed rapid video and CD production and sharing and broadcast channels like TBN's re-airing of Bynum's "No More Sheets" sermon replicated the narrative of a broken Black female body made whole by the word. White and Black audiences alike were moved by its testimonial-style revelations and its authenticity as a Black Christian woman's story. Given Clinton-era readings of the Black body, Bynum's story of sexual deviance reformed only by embracing a paternalistic theology of God followed American sensibilities regarding Black women's bodies. By wearing the vestiges of purity in her clothing and language, Bynum demonstrated to Black and white church goers, themselves influenced by both this national climate and historic beliefs regarding Black bodies, that Bynum's Black female body, troubled as it was, was deserving of redemption.

I vividly remember a church trip from our home church in Rochester, New York, to Daytona Beach, Florida. Our group of about seventy members consisted of an almost equal smattering of seniors, middle-aged, young adult, and youth members. As part of a holiness-Pentecostal denomination that espoused, at times with an unsettling severity, a doctrine of sexual prohibition, my childhood and teen years were filled with the hushed gossip of adults relating stories of the sexual woes of other church members. Raised in the shadows of such contradictions, it was difficult for me to make sense of why a video of "No More Sheets" was selected as intergenerational viewing as we traveled along I-70 headed south. We believed in having sex secretly, despising its desires in our members, and then punishing it openly.

There was the unmarried preacher who had been "sat down" when it was learned he had contracted HIV. A teenage friend would relate to me both her sadness over being silenced during the pregnancy of her first child and her difficulty in remaining still whenever the church service became particularly hot. "The spirit be hitting me and I be trying to be still. But I be feeling it," she sadly remarked. Her body, like those of so many other Black women in our congregation, seemed to betray her. In her sexual and spiritual desires, her body refused to obey the delimitations placed on it by our Black church. And then there were the rumors that the balcony of one of our sister churches, though it overlooked a city of the faithful below, sometimes doubled as a make-out mountain. Its darkened heights hid sexual rendezvous of all orientations. From groping sessions to oral pleasures, the church had borne many of our secrets in its walls. It had also doled out punitive measures for those found in errancy.

Bynum created a space, troubled though it was, in which the sexual lives of Black churchgoers could come out from their shadowy hiding places and be centered instead in one of the most sacred parts of our liturgical traditions: preaching. As Keri Day (2017) has analyzed it, for a mostly Black female audience Bynum offered a "vocabulary of self-worth, a religio-cultural grammar that allowed them to be reclaimed and redeemed as worthy and pure in a white society (and in many black church spaces) that defined them as fundamentally impure" (para. 2). A few years prior to Bynum's "No More Sheets" sermon, the 1996 Telecommunications Act, which allowed unfettered media ownership, made media conglomerates out of some companies almost overnight. As companies were allowed to own multiple media entities, consumers were increasingly offered a bundled media experience (e.g., cable television, internet services, or mobile devices).

As Jackie Hill-Perry sat watching "Doo Wop" in the early years of the millennium, and was moved by its imagery, its airing on her television was not unlike similar older Black Christian women who encountered Juanita Bynum's message through passive media encounters. Yet Hill-Perry and many other digital Black Christians benefited from the more participatory role that media convergence allowed. This group of digital Black Christians moved, as Jonathan Walton's 2009 book title instructs, from the *Watch This!* of Black televangelists, to the "watch me" style of online ministries. Hill-Perry and other creatives invited viewers close into their intimate lives, to focus on their material existence, which included their bodies. The bodily narratives of creatives filled YouTube spoken word performances.

YouTube and the Digital Black Christian Body: Two Examples

The digital testimony of Jackie Hill-Perry highlights the unique racial, gender, and economic dynamics of digital Black Christian approaches to the body and sexuality. Older Black mentors (who provide extensive guidance on how LGBTQIAs can transition into heterosexuality) and YouTube performance clips provide an alternative to more formalized forms of conversion therapy—clinical attempts at altering one's sexuality. Mostly white Christian accounts of conversion therapy often include any number of pseudoscientific interventions aimed at assisting clients in altering their sexual orientation. Jackie, however, details the influence of both YouTube and informal young Black adult guides in her transition from lesbianism to heteronormative behavior. Earlier in this volume I covered the role of mentor-like figures in discussing digital discipleship. The role of online spaces, coupled with such mentorship, has been overlooked as a patterned intervention into practices considered sexually deviant in Black religious circles. Such spaces are important sites to visit in order to understand why digital Black Christians retreat to YouTube to seek therapy and how they construct meaningful spaces for themselves once there.

The work of Hill-Perry in many ways fulfilled a deep need in the sexual discourse among digital Black Christians. Despite a troubling approach, she maps poor queer Blackness and Black experience onto the YouTube space through her intimate hip hop appeal to other digital Black Christians. This kind of intimacy is viewable in such Hill-Perry poems as her "My Life as a Stud" and "Jig-a-boo" (2012).

The testimony of Jackie Hill-Perry was first introduced to digital Black Christian audiences via her YouTube performance for the 2009 Rhetoric spoken-word event. By 2008, Rhetoric, a part of the Passion for Christ Movement (P4CM), while still unknown to many, had moved past its even humbler beginnings to feature more prominent acts and larger venues. Hill-Perry's performance there of "My Life as a Stud" further bolstered Rhetoric's appeal among digital Black Christians ("stud" is a Black vernacular term for a masculine lesbian). The poem details her move from lesbian identity to heterosexuality.

Following the digital upload of her performance and its millions of views and shares, Hill-Perry became a popular, in-demand digital artist. She is routinely called upon to speak and write about her story, appearing on the 700 Club and in the *Washington Post*, and regularly headlining some of the largest Christian conferences in the nation. Her prominence among digital Black Christians grew, ensuring that her path from lesbianism to heterosexuality would become a model for others who hope to emulate her transition.

Spoken word poems like Hill-Perry's work offered digital Black Christians an alternative to the more formalized, though often white Christian–led, forms of conversion therapy, which have historically included a wide range of approaches including group therapy, aversive treatments, masturbatory reconditioning, and, in extreme cases, lobotomies. In recent years, accounts regarding the harms of conversion therapy have emerged in films like *Cure for Love* (2008) and *Boy Erased* (2018), and from former proponents of its approaches like the past leader of the Journey to Manhood organization, David Matheson. Yet often absent from such media portrayals of conversion therapy are the differences in participation rates among racial and economic groups in such programs. This is an essential element for understanding why Hill-Perry entered the digital space both to seek guidance on her new transition and to offer her digital testimony to other digital Black Christians.

Formal programs of conversion therapy often require an economic investment along with access to clinicians trained in such techniques. Economic challenges, along with Black communities long-standing suspicion of numerous forms of medical treatment, often preclude young Black Christians from participation in conversion therapy. This accounts for why Black gender-questioning youth are rarely counted among conversion therapy clients, opting instead for informal and more accessible alternatives. This may also be attributable to Black ways of knowing and accessing the spirit that are neither acknowledged nor fully embraced in predominantly white circles. In addition to these factors, despite creatives' connections to white evangelicalism, conversion therapy remained off limits to them for other reasons.

Many such programs, like the National Association for Research and Therapy of Homosexuality (NARTH, now called the Alliance for Therapeutic Choice and Scientific Integrity), operated initially in deep connection with the Church of Latter-Day Saints. African Americans' affiliation with white evangelicalism, however, came largely through Baptist traditions like the Southern Baptist Convention or through other Protestant special-interest groups and ministries like Focus on the Family. Nor were organizations like NARTH particularly focused on outreach to groups of color.

A year prior to Hill-Perry's popular YouTube poem, NARTH published a scathing critique of the civil rights, women's rights, and gay rights movements. Written by one of the organization's Science Advisory Committee members, Gerald Schoenewolf (2005), it described "Africa at the time of slavery" as "primarily a jungle. . . . Life there was savage . . . and those brought to America, and other countries, were in many ways better off."[2] Amid calls by Truth Wins Out—an LGBTQIA advocacy group—for Focus on the Family to disinvite NARTH founder Joseph Nicolosi from its conference in August of that year, Schoenewolf's comments were deleted from NARTH's website, though Nicolosi still appeared as planned. Hill-Perry had no connections with NARTH, but she has continued to appear with Focus on the Family at conferences and other ministry engagements. Focus on the Family's own connection to NARTH reveals the distant relationship between the creatives discussed here and conversion therapy groups. Their own path to conversion therapy, however, is more closely framed by their own racial context. Many accounts of Black youths' conversions from homosexuality show that they happened through personal encounters, informally led by their church or pastors; others, as in Hill-Perry's case, transpired online.

Following her conversion in 2008, Hill-Perry describes surfing the web for Christian content and encountering an evangelism event led by P4CM leader Santoria. The digital encounter led her to Los Angeles, California, where she lived with Santoria for a year, was discipled by her, and "learn[ed] how to die to so much more than" homosexuality (Hill-Perry 2018, 101). The role of YouTube in mediating her faith continued the following year when she decided to share her testimony with audiences via P4CM's video post of "My Life as a Stud." Hill-Perry's inclusion of her own sensory experiences as a lesbian woman in the poem bore witness to the stories of Black, same-sex-loving women excluded from mostly white Christian as well as Black Church narratives and in popular media accounts of the same. While her readings of same-sex bodies are mostly affirming, she uses this stance to critique same-sex practices. Her approach adds nuance to digital Black Christian beliefs regarding sexuality.

YouTube Performance Clip 1: "My Life as a Stud"

"My Life as a Stud" (Hill-Perry 2010) is raw in its discussion of same-sex eroticism. It begins with the line, "I remember the first time I kissed her." Hill-Perry's epistemologies of "been there, known her" resonated with an audience whose sexual experiences had been hushed in the pews and pulpits of more than a few Black churches. And while they operated on the margins of Black churches, truth be told, they made up the fabric of those holy sepulchers. In *Sexuality and the Black Church*, Kelly Brown Douglas (1999) opines that Black churches' silence regarding the presence and concerns of LGBTQIA people in their midst is a byproduct of white racism. Acknowledging the diverse sexual orientations of Black people, for many, confirms historic readings of the Black body's social deviance. Yet Hill-Perry attempts to describe the beauty of same-sex love in a digital Christian context that usually ascribes shame to their experiences. The YouTube clip provides a transient therapeutic space for many digital Black Christians who, like Hill-Perry, have been silenced in Black Church spaces because of their sexuality. She does not, to be clear, affirm lesbian identities. Yet this space of knowing and being known is richly meaningful for those made to feel invisible or shunned in the Black Church. Commenters' responses range from gratitude to

Hill-Perry for sharing her struggles in the body to similar testimonies regarding their own desire to be free. Despite the openness of the forum, these comments often read as personal and deeply revealing reflections and confessions. They talk back to Hill-Perry, much like the redeemed (those who are certain of their convictions and conversion) do in Black churches following prayer services or altar calls. Hill-Perry's digital audience recognizes YouTube as a healing space and her poem acts as the catalyst in their own transformation. Given the sensitive and sometimes personal nature of their responses, commenters' profile names are anonymized in the following examples (found on Hill-Perry 2010):

Commenter 1:
This poem and testimony hit home. I teared up when the stud in the room stood up, because I know the pain too. God bless you Jackie for your obedience.

Commenter 2:
This .. is the poem that changed my life Jackie thank you thank you for this truth.. I was [a] full and complete stud when I stumbled upon this jewel.. that Jesus used to transform [my] life lol I even tried to cut off [my genitals] twice.. but I couldn't it was life.. I Thank You for being part of the process that set me free .. of [what] I thought was he.. is really she.. Thank You Mrs. Hill.. ⛪ P.S. Help Cometh From The Hills

Commenter 3:
Wow . . . this jus made me realize since iv been with my girlfriend, my relationship with God is not how it used to be. Dang I need to pray, read and believe.

Commenter 4:
EVEN AS A MALE EX-HOMOSEXUAL I CAN RELATE TO JACKIE IN SO MANY WAYS. I THANK HIM FOR DELIVERING ME!!!

Commenter 5:
Wow, I don't even know what to write. I am a Christian and have battled with Homosexuality my entire life. I have always been active in the church and God has always made Himself present in my life. I am a leader in my

church and have, for the first time started formally dating another man. I love him but my desire for God is so much stronger and is calling me to pull away from such sin. I want for my partner to be my Brother because I see myself in him. This video is a blessing. Pray for me!

The therapeutic space elicited by Hill-Perry's testimony is a byproduct both of the YouTube context and Hill-Perry's authenticity and autonomy in relating her own lesbian experiences and spiritual transformation. She remains at the center of her own narrative in a way that feels relatable to her audience. When the Black Church enters this same YouTube context it does not play nearly as well to digital audiences. Later viral portrayals of conversions when occurring in the context of the Black Church lack both this self-narration and thus believability, and have consequently not been as well received as "My Life as a Stud."

A key example: in February 2014, twenty-six-year-old Andrew Caldwell claimed he was delivered from homosexuality during the Church of God in Christ's annual Holy Convocation event (Welcome 2 Church 2014). His proclamation that he had been "delivert" and didn't "like mens no more" filled memes and spoof videos for weeks afterward. It became acceptable to deride Caldwell given both his "nonstandard" use of language and the farce of his conversion. Yet commentors' criticisms were also meant to deride the Black Church and its antiquated beliefs regarding homosexuality and spiritual practices around deliverance from homosexuality, as denoted in the following comments (Welcome 2 Church 2014):

Commenter 1:
And my mother wonder why I don't go to church anymore!

Commenter 2:
What a disgrace to God. Every single person in this clip is a disingenuous liar exploiting religion for personal greed and power.

Commenter 3:
I have never seen such ridiculousness in my life. You can't pray the gay out of anyone. He will always be gay.

Commenter 4:
> This is mockery. . . . smh!!!! I'm a firm believer, but u can tell when a person is making a mockery. This pastor should be ashamed of himself.

Commenter 5:
> Oh my GOD that is the funniest shit I ever seen LOL!!!

Caldwell's conversion was preceded by derogatory comments from Bishop Earl Carter regarding both women and gay men. At one point, Carter described gay men present at the conference as "sissies" and said, "homosexuals just walking around here with your pocketbooks, and your tight pants and your bowties, and you're walking like a girl—you need deliverance!" (Carter 2014). For many digital Black Christians these staid, even shameful characterizations of certain groups within Black churches replicated harmful readings of the Black body that they were far too familiar with.

Caldwell later regretted his participation in the service, saying "they think you can preach homosexuality away in the Church of God in Christ and you can't . . ." (NBC 12 News 2015). Recently, in an attempt to "show" followers that he was, in fact, no longer gay, Caldwell posted a string of videos with his new girlfriend(s) (Blair 2018). Like Caldwell, for many digital Black Christians, the internet has provided a space not only for finding acceptance as LGBTQIA folk, but for linking them with resources, as it did for Jackie Hill-Perry, on how to transition into new, heterosexual identities by "wearing" heterosexuality. Beyond YouTube, other social media sites like Instagram allow them space to try out, to perform their new heterosexual identities. Hill-Perry's story is a similar tale of a digital Black Christian both locating and performing a new straight identity through online guidance. Unlike Caldwell, however, her testimony's distance from the Black Church and self-narration allowed "My Life as a Stud" to be taken seriously by YouTube commenters.

Hill-Perry's description of her outward appearance places further distance between her and the Black Church. She contrasts her last time in a church with a description of her hip hop clothing, thus situating her hip hop body as beyond the care and concern of the Black Church.

> His [Hill-Perry's father] funeral was the last time I stepped
> foot into a church
> I refused to deal
> with the eyes looking down on this deep
> voice masculine girl
> yet couldn't see
> past my face to pray
> past the pants
> falling past my waist
> past the fitted
> caps and the braids.

Hill-Perry's account makes clear that her lesbian body found no home or love in the Black Church. Through *pretexting the body*, in this way, putting on hip hop style, she demonstrates Black churches' inability to love LGBTQIA folk. In other interviews, Hill-Perry describes briefly locating this kind of love and acceptance in the gay community. She does not leave this awareness or common ethos behind once moving back into Christian spaces. Instead, her experiences as a lesbian woman shape how she both embodies a hybrid of this identity in the Christian communities she joins. She detailed her perspective in a 2018 interview on the *Truth's Table* podcast:

> What's been helpful for me to communicate to the Christian church is how much the gay community is an actual community. Because it's an actual community it can be terrifying to say "Oh, come up out of that community and join ours even though we don't look communal . . . Especially for me. I hadn't seen Christians look like Christians. I hadn't seen the church as described in the scripture. And so, all I thought church was was [sic] y'all show up, yell and shout, call out some sins and everybody leave the same way. What I saw [in the gay community was] the language we spoke to each other was deep . . . kind of like our own type of native tongue . . . There was the shared experience of what it feels like to be out . . . especially in your Black family, like the terror of that and the shame that can come out of it . . . So I think I've tried to impart that experience in the experiences of the church. (*Truth's Table* 2018)

Hill-Perry thus reveals that her past experiences within Black churches lacked a certain authenticity and transformative ability. Her call for a better Christian community, then, is itself a critique of the experiences of same-sex loving Black bodies in Black churches. In "My Life as a Stud," Hill-Perry conceals in her imagery the same critique of the church and its dissension of LGBTQIA persons. Yet, along with critique, Hill-Perry's work also presses for a new epistemological understanding of the Black body.

In wearing hip hop in her language, she constructs a notion of digital Black Christian identity that lies at the intersections of Christianity and hip hop. It is evident from their response that her audience fully understands that she is pointing to a shared digital Black Christian identity. It is one that moves beyond a simple critique of Black Church practices. She describes in graphic detail her first sexual encounter with her girlfriend, in which she uses a strap-on. She now figuratively disrobes from the hip hop ensemble she had put on earlier in the poem. The clothes here become symbolic reminders of her attempts to conceal her true identity, as she only used "the big clothes to hide behind." In a later interview she states that "putting on the clothes . . . covered up the hurt little girl I was on the inside" (Hill-Perry 2010). For Hill-Perry, wearing hip hop was bound up in wearing gender. She reads well the male-driven bravado of hip hop music and fashion and seeks to inscribe her own body with its meaning and force. Yet by the poem's end it becomes apparent that hip hop, much like the Black Church, offers little in the way of refuge for Hill-Perry. With neither to return to, she sets out to construct a new site of digital Black faith.

Acts of pretexting like this have been misinterpreted as fraudulent or misguided returns to a sort of religious captivity. However, this would be a purely superficial and inaccurate reading of Hill-Perry's body work. In earlier works like *Black Noise*, Tricia Rose (1994) highlights the challenges faced by female emcees in male-dominated hip hop spaces. Rose notes female artists' attempts to fit in with male artists while employing unique strategies to address misogyny. Similarly, creatives like Hill-Perry make sartorial, ideological, and artistic moves to "fit in," in order to tell painful truths and critique the spaces (both of hip hop and the Black Church) from which they come as a way of serving notice to other creatives that they are down for the task of mapping out new religious terrain.

Through pretexting, Hill-Perry is able to situate gays, lesbians, trans, and queer folk in a common Black Christian experience in socially affirming ways and asks us as scholarly readers to sit with the real experiences of LGBTQIA folk who desire to fall elsewhere on the spectrum, mostly in heteronormative roles. Through the material culture of hip hop, its masculine style of dress and linguistic play, Hill-Perry offers Black Christians a broader view of the functions and possibilities of the Black female body and ways of being a woman in Christian faith. She is both intentional in this project and aware of the way it pushes up against racial-heterogenous constructs of white Christian femininity. In her autobiography, Hill-Perry (2018, 116) writes, "By looking to God's word for how to be a woman, I found what God intended when he gave me this call. God's image is what womanhood was born out of. Not the 1950s polaroid of white women baking cookies . . ." By thus rejecting white femininity, Hill-Perry instead positions herself—her female, same-sex loving, hip hop body—as a reflection of God, giving Black Christians more ways of being in hip hop while affirming LGBTQIA folks' legitimacy and belonging in Christian spaces. This points to the sort of embodied discourse where the insertion of the Black female body in the dialogue, even one wrought with as many contradictions as Hill-Perry's, redirects established epistemologies of the Black body in Christian spaces and seeks to move religious folk toward freedom. Female creatives respond, in white churches, Black churches, and hip hop, to injurious cultural stereotypes of what the female body represents and seek to serve notice to onlookers that their own bodies (much like Juanita Bynum's earlier sermon) can be inscribed with new spiritual meaning. Such pretexting is a performance of liberation in the body. The female creative is saying, as Anne Julie Cooper ([1892] 2017) might have put it, "This is what a free body looks like. Come get free."

While she does not fit the traditional mold, in percussive ways, Hill-Perry takes on the womanist task of making room for her own narrative in Black and white Christian spaces and in her own digital space. She is guided by her experience with women she has loved both sexually and nonsexually. She describes herself and her mother as not fitting any of the constructs of white Christian femininity as outlined in contemporary Christian literature. Instead, in the previously cited interview on the

Truth's Table (2018) podcast, Jackie locates her mother in Black women's care work of "cutting the grass, going to work, making sure I was loved and affirmed." Wearing hip hop, then, post-conversion, becomes a way of loving the Black femaleness of her body. She says in the same podcast interview, "I don't like dresses, I have a heavy voice . . . I'm just going to be myself. He's given me this personality and the context in which I grew up in to see womanhood differently. Black women are different. Period. And I love it!" (*Truth's Table* 2018).

And while some critics opine that Hill-Perry's work does not go far enough—many desire a full affirmation of gay and lesbian folk in Christian spaces—it does seek to acknowledge and normalize gay and lesbian practices and the desires of LGBTQIA Christians. While she does not describe it as such, Hill-Perry can even be considered to be making room for bisexual folk in owning her own continued desire for both her husband and other women.

YouTube Performance Clip 2: "Jig-a-boo"

In performances like "Jig-a-boo," Hill-Perry's (2012) actual visual presentation in hip hop clothing offers yet another reading of the Black female body. Hill-Perry's performance is richly layered, as she performs a poem critiquing "jig-a-boo" Black Church preachers at a multiracial church with a mostly digital Black Christian audience for the 2015 P4CM/Rhetoric spoken-word event. That Hill-Perry settles on cornrows, large diamond earrings and chain, a crew-neck, button-down shirt, fitted jeans, and a pair of Jordans reads its own grammar onto her performance. By "wearing hip hop" in a temporarily contrived digital Black Christian space, she signals to the audience that it can trust the veracity of her critiques of the Black Church. After all, she is here positioning herself as both an insider and outsider in relation to it. As with "My Life as a Stud," later responses to the video upload of the performance are filled with agreement and shared understanding among digital Black Christians. Yet the fluidity of Blackness and gender makes this a moving target, particularly online. As easily as Hill-Perry affirms contemporary Black female bodies (her own included), she also desires to dismantle them in her readings of Black bodies that exhibit a historical distance from her own. In order to fully understand the bilateral nature of Hill-Perry's bodily and linguistic performance, "Jig-a-boo" must then be triangulated with other discourse on the female body and Blackness in her autobiography *Gay Girl, Good God*. A particularly useful example appears nearly halfway into the volume as she discusses her decision to end her relationship with her girlfriend, following her conversion.

> She was the eye Jesus said to gouge out and the right hand He commanded me to cut off (Matthew 5:29–30). Though it was as painful as the extreme act of removing a part of the body, it was better for me to lose her than to lose my soul. I just . . . gotta live for God now, I said with a tear-broken voice, ending us and what felt like my own undoing. (Hill-Perry 2018, 108)

Through the use of stark biblical imagery, Hill-Perry metaphorically dismantles the body of her girlfriend. There is a highly problematic bend toward violence against women in her description of her exit from lesbianism and in her subsequent rap lyrics as featured on *The Art of Joy* (Hill-Perry 2014a). In depicting her ex as the excision of an offending part of her anatomy, she declares violence on the Black female body. It is a current of thought that runs through much of her rap lyrics, in which women are often poised as "troubled and empty hearted" for their bad decisions, "filthy since Genesis," or "schizo and fearful." For Hill-Perry the abjection of all things lesbian and her entry into "Christian womanhood" negatively frames womanhood and women, replicating some of the same harmful delimitations on Black Christianity I discussed earlier about the Black Church. On one hand it seems out of character, given her wholesale love of Black womanhood as expressed in the aforementioned interviews. However, the percussive strategies of pretexting that Hill-Perry employs come with significant limitations on her reading of her own body. Evelynn Hammonds (2004) notes that lesbian women in Black Church spaces are often viewed as deviant within deviant behavior, given the discrimination they face first because of their gender coupled with their sexual orientation. Brittany Cooper (2019, 15) writes, "We live in a world that tells women to distrust other women. And those of us who do dare to love other women hard are taught to distrust our impulses, to see that love as queer and wrong." As Hill-Perry attempts to disentangle herself from negative constructs regarding her sexuality, she overlooks its meaning for her gender. Still, the pretexting Hill-Perry engages in makes violence against women nearly always necessary. This violence, as Audre Lorde ([1984] 2007, 37) pointed out, attempts to destroy the "visible face of [one's own] self-rejection."

Hill-Perry's lyrical choices may also be attributable to her being one of only a handful of prominent female Christian hip hop (CHH) artists. Hill-Perry reflects male CHH artists' portrayals of women. Hill-Perry thus does away with the well-worn Christian reparative therapy model, in which in order to be a *real* woman one must love a man, and replaces it with a model in which to be a woman one must treat women *like* a man. This is itself a toneless minstrel-ization of Black masculinity, a performance in which the brutal Black buck imposes violence on the female body. And it warrants the same critique of hypermasculinity offered of other hip hop artists. Yet Hill-Perry goes unnoticed because among digital Black Christians, as has been noted by Michael Eric Dyson (2008), in some ways the sensibilities of hip hop and the Black Church have historically aligned, here in the deprecation of Black female bodies. Hill-Perry continues this tradition in ways acceptable to digital Black Christians because, as Joan Morgan and Mark Anthony Neal (2006, 239) opine regarding hip hop, the same is true of the Black Church: "it isn't doing something to Black women that American society isn't already doing to Black women." And so Jackie Hill-Perry raises no eyebrows in her sometimes violent reading of the female body.

The way Hill-Perry takes up Blackness in her work also offers an important reading of the Black Christian female body. Hip hop's link to young urban Black life and culture has married the two with social deviance in media as well as both white and Black Church portrayals. Because of this, wearing hip hop reads deprecating notions of Blackness back onto the body, particularly in the white evangelical circles frequented by digital Black Christians like Hill-Perry. Nancy Wolgemuth (née DeMoss), a central figure in reigniting the Women's Purity movement, first discipled Hill-Perry through her writings and continues to act as her mentor. Hill-Perry asked Wolgemuth to write the foreword to *Gay Girl, Good God*. Like the cult of true womanhood that partly inspired their movement, Nancy manages to cast herself as a pure white woman against Hill-Perry's Black hip hop body. She opens the foreword to *Gay Girl, Good God* by saying,

> Jackie Hill-Perry and I could hardly have more disparate backgrounds. She is a millennial; I am a boomer. She is black, and I am white. She was raised by a single mom and disregarded by an absentee dad who had no idea how to love her. I was parented by a happily married, attentive mom and dad who adored each other and their children. (Wolgemuth, in Hill-Perry 2018, xi)

Wolgemuth's description in her foreword of her own alleged naïveté regarding the meaning of the word "homosexual" and hip hop language used by Jackie, like "dope," reminds the reader of her virtue against Jackie's Black body (in Hill-Perry's own book). Hill-Perry duplicates these same troubling readings of Blackness further in her autobiography and in her poem "Jig-a-boo." It is interesting to note once again that Hill-Perry's autobiography was issued by the same publishing house as Lecrae's autobiography, B&H Publishing, led by the mostly white Southern Baptist Convention. As with *Unashamed*, this context seems to influence the way Blackness shows up in *Gay Girl, Good God*. Racial identity is assumed through references to Black cultural practices, yet largely undiscussed as significant in shaping her early life. Where the word "Black" itself appears, it is usually associated with a negative experience or emotion. While digital spoken word allows Jackie Hill-Perry the latitude to redefine gay and lesbian identity in Black Christian spaces, Blackness remains rather flatly assembled, described through caricatures of Black Church practice in her poetry.

Toward the top of "Jig-a-boo" Hill-Perry (2012) defines "jig-a-boo Christians" as "people with a holy facade like a white face painted over their negro colored heart." While the etymology of the word *jig-a-boo* dates back to the 1700s, Hill-Perry uses its derisive connotation against Christians who are receptive to millennial-era prosperity doctrines. It is a direct critique of just the sort of word-of-faith Black preaching circle that produced Juanita Bynum. Collapsing the predominantly white antebellum and the Black post-antebellum minstrel practice, Hill-Perry describes an ambiguous group of Black performers "dancing for quarters, nickels, and dimes." Hill-Perry moves the historical goalpost backwards and forwards, in cautioning her mostly Black audience that, "just like your ancestors . . . [you] are still enslaved." In driving her point home, Hill-Perry fills her poem with all of the imagery of American enslavement to represent spiritual bondage. In an unfortunate grab for alliteration, she humanizes God in the person of a white slave master, rebuking, by whipping, his slaves, much like God rebukes Christian believers. She says, "You'd rather hide behind your old Negro spiritual worship songs because you can't stand the Master's whippings" (Hill-Perry 2012).

Recalling, like other digital Black Christians mentioned earlier, the collective memories of Black film and television broadcasts, Hill-Perry references *Roots* and *Amistad*. Yet she employs such films differently than Lecrae does. She describes them as slave narratives Christians must relinquish in order to develop spiritually. While never calling the Black Church or Black preachers by name, she mimics, to the laughter of the audience, the heavy breathing and whooping of Black preaching styles. She then contrasts this style—much as in Wolgemuth's description of her own "plain intellectual style of teaching"—with the Apostle Paul's "preaching which is plain and void of clever and persuasive words" (Hill-Perry 2018, xi). With references to the underground railroad, the Million Man March, and the Thirteenth Amendment, Hill-Perry argues for a move toward freedom from past histories of oppression. It is clear that her theology is one of progress, imploring her audience not to return to the failures of their ancestors, eschewing historical Black Church practices, and directing the listener to the suffering of Christ over and against the lesser suffering of Blacks.

Conclusion: Intimacy through Identity and Visibility

Like the work of Juanita Bynum before her, Jackie Hill-Perry's writing and performances draw digital Black Christian women into a deeply felt intimacy through her successful attempts at making the Black body visible. Yet such visibility comes at a high cost to the Black female body in Hill-Perry's work. From James Cone (1969, 1970) to Delores Williams (1993), Black liberation and womanist thinkers have argued for the necessity of a theology that places Christ in the midst of Black lived reality. Jackie Hill-Perry reverses this approach in her strategy of moving Him out and away from Black practices. By resituating LGBTQIA bodies in more affirming ways in Christian and digital spaces, it seems at first glance that Hill-Perry is envisioning perhaps an overhaul of the Black Church–based way in which Juanita Bynum takes up the body. Yet in reaffirming injurious tropes regarding Blackness and violence against Black women's bodies we find a strain of thought that has gained significant currency among digital Black Christians and borrows heavily from white Christian and Black Church spaces, even while wearing hip hop to do so.

Pretexting reflects creatives' deep regard for personally realizing the divine value in a historically devalued Black body. This is not without deep flaws, however. By wearing hip hop, Hill-Perry moved against Juanita Bynum–style televangelists of the late twentieth century. Yet in offering listeners an identity/secondary Blackness—a performance of Blackness, Christianity and gender through hip hop—creatives like Hill-Perry fail to discuss the capitalist and patriarchal systems that shaped hip hop culture. Like Black female televangelists before her, her religious proscriptions are espoused as universal pathways to spiritual freedom. In truth, like the present sex-based "e-vangelists," the Black female televangelists of the past often projected their particular sexual struggles onto their audiences. Womanist scholar Melva Sampson (2017) argues that women can be both "assailant and victim," collaborating with systems of oppression within the Black Church. Even as Hill-Perry did incredible work in positioning same-sex loving bodies more centrally in Black Church spaces, as in "My Life as a Stud," it came at the expense of violence and deprecating readings of the Black body, as in "Jig-a-Boo." The work of Hill-Perry reveals the way digital Black Christianity perpetuated the same harmful beliefs of the Black Church regarding the Black body in digital spaces.

Yet, much like Joseph Solomon, creatives continue to evolve and relocate their Christian identity within Black Church rhetorical practices online. This was evident in Jackie Hill-Perry's March 23, 2018, Instagram sermon clip by the late senior bishop of the Church of God in Christ, Rev. Gilbert Patterson. Hill-Perry's video post included the following caption:

> *Jackiehillperry* I know it's a common trait of young-biblically sound African American Christians to look down on the older generation of Saints

that went before us (I've made this mistake myself). We start going to churches that teach the word a little calmer and we start thinking that that's the ONLY way & the "solid" way but don't be fooled. Many of the Preachers and Saints that have gone before us are just as biblical and as worthy of our honor as we give to the majority culture theologians that we enjoy quoting. They may not say the word "atonement" too often, but they sure know that Jesus paid a debt that we owed. And you can bet, when the Gospel is preached, whether it's simple or academic, Jesus is glorified.

Jackie Hill-Perry's celebration of the Black Church rhetorical tradition hints toward the argument of this book, in which digital Black Christians come full circle, both affirming and reconstructing the very notion of the Black Church.

4

Work

The Story of Natalie and Beleaf

I asked her, "How much is it worth for me to be away." She said, "Nothing. There's not an amount that can rationalize you being gone." I said, That's it. I'm done.
—Interview with Beleaf Melanin[1]

KB [rapper] and I wanted to have ownership. We wanted to provide opportunities for our people to be artistically, spiritually, and financially free and that comes with sacrifice and ownership.
One day he realized that he couldn't pass down his catalogue of music to his kids because he didn't own it. I realized that I would always be a means to someone else's end. So, we started our own company.
—Interview with Natalie Lauren Sims[2]

The complex and often lopsided entry of Black creatives into the digital marketplace has its unique challenges. This chapter details the complex cost of working online while Black, young, and Christian, and the multiple strategies creatives employ to navigate economic and social challenges to their digital Black labor.

As a common ethos, Black Lives Matter (BLM) is integral to this process. The BLM movement has been popularly described as separate from the Black Church. Yet young Black Christians' online engagement with BLM evinces other connections between contemporary Black Christianity and a Black movement largely touted as nonreligious (Tesfamariam 2015). The relationship between digital Black Christians and BLM remains complicated at best, as Alissa Richardson's interview (2020) with Christian activist Ieisha Evans demonstrates in "The 'Good News': How the Gospel of Anti-Respectability Is Shaping Black Millennial Christian Podcasting." Yet the influence of young Black Christians on the movement, and vice versa, is significant. As in the phrase "Black Lives *Matter*," creatives consistently discuss "worth" and "value" in the digital economy, as in "the worth of" other people, and by extension themselves—often as being "worth more than that." Such discussions revealed times in which creatives felt they did not "matter." In our interviews some creatives also expressed intense emotions associated with being made to feel "worth-less." Such ongoing "housewifization" in the digital, as Christian Fuchs (2018) calls it, remains dependent on surplus value; the super-exploitation of workers' labor for the benefit of capitalists' entities. As Karl Marx ([1862–63] 1969) first described it, such a process ensures that workers never receive the full value of their labor. Instead labor takes on its own value or surplus, the worth of which is owned by the employer. This explains creatives' feelings of worthlessness.

Media scholars Kathleen Kuehn and Thomas Corrigan (2013, 9–13) describes hope labor as free digital work done in hopes of gaining future monetary work. Kuehn's work accentuates how devaluing of artists in the digital economy occurs across racial lines. However, this reality is more acutely felt by Black creatives, whose additional forms of labor are often invisible. Given historically racist labor practices in America, creatives' reality is far more oppressive than the sort of "housewifization" that Fuchs (2018) describes. As Angela Davis (1981) points out, "since Black women as workers could not be treated as the 'weaker sex' or the 'housewife,' Black men could not be candidates for the figure of 'family head' . . . After all, [Black] men, women, and children alike were all 'providers' for the slaveholding class" (2). Davis's analysis is essential for understanding the gendered dynamics of both male and female creative labor. Born out of a history of trauma, the affective forms of labor that creatives participate in often call on them to 'perform' or reveal such trauma in order to elicit feelings of intimacy and (financial) support from followers. Additionally, their historic exploitation as care workers places them at heightened vulnerability for exploitation and the expectation of their free labor. In the digital in the way Beleaf, a self-proclaimed stay-at-home Dad, attends to the domestic life of his family in the most popular clips of his YouTube show "Beleaf in Fatherhood" and in Natalie's persistent "grooming" of young artists, we see fluid racial-gender dynamics of their labor and what makes its value just as transient. To be clear, emotional labor, affective labor, and care work have become identifiers of women's work. Feminist scholarship thus works out of this understanding and has provided us with some of the richest resources on the topic of labor. Creatives cross this storied gendered terrain as they grapple with the realities of Black bodies' subjection to capitalism and seek new value or matter for those bodies.

In speaking of "matter," some of the interview sessions for this book operated as a cathartic space in which creatives revealed the intimate details of their workplace traumas. Those moments led me to investigate further what is traditionally called "work" and the multiple ways Black Christian bodies are coded (or left uncoded) in the digital workplace. Christina Sharpe (2016) describes the "sense and awareness of precarity; the precarities of the afterlives of slavery" that African Americans face even as they ascend the economic ladder from working class to middle class (5). Their work remains encoded with a unique set of concerns and sensibilities related to histories of trauma and located in present bouts of scarcity and death. In a moving description of her care for her brother during his final moments, Sharpe notes,

> What does it mean to defend the dead? To tend to the Black dead and dying: to tend to the Black person, to Black people, always living in the push toward our death? It means work. It is work: hard emotional, physical, and intellectual work that demands vigilant attendance to the needs of the dying, to ease their way, and also to the needs of the living. Vigilance, too, because any and everywhere we are, medical and other professionals treat Black patients differently: often they don't listen to the concerns of patients and their families; they ration palliative medicine, or deny them access to it altogether. While there are multiple reasons for this . . . , experience and research tell us "'people assume that, relative to whites, blacks feel less pain because they have faced more hardship.' . . . Because they are believed to be less sensitive to pain, black people are forced to endure more pain" . . . . We had to *work* to make sure that Stephen was as comfortable as possible." (10; emphasis added)

Sharpe's description underscores the difficulty, the hard "work" that it took to make her brother's Black life "matter" to health professionals.

Her meditation elicits an important question for the scholarly reader: how do we account for and take account of the hidden work of Black people in America? This question is of particular concern for digital Black Christians, as the digital context was built upon and continues to reflect the same structural forms of racism that Sharpe notes were born "in the wake" of slavery. Digital Black Christians, too, must fight to ensure that their "hard emotional, physical, and intellectual work" matters.

Historically, there has been considerable slippage in how Western capitalism catalogs Black labor. The emotional labor of creatives often goes uncoded as work, and thus creatives, at times, feel "worth less." The intimate revelations that occurred in the interview setting prompted me to question why creatives might be inclined to reveal painful truths in our conversations. I believe it has much to do with our shared Black subjectivity, that is, interviewees' assumptions that unlike in the digital workspace, we hold an intimacy in our shared experiences with white racism. As noted earlier, intimacy among Blacks has always been a contested and deeply political affair. The reader should be reminded of Candice Jenkins's (2007) assessment that "African American subjects have a complex relationship to the exposure of intimacy, and to its peculiar vulnerabilities, because of the vulnerability that many Blacks already experience through racial identity and its associated dangers" (4). Jenkins argues that Blacks hold tightly to traditional notions of respectability in an attempt to live down harmful stereotypes of overly sexualized Black bodies. The digital workplace holds this same site of vulnerability and risk of exposure for digital Black Christians. Through webwork, creatives must balance their desire to seem authentic online without revealing so much that could be endangered. Unfortunately, through such performances, what is left unknown is work performed in response to racism and sexism and the emotional toll it often takes on them. Mindful of Sharpe's (2016) approach to what she calls *wake work*, this chapter interrogates this grey area in the digital labor economy in which "we, Black people everywhere and anywhere we are, still produce in, into, and through the wake an insistence on existing: we insist Black being into the wake . . ." (11). With particular attention to their notion of the "Christian faith," I am mainly concerned with all the ways digital Black Christians *insist* their existence upon the digital space through *woke economies*—monetarily compensated responses to structural and personal inequality.

In recent years, the notion of "woke capitalism" has emerged in which corporations seek to attract customers through value-centered approaches to consumer marketing, as in Dove Soap's "Real Beauty" campaign (Dove 2020). In the summer of 2020, corporations like The North Face (against Facebook) and Nike and FedEx (against the Washington Redskins) canceled either advertising or other proceeds over issues of bias. With tremendous variation and mindful of their religious beliefs, the Black content creators studied in this volume also participate in the aims of such "conscious while capitalists" efforts. In essence, this chapter asks: in a hostile capitalist economy, how do digital Black Christians recode and uncode their labor in an attempt to be seen and heard in ways that are meaningful to them? In this process, I am myself seeking to recode the meaning of young Black Christian bodies and labor to allow new ways of reading digital Black Christians.

Allowing my guides to lead enables the reader to see that the process and attainment of visibility and self-worth is marked by increased intimacy with digital co-workers, friends, and other Christians. In short, contrary to pessimistic claims that young Black adults may be falling away from the "faith" and/or human relationships, the digital labor context in which creatives develop religious practices drives their intense desire for more and not less intimate human and divine contact. The stories of Beleaf and Natalie substantiate this point.

The Hidden Cost of Digital Black Christian Labor

The creatives selected for participation in this two-year study represent diverse geographies. They hail from small towns like Tulsa, Oklahoma, and Fort Hood, Texas, major metropoles like Chicago, Illinois, and Los Angeles, California, and mid-sized cities like San Diego, California. Though they come from such a wide variety of places, they are connected in their common experiences of internet usage. As we have seen, digital technology allows meaningful online space for shared affirmation among digital Black Christians. Earlier, it was out of such safe online spaces as Myspace that young Blacks established communal expressions of Blackness. But, as Mizuko Ito et al. (2010) note, there is a direct correlation between "hanging out, messing around, and geeking out." Social platforms that gave digital Black Christians, in their teens, a space to dialogue on communally held beliefs and experiences in Black Christianity have given way in their adult lives to highly skilled digital practices. Yet, as the story of Natalie Lauren Sims and Beleaf Melanin reveals, for young Black Christians, there are a number of hidden costs to joining the labor market through such platforms and under these terms.

The creatives I have interviewed discuss their initial leisurely online practices or activities as marked by curiosity. Many have commented in terms such as "I wanted to see what was out there," or "One day I was just searching for a new . . . (song, sermon, etc.)." My guides understood these moments of discovery relationally. It was in periods of religious development and negative church experiences that their online curiosity grew. Joseph Solomon recalled his desire to "know more" than what the church of his childhood had taught him. This led him to an online search of sermons on Christian theology and eventually to his decision to enroll in a seminary. The online environment thus became an alternative to the physical realities of the Black Church. Yet creatives like Solomon do not become lost in the digital world. Rather, seeing what's out there typically leads to a heightened desire for greater visibility of one's self. DJ Wade-O describes in our interview his first time hearing gospel rap: "I was like "Man, if I could just get this in the hands of my friends . . ." His trek into the world of Christian hip hop led to Wade-O becoming one of the most popular and influential DJs in the genre. He is not alone in this experience.

Through his promotional assistance, Andwele Williams, marketing director of the Passion for Christ Movement (P4CM), has helped ignite the careers of several of the digital Black Christians discussed in this book. It was in a crowded café in 2009 that he attended the very first Lyricist Lounge, which later became Rhetoric—the largest Christian spoken-word event in the United States. A certain awe could be heard in his voice when he talked about that early event in our interview: "I just thought if people could hear this, this would change the world." More than ten years later, his words may read as self-aggrandizing. Yet his initial encounter occurred just as the popularity of Russell Simmons's HBO television series *Def Poetry Jam* was beginning to wane and conscious hip hop seemed to be searching for a new medium.[3] Cross Movement Records, though popular among a number of digital Black

Christians, remained a largely underground name. Albums like rapper Mase's *Welcome Back* (2004) tried to offer a positive and overtly Christian message. Though it initially did well on the charts, music critics did not warm to it. Earlier in 1997, gospel recording artists such as Kirk Franklin moved the gospel music genre further toward young Black hip hop culture, through cameo rap appearances of artists like Salt of Salt-n-Pepa (Franklin 1997) and later with popular Christian rappers like Da Truth (Franklin 2007). Yet there remained a void in Black hip hop-style Christian crossover culture that artists like Lecrae had only just begun to fill with his 2004 release *Real Talk*. It was not a stretch to think that Christian spoken word, which many of its artists had long considered the fifth pillar (knowledge) of hip hop, could fill that void.

The room that Andwele describes was a darkened converted warehouse in downtown Los Angeles. He attended Lyricist Lounge on one of his first dates with the woman who is now his wife, who is also a poet. Young Black Christians packed the audience, sat along the stage and crowded near the exits, listening closely as each poet performed. Between poems, someone developed a chant, which Andwele remembers going something like "Wha-aats his name?" The crowd responded "Je-sus!," louder with each repetition. Andwele had grown up in a more reserved Black Methodist church. He had heard many of the same theologies from his own tradition posited in the words of poets. But it was the visceral and rhythmic drive of the chanting together with the conviction of the poets and the energy of the audience that created an altogether different experience for him from the experience he'd had at his home church. It was the most authentic encounter with the divine he had ever felt, and he wanted to share it with others. His decision a few years later to take over as marketing director confirmed this desire and led him to social media. It was his passion to reach others and to provide platforms for digital Black Christians who, though a bit younger than him (he jokingly calls himself "an elder statesman" in P4CM) were, like him, committed to ministering through digital platforms.

As we have seen, creatives' exposure to Christian content beyond their Black Church, whether through digital sound, physical meeting locations, or online videos, ignited their desire to promote their newly acquired knowledge still further. For many of these creatives, skills acquisition took the form of online tinkering, searching through how-to videos or trying their hand at developing platforms for podcasting. Like Andwele and DJ Wade-O, they often reached back to teach, train, and provide platforms for those younger than themselves. Because each stage of their digital development was marked by very personal and religious interests, it is possible to overlook the considerable work it took to acquire those skills. Yet in moving from seeing to online tinkering to being seen, creatives developed highly desirable skills in the digital labor economy. Indeed, all the creatives interviewed make some, if not the majority, of their annual income from digital labor. In this, their experiences are largely consistent with all young adult Blacks in the digital economy.

In recent years, a number of digital platforms have provided work opportunities for a diverse labor market. Jobs like survey-taking, ridehailing, delivery services, and social media brand promotion provide a few common examples of online possibilities for work. While this offers flexibility and autonomy for many, as has been the case historically, Black labor online has a number of hidden costs. A 2016 Pew Research study found that young adult African Americans and Latinxs were more likely to perform gig work than whites, while fewer opportunities exist for consistent and stable employment for young Black and brown people. In addition, when securing such jobs, compared to their white counterparts African Americans are more likely to fulfill jobs requiring physical labor, such as ride hailing. On average, lower-income Americans (those with annual household incomes of $30,000 or less) are more than twice as likely to engage in what is known as technology-enabled gig work (Pew Research Center 2016).

For the Black Christian creatives studied here, the situation is even more complex. Legitimizing Black artistic labor, particularly as intellectual production—from late nineteenth-century Black minstrel performances, chitlin' circuit plays, and artists of the Harlem Renaissance, to more recent examples, like white pushback over *Black Panther*'s Oscar consideration—has always been tedious. Young Black workers continue to be cast as the "brute" in the digital labor economy, able to fulfill physical tasks while much less likely to be considered for intellectual roles such as social media influencer, YouTube personality, or online brand promoter. Digital labor, and its "playbor" economies (hobbies or play turned work), further call into question the legitimacy of their work.

Labor union calls for more or any pay often represent only white artists' interests or simply fall on deaf ears in an economy that privileges overproduction (i.e., payment for number of tweets) and underpayment ($3 to $10 per 1,000 views on YouTube) (Geyser 2016). Monetizing one's passion presents further challenges given creatives' religious beliefs regarding money and ministry. Widespread criticism of Christian fundraising activities and prosperity theologies makes receiving monetary compensation—or "getting those coins" as one creative describes it—an additional and negative burden for digital Black Christians who desire (and deserve) financial compensation. That many operate beyond traditional Black church roles of pastor or evangelist complicates their position and acceptance in the wider Christian economy. The following introduction to the life and work of Beleaf and Natalie bears out such realities.

Beleaf

A rapper, lyricist, and YouTube personality, Beleaf's real name is Glen Henry. My first interview with him occurred just eight months after his decision to leave rap music. Today Beleaf produces beats and lyrics for some of Christian hip hop's most prominent voices, like Andy Mineo. The artist first gained notoriety as a DJ and lyricist for a group called BREAX in 2008. Ultimately, BREAX disbanded and Beleaf joined rappers Ruslan and John Givez to form Dream Junkies. The group released their first album in 2014, followed by their more popular album titled *Good Religion* in 2016. Beleaf also hosts a popular YouTube channel called *Beleaf in Fatherhood*. Since the channel's first upload in August 2015, *Beleaf in Fatherhood* has continued to attract a niche following. Both his discussion of the ups and downs of being a stay-at-home parent and his celebration of Black fatherhood have resonated with his audience. The success of *Beleaf in Fatherhood* has earned Glen 203,000 subscribers (as of this writing) and featured commercial spots with companies like Apple, Pampers, Disney, and Hello Fresh. Through creative approaches to brand promotion, he continues to use multiple social media platforms to sell clothing, hair accessories, electronics, other lifestyle products, and his own creative work.

Glen Henry was just nineteen years old when his father suggested he move with him to Escondido, California, following Glen's revelation that he was battling suicidal thoughts. When he arrived in California, his first job was as a sales associate for Men's Warehouse. There he learned how to "control the stage, how to sell yourself . . . I had to learn how to do this to get money." Beleaf has been developing shrewd marketing techniques to sell himself and earn money ever since then.

As he told me in our interview, the products he promotes must align with his family's beliefs and values. At the center of his beliefs is his faith. By pairing products with lifestyle choices, Beleaf is essentially selling his faith. The transactional nature of this process and its benefits and challenges is revealed in a close reading of an average work week for Beleaf, to which we will turn after introducing Natalie Lauren Sims.

Natalie Lauren Sims

Born on June 25, 1984, Natalie Lauren Sims is a woman of multiple talents. The singer, rapper, and song-rapper has more recently been working as an A&R rep or creative guide, as she calls herself. It was in her childhood home of Tulsa, Oklahoma, that Natalie first developed a love of music. Natalie is unabashed in testifying to the fact that hip hop was her first musical love. "I was the kid freestyling during lunch and writing raps. My friend Franny and I use to freestyle into one side of her earphones to Ginuwine tape instrumentals," says Natalie. Her musical tastes also included Anita Baker and Norah Coles. Natalie notes with a smile that the songs of Cole were "one of the few songs I remember hearing as a child," from her mother. There was also the deep passionate way her cousin Vergie Mae would belt out,

> Oooohhh, Iiii-ii—iiiiii,
> I lo-oove to praise His name"

"I love that song, it feels like home," Natalie remarked in our interview. The song "I Love to Praise Him" was most famously recorded by the Mississippi Mass Choir began in 1988. It conjures all the foot-stomping, deep Southern gospel roots Natalie grew up with. Such songs pull her back to her childhood, back to Bixby Snake Creek, Oklahoma, at her Big Granny's church where beautiful hymns elicited the full-throated raspy praise of the whole congregation, as little Natalie rocked along.

It was her uncle, Wayman Tisdale, who exposed her to music and the possibility of pursuing it as a career when she was merely fourteen. It was at this same age that Natalie experienced another transformative event in her life. One evening, following a revival service, she remembers praying fervently to God. She had decided, she told God, to judge His veracity by His ability to heal her body. Natalie routinely suffered from a number of large tumors, which often left her body racked with pain. She remembers "suddenly being healed of the tumors in my body . . . He did [it], and I believed from that date forward."

These two transformative events—her uncle's musical influence and being healed from tumors—shaped Natalie's lifelong trajectory. From that point on, faith and art would always be inextricably linked for Natalie. At the age of seventeen, she set out for Tampa, Florida, where she attended college for a time, often performing under the name Suzy Rock. She lived for a time in Tampa and worked with the rappers HGA (His Glory Alone) and KB, a close friend.

Sims's desire to write crossover music found significant mentorship through her connection to then-popular gospel singers Deitrick Haddon and his then-wife Damita Haddon (now Chandler). Earlier, we saw Juanita Bynum's digital connections to other female creatives like Jackie Hill-Perry. Sims's own connection to Bynum was more directly linked to digital employment. In 2007 she moved to Atlanta, Georgia, to work as a graphic and web designer for Bynum. Connecting with the Haddons, who were rising gospel stars, Natalie lived with the two for a time in their Atlanta home, learning the craft and carefully watching their process of musical creation. That time was instrumental in shaping Natalie as a songwriter. Most days consisted of her writing and singing together with the couple and members of their popular Christian group Voices of Unity. Voices of Unity, begun in 1995, was the outgrowth of Deitrick and Damita's artistic talents. Just after the release of the group's first commercial release, "Come Into This House," the pair married. By 2005, Deitrick and Damita had signed to major record labels and received recognition for their signature R&B gospel sound.

Sims began working with Lecrae and developed album covers and music for Voices of Unity in 2011 and for Juanita Bynum. She eventually signed to Juanita Bynum's label. During that time she shared producers and developed a friendship in the studio with Iggy Azalea, FKi 1st, and

Jon Jon Traxx. A few years later, Natalie appeared on and wrote music for Iggy Azalea's *The New Classic*. Her writing can be heard on songs like "Bounce," "Work" and "New Bitch." Her other writing credits include songs for KeKe Palmer and Chris Brown, and she provides artistic guidance and production for friend and client Joseph Solomon through her company founded with Jon Jon Traxx and KB.

From her time as Suzy Rock to her present-day work as Natalie Lauren Sims, Natalie has continued to evolve. Her greatest passion and current job includes grooming and marketing new artists. This role has its challenges. Brittney Cooper (2015) discusses at length the emotional labor Black women, in particular, are often expected to perform in professional spaces. The story of Natalie Lauren Sims demonstrates this reality. In our interview Sims discusses her unique position as a woman in a male dominated artform and her attempts to circumvent the negative aspects of this reality. In the process, her Christian beliefs connected to visibility and worth are revealed.

In the next section, I incorporate eleven Twitter and/or Instagram posts to give a glimpse into the average work week of digital Black Christians. I provide day-in-the-life ethnographies of Beleaf Melanin and Natalie Lauren Sims to show the kinds of complexities they face and how they address them in a way that preserves their notion of their intrinsic self-worth in a digital marketplace that undervalues Black labor.

Selling the Struggle: Process as Product

The Digital Work Week: Day 1

What is seen as success is all a facade. Because success isn't seen. It stands basically unaccounted for. It's the midnight grind, the sleep deprivation. The breaking point. Learning to shift your weight when life tries to knock you down. Weeping while your kids watch. Weeping alone. Weeping in front of your spouse. Being fed up of being broke. Collecting bottles to eat. Selling your art for dirt cheap to afford gas to take your son to get surgery. Waiting. Waiting again. Waiting for your friends or family to believe in you. Waiting for a door to open and it never does only to realize that you are the door. You can aspire to have all the things the people you adore have at their disposal but before you do that, ask for their pain. Success is painful and I'm loving how it feels.

James 1:2 Consider it pure joy, my brothers and sisters, [a] whenever you face trials of many kinds, 3 because you know that the testing of your faith produces perseverance. 4 Let perseverance finish its work so that you may be mature and complete, not lacking anything.
—@beleafmel

Don't let Mondays punk you! Lately I've been overwhelmed with work and not knowing how to balance clients, craft and plant obsession! I always question whether or not I'm a good friend or a workaholic and why they put up with my ish. It's hard to admit I just don't have it in me at times to be present. It's even harder to admit I say yes to more than I can handle. Im learning Honesty about my capacity allows me the freedom to grow and figure things out as I go! With that being said, my Monday will be hard, finding balance will feel impossible but I'm committed to showing up for the hard shit.

Let's Go!
—@natalielaurensims

The Digital Work Week: Day 2

Celebrating in 8 hours. #beleafinfatherhood #youtube100k December 7, 2016 . . .

This year has been monumental.
- We had our baby Anaya!
- Theo made the #shotoniphone world gallery
- @mrsmelanin became SAH Mom
- I Started speaking landed a TEDx Talk -Put out my last Album #InFatherhood
- Started the year at 17k subs ended at 72k Extremely #Grateful
—@beleafmel

find your safe space and stay there as long as you need. Don't limit your process to a shareable end result or a unrealistic timeline. Give yourself time to undo & time to become.

And Thoughts On Being Present, Today
rest + restore +create + return when you're ready.
—@natalielaurensims

For several reasons, as we have discussed, the Instagram environment and its "me-centered" representations provide fertile ground for celebrity cultures. Followers are drawn to the personalities and seeming affluence (whether of social standing or monetary value) of those they follow. The backlash over Kylie Jenner's inclusion in a 2019 *Forbes* article listing Jenner among "self-made" women in some ways overlooked this dynamic of Instagram celebrity (Robehmed 2019). Jenner was, however, able to point to the intense effort required to build herself as an online brand through carefully staged visual representations of herself and her work and through cross-platform promotions. Jenner's "come-up" story is largely revealed in her ability to boast 132 million Instagram followers.

Beleaf's success is noted in the similar numbers of his online followers (see the "Digital Work Week: Day 2" section, above). From his channel's beginning, viewership has grown from thousands to millions of views for some of his most popular episodes. Yet this "success" represents the continued struggle for himself and creatives like him. What goes unmentioned in Jenner's description is the role of both white privilege and generational wealth in partly accounting for her meteoritic rise on social media platforms. Having neither of these to rely on, Beleaf's come-up (sponsorship and viewership royalties, Patreon[1] contributions, etc.) undergird what he described as the "pain" of his success. His catalog of struggles is full of weeping, poverty, unfair wages, and sleep deprivation. The online work environment, while providing numerous avenues for success, has taken an emotional toll on each of the creatives documented here.

For Natalie Lauren Sims, "rest + restore + create + return when you're ready" is the key. On the surface, such advice can seem insipid. Yet Lauren's Day 1 advice reveals her own struggle to do the same. She noted in our interview that "I really need some new inspiration, low key. Which is why I'm about to take 2019 and step back from the business to really be a student again." Her own health, work, and family challenges pushed her toward that decision. The Instagram life of such creatives provides a shared moment of revelation when the user offers advice on their creative process. Such "sharing" of advice is work in itself. Natalie's full-time gig, after all, is grooming artists. Her Day 2 post falls within that work description as she both reveals and sells her product, that is, her process (remember that prospective clients could well make up the "invisible audience").

Though Natalie's approach is different from Beleaf's, both have in common the experience of the trauma of life challenges, as well as showing their upward mobility—Beleaf in his promotions for Stich Fix, an online clothing retailer, and Lauren through the promotion of rest, a privileged commodity in the digital labor economy. The delicate balance between struggle and come-up that creatives employ online conceals deeper issues of emotional trauma historically endured by digital Black Christians and continued, though in a different form, in the present digital economy.

Selling Sadness: The Centrality of (Black) Depression in the Digital Economy

The Digital Work Week: Day 3

After he apologized to me for lying and telling some of our friends that we watched TV all day and he was forced to cook his own meals . . . ☺

He said "Dad I want to talk to you." I looked at my 5 year old son and said "Go ahead . . ." he went on to tell me that I work too much and that's why he told the lie.

He explained "All you do is work and go to the computer and get on the airplane and make some videos and work with @frankpuppet (bts) and do things. You have to make more time with your family . . ." •I WAS TRIGGERED!

The audacity of this little person coming at me like this picked at my ego But I low-key was proud. This was very brave of him. . . . he was telling me on behalf of his siblings that I wasn't being present. This is [the] type of relationship I want us to have, that he could come and tell me things that bother him. He is growing up and I'm sitting there #childish just looking like ☺

Now, as far as I'm concerned, I'm very present he doesn't know what it's like to have a father that works for most of the day then comes home grumpy and he shouldn't know what it's like, I've been saying that I'm going to take the time off I need but I'm swinging from deadline to deadline and failing at that.

The last thing I wanted was for my children to have to give me the "hey dude, you kinda trash" talk. If you've wondered why [I] haven't posted on @YouTube it's because I'm working on my #creatorforchange project

but you can listen to this whole conversation between Theo and I on my Patreon Page. Link is in my bio.
 —@beleafmel

It's okay if you're not okay.
 I share this experience as an invitation to all my friends and family who are in a season of blooming and breaking all at once. I am here with you learning to laugh and cry with the same breath. This is a safe space to admit we are all Learning to be okay, when it's not okay. All seasons deserve your presence. To all those fighting to live, I pray you continue! Video shot with @apple iPhone.
 —@natalielaurensims

Day 3 more poignantly reveals the emotional challenges creatives face in the digital workplace even as they access this space to catalog such challenges. In the video accompanying Lauren's Day 3 post on November 8, 2019, she chronicles her trip home to Tulsa, Oklahoma. While she is experiencing several successes in her professional career (e.g., launching a shampoo line, finishing a music video shoot, signing to a major recording label), it has been a tumultuous few months for her family, full of "just a whole bunch of shit," according to Sims. Quite tragically, she has just learned of the death of her paternal uncle from an apparent suicide on October 18, 2019. On November 2, 2019, she writes an Instagram poem in his memory:

> Maybe no one taught you to cry
> I know tears have always been an acquired taste for black men.
> Who told you sadness was a soft color for girls only.
> I guess no one taught you how to
> interrogate your pain,
> How to reach down its throat until it coughed up the truth and took
>   you to its home . . .
> No one showed you how to find where it hurts.
> Ain't nobody gone teach us how to heal.
> I can only remember your smile
> and today that's what I'll hold on to.
> Today we will Honor you.

> We will Sing your Name.
> Suicide doesn't make you a weak man, or a selfish one, Just a man.
> Just a human, who had no language or levy
> for all the tears they said didn't belong to you.
> But God knew and he's bottled them up.
> We don't grieve as those who have no hope.
> but we have a Savior, a man of sorrow
> who shed your tears as His own and has exchanged them for Joy.
> Uncle Glen, we love you and will miss you.

Later, in a revealing conversation with her father, viewers learn that "Uncle Glen" exhibited many signs of depression and had reached out to multiple family members. In an Instagram video posted on November 8, 2019, Sims's father shares his own battle with depression and therapy since adolescence and his more recent feelings of being "down in the dumps" after learning of his diagnosis with prostate cancer. He says, "I can't even connect with God right now. I'm going to have him [doctor] increase my medication." Natalie too has suffered from depression. In fact, more than half of this study's participants battle mental disease. Their struggles are often exacerbated by their digital labor.

Describing his present battle with depression, Beleaf says, "Even now, it gets very hard as an entrepreneur because everything's on you. You meditate on those thoughts and it just goes deep into your brain." Without naming it, the role of depression in his life is an unspoken part of his Day 3 post. Note the use of emotion-centered language. Words like "TRIGGERED," "grumpy," "failing," "trash," and even the go-to emoji for such situations, "😩," reveals a battle against anger, feelings of worthlessness, anxiety, and tiredness—all of which are signs of clinical depression. Many creatives like Beleaf often perform multiple functions, among them videographer, photographer, chef, director, and brand manager, to name a few, in order to produce a single webisode or provide a complete podcast for their viewers. As discussed in the introduction to this chapter, such worker production represents what Karl Marx described as surplus value in *Das Kapital* ([1867] 1894) and *Theories of Surplus Value* ([1862–63] 1969). Other corporate entities like YouTube will receive a greater benefit from his labor than Beleaf ever will. Paying into such economies of hope feels daunting at times. The success or failure of such endeavors rests totally on him. Certainly, the digital marketplace is not the sole catalyst of creatives' mental health disorders. Yet it is a potent trigger for digital Black Christians with a history of stress exposure. Beleaf's early life is indicative of this fact.

Beleaf began his battle with depression in early childhood. His first suicidal thought came at age nine. A victim of physical abuse by his mother, he often thought of ending his life. Beleaf (2020) says in an interview on the *TruthSeekah* podcast, "I went through PTSD. Even at 19, I'd wake up flinching, like someone was going to break in the door and hit me." The violence he experienced at home in some ways muted the wave of violence occurring in his neighborhood of Berry Paul Lane in Baltimore, Maryland.

While the rate of mental illness is nearly equal between whites and Blacks of all ages, African Americans are far less likely to acknowledge and seek treatment for it. The numbers are particularly staggering for Black males. Only 6.6 percent actually seek out treatment (Ward et al. 2013). For young adults, overall numbers for seeking treatment are even lower. This is particularly disturbing given the amount of mental health information available to young adults (who are the highest population of internet users) online. Indicators for mental illness typically begin during adolescence and continue into young adulthood. Digital Black Christians exhibit even higher rates of depression than white youth of the same age as a result of increased stress exposure. The realities of inner-city violence and early exposure to drug culture, as exhibited in the lives of some of the creatives studied here, are often one significant known cause. The stigma associated with health care coupled with lack of access to health coverage and mental health information in certain communities likewise often contributes to African Americans' awareness of help options and decision to seek it or not.

Additionally, digital Black Christians in both urban and suburban environments often suffer acutely as a result of both systemic and individual acts of racism. There is a direct link between such stress exposures and the higher rates of depression among young adult Blacks like Beleaf.[5] Both the consistency and proximity with which some of the creatives studied here experienced personal and community violence normalizes such trauma. In recent years, creatives' online presence has duplicated early exposure to violence against African Americans. As discussed earlier, in an open letter to the *Huffington Post* website, Lecrae Moore (2016a) attributes a recent depressive episode, in part, to displays of police brutality on social media platforms that triggered memories of violence in his childhood as well as self-criticisms regarding his worth as a Christian and human being. As Chapter 3 attests regarding Jackie's social media responses, fan/follower responses on social media and the multiple ways creatives respond to them affects creatives' individual feelings of self-esteem and value. When one's value is attacked online, depression or depressive episodes are more likely among creatives.[6] Unlike Natalie Lauren Sims's father, as we shall see, in the absence of clinical treatment many young Black males develop self-prescribed alternatives and/or other coping mechanisms, and carry such coping strategies with them into the digital work environment.

As Beleaf grew older, he learned to keep his head down and stay out of trouble as much as possible. Yet turmoil in his city and his home affected his mental well-being. A high school friend advised him when he walked through the sometimes violent streets of Baltimore to keep his head low and concentrate on his feet as he walked in order to keep himself safe. It was while heeding that advice one day that he found at his feet a CD by rapper Black Thought, lead emcee for the Roots. It was still safely wrapped inside its case. He picked it up and put it in the CD player he always carried and played it to mute the chaotic world around him. The first lyrics he remembers hearing were:

> What if you could just disappear
> What if no one knew you was even here

He stopped abruptly and his head snapped upward. It seemed as though the lyrics had jolted him out of a very deep fog. Those words felt like the solution to all of his problems. What if he could *just disappear*. That moment was the beginning of period when he could not shake the desire to end his own life. He says, "Those were really dark times for me." Other creatives' interviews are filled with the same words, "darkness" and "death," in both their descriptions of mood and their discussions of pivotal life experiences. Like Beleaf, the digital context becomes the ground and workplace in which they process such trauma into adulthood.

Yet, in his teens, nightfall lingered in his every waking thought as he battled a monster he could not yet rightly name: depression. It is no coincidence, then, that hip hop, the soundtrack to his depressive episodes, offered the same digital antidote to his mental illness. Through it, creatives like Beleaf have learned to employ strategies of rebranding and therapy to combat mental illness in the digital workplace.[7]

Rebranding Strategies

Very little empirical attention has been paid to the correlation between young Black adults' religious practices, use of digital technology, and rates of mental illness. Yet the creatives here document an intertwined and complicated relationship with the three. Technology, religion, and mental illness inform each other, depression being both fueled and abated through technology and religious practices taken together. Still, through digital postings of music, digital creation of art, and several other artistic and curatorial projects, creatives have rebranded their history of trauma as appealing testimonies within the Christian marketplace. Angela Davis (1981), as noted earlier, discusses the precarious position this places Black laborers in as they become "providers" for the white capitalists' economy. In this instance they fulfill the desires of white audiences, providing them with a way of both experiencing their fantasies and conquering their fears associated with Black life. For creatives, trafficking in trauma at times leaves them in the cyclic role of producing, revealing, and sharing Black pain as the market demands. It is emotionally challenging and highly rewarding, both in building intimacy with followers and fans and in gaining monetary support. Such intimacies revealed through postings or digital music files about past suicide attempts represents the sort of affective labor that political theorist Michael Hardt (1999, 96) notes "produces social networks, forms of community, and biopower."

Many male creatives, like Beleaf, have developed shrewd ways of either masking their mental illness or allowing it to fuel their hip hop work. For Beleaf, such fueling is apparent in the often dark environment he created in his music. In the 2014 song "Depressed," on his first solo album, *Red Pills + Black Sugar*, Beleaf details the cyclical battle with depression that spawned his addiction to marijuana. The same album (2014) includes the song "Suicide Roll." In the chorus, he repeats "I've been thinking about killin' myself." Listing the various means he is thinking about using to bring about his demise, Beleaf suggest pills, hanging himself, or cutting his own throat. Yet even these darker moments became part of his brand. Beleaf used his skills in music production to create short commercials and online videos, which subscribers and sponsors could pay to see. As his subscriber numbers (see the Day 2 section) continued to rise, Beleaf noticed that viewers enjoyed hearing his whole "story." "People will tell you who you are to them," he noted in our interview. Stories regarding Black fatherhood, battles with depression, and other life challenges greatly appealed to his viewers. In response, Beleaf began providing his digital audience with more of that kind of content. As in his performance of struggle and come-up in his Day 1 posts, Beleaf intentionally designed his story in marketable ways. Deciding to duplicate multiple performances of a particular aspect of oneself is central to the process of rebranding and thus of controlling one's own digital narrative.

Therapeutic Strategies

Strategies to combat depression, exacerbated by the onset of digital and physical stress exposure in adulthood, has led some creatives to therapy. Most interviewees speak openly about their reliance on some form of counseling or therapy. This is true for Preston Perry, a self-described "little black boy from the South Side of Chicago." Preston describes attending counseling sessions with his wife Jackie Hill-Perry, the subject of the previous chapter. The benefits of marriage counseling has, in many Christian circles, become an appreciated and valid social practice leading up to marriage, and sometimes includes ongoing support groups and conferences. What has received a lot less attention is the value of individual counseling.

Non-church gatherings, both online, as in P4CM's talk show (which centers largely on dating and relationship advice for its mostly digital Black Christian female audience), or located physically, as in the popular Christian spoken-word tour titled Poets in Autumn (PIA), provide varying degrees of informal counseling to their young Black Christian audience. The latter PIA event can be described as a therapeutic space in and of itself.

On an unusually warm fall day in September 2018, I joined the PIA audience for a performance at Peel Pentecostal Tabernacle, in the town of Brampton just outside of Toronto, Canada. The Tabernacle lived up to its name. It is a large and imposing structure; the stately building and surrounding parking lot takes up nearly an acre of its corner lot. Tonight, however, the building serves as a mere backdrop. Of greater interest is the line of mostly twenty-something Blacks wrapped around the buildings' exterior. The PIA tour has already played to sold-out shows in cities like New York and Chicago. There is a giddy anticipation among ticketholders as they wait for the doors to open. This event may be at a church, but it is clear that these young adults are not here for "church." In fact, for the most part participants seem to be performing non-church personas in this space. Young women fix their hair and makeup in the bathroom with the anticipation of meeting someone or perhaps hooking up. Others can be seen rifling through the extensive display of PIA tees, hoodies, and other merchandise. Another quite substantial group is couples holding hands, perhaps out for a date night. Tonight is not meant for corporate worship. It is a night for individual encounters.

As I make my way to my seat, I attempt to employ my fieldwork training. But the consummate ethnographer in search of Clifford Geertz's (1973) "thick description" instead finds John L. Jackson's (2013) "thin description." My attempts at participant observation are thwarted at every turn as I smile and try to talk up those seated around me—"to read the room" as it were. Later, in writing up my fieldnotes, I reflect on the overall difficulty in doing just that—"talking folks up." I surmise that this evening was not designed for that. Tonight is the physical outgrowth of the sort of digital discipleship described earlier. Having engaged in what felt like very intimate ways with these artists' online personas, audience members are not inclined to greet their neighbor or make new acquaintances. They are here to engage with the artists. Knowing this, Kingdom Promotions, the company hosting this event, has even offered VIP tickets, which allow fans early admission, photo ops with artists, and a private Q&A. The closer the better. The digital context has led them to believe that the therapist-client relationship begun in YouTube postings extends to this real-life encounter. No one murmurs or moves. Audience members look straight ahead, seeking words of wisdom from each poet. The therapeutic moment is made ever more layered, more complex as performers like Joseph Solomon and Preston Perry begin discussions regarding depression and therapy.

In his performance to an intently listening audience of over two thousand digital Black Christians, Preston recalls the moment his therapist called him back into the room following a marriage counseling session with his wife Jackie. The therapist suggested he come back alone because, in her professional opinion, Preston exhibited the signs of someone battling PTSD. He had stared down the barrel of a gun more times than he could count in his South Side Chicago neighborhood. Perry had even seen a woman fully decapitated by the gun blast of a scorned lover just in front of his stoop. Yet, since becoming a Christian, he had not considered the effects of such traumatic experiences on his mental health. Following a year in therapy, Preston Perry posted a new poem on September 2019 as part of that year's PIA tour. He described his changed attitude regarding how Black men deal with depression. In the piece, titled "Who Gives a Black Man Permission to Feel? (An Ode to Uncle Stan)," Preston recalls a discussion with his uncle following the loss of a male relative to gun violence:

> "It's time for you to be
> strong for your family. Your mother
> doesn't need a weak man in the house at
> this time." My tear ducts dried up and
> became a deserted land
> And in all my
> years the men of my life have taught me
> that my emotions is a disease
> Because where I'm from showing the wrong
> emotions might get you killed
> or worse, you will live in the shame of
> being human. (Apologetics with Preston Perry 2019)

Like Beleaf, Preston realizes only in adulthood that his inability to express his emotions in healthy ways is attributable to early-life messaging that dissuaded him from such "unmanly" practices. This also contributed to his bouts of depression. For this performance, Preston sports a cream-colored hoodie, the words "Jesus & Therapy" stenciled across the front. Its caption is as much a part of this digital performance as the poem itself. Creatives like Perry, while at work, debunk the notion that real faith abhors clinical care. Such moments provide a seamless message between digital and physical audiences, a message enhanced with details about where one can receive therapy or treatment, be it through a YouTube post, spoken-word events, or a clinician's couch. Digital Black Christian Cristin Dent (2019) describes the crowd's response to Preston's poem in a YouTube post: "We were just snapping and 'ooooing' and 'ahhhhing!' Because it was like 'Finally! Somebody is talking about this!'"

It also provides a soft critique of the Black Christianity of previous generations. While rarely acknowledging the question of spatial and economic access to clinical care, creatives do push back against perceived and real stigmas in Black communities regarding counseling. In introducing his poem at the 2019 Poets In Autumn event, Preston says, "I think a lot of times, particularly in the African American church, we can look at counseling and look at their appeal as if somebody is saying that Jesus isn't enough. And that's just not the case" (Apologetics with Preston Perry 2019). He closes his poem in affirmation of a new model for the digital Black Christian in which God ordains and even employs therapy to ensure healthy Christian living:

> This last year God has shown me
> that it's not just His job to make me
> His
> but He's using therapy to make me
> whole.

As I mentioned earlier in describing YouTube responses to Jackie Hill-Perry's poems, the space to post a comment in response to her words can be seen as a therapeutic space in itself. As Preston tells his story, he both affirms the value of a "little Black Boy from Chicago's South Side" and the value of all such Black boys. The hyper-mediatized context (through sharing, reposting, viewer count, to name a few modes of message amplification) in which such affirmation occurs allows for the constant restating of an important truth, that is, that "little Black boys from Chicago" matter, among digital Black Christians who watch the live performance of Preston's poem on YouTube.

Commenter 1:
   Thank you so much brother Preston for encouraging our race to feel. Addressing the most critical thing, dignity. Dignity was stripped off our

parents and it has to cease now. Your story telling, brother, is impeccable. Men are allowed to feel too.

Commenter 2:
Touched my soul on this one iseen him do this live and i teared up.

Commenter 2:
Wow!! I am a single Mom raising a son . . . thank you for this poem . . . from South Africa.

Natalie Lauren Sims's approach to therapy is markedly different. While she is a firm advocate of receiving clinical counseling, she also incorporates other daily practices aimed at combating both digital and physical stressors. In an Instagram video post on June 28, 2019, she says, "As someone who suffered from extreme anxiety and panic attacks, meditation is the number one tool my therapist recommended to be aware of myself and know when those panic moments are about to happen." In her most recent album, simply titled *Meditate* (2019), Natalie encourages listeners to: "Take time / meditate/ On the most high / levitate."

Natalie combines Eastern practices like meditation, mindfulness, and yoga and is influenced by the work of alternative medicine advocate Deepak Chopra. Her Day 1 post hints at such practices without mentioning them by name. Her argument that meditation is prevalent in most cultures and religions provides her the ground to claim it as part of healthy Christian practice. This stance is not without its objectors, however. Her post describing her own meditation practices drew stiff criticism from some commenters, who warned her against such "occult practices."

Sims says she once considered such beliefs to be rooted in "ignorance." In the post accompanying her June 28, 2019, video, she explains her beliefs regarding meditation by saying "My first experience with meditation was watching Angela Bassett play Tina Turner on *What's Love Got To Do With It* . . . basically I knew nothing about the practice, except it wasn't for me[—] and I was so wrong!" Initially, the mediatized introduction to meditation read as "different" or "strange" to Natalie within her mostly Christian context. Yet through therapy she was able to broaden her beliefs, incorporating new approaches to digital media supportive of meditation. Like Preston, she now uses the online space to act as an advocate for practices stigmatized in her home community. Their testimonies become important "products," as they sell and/or promote therapy to other digital Black Christians. This is vital work, particularly in a digital marketplace that measures worth in terms of monetary value. Creatives push back against that notion with work that yields alternative dividends, here specifically valuing the Black mind and body. The payoff comes in their own mental health and the collective mental health of those digital Black Christians who heed their messages.

In a 2018 interview by *Trackstarz*, Natalie described battling deep anxiety and panic attacks as she sought to provide A&R representation for eight artists on Reach Records. "At that time . . . I'm in a publishing deal, so I'm still writing. So . . . including myself . . . those are eight humans with eight different lives with eight different problems and craziness and opinions. And I just did not care for myself well." Her digital work around promoting artists was equally daunting. In our own interview, Natalie describes her work as including "running ads all day, tracking the use and engagement of followers, [and] predicting [the] social trends of our audience" (*Trackstarz* 2018).

That time encouraged her to begin what she calls Creative RX, assisting other creatives, including herself, in developing better self-care practices. She combines spiritual, mental, and emotional care goals to help artists survive in the music industry. For Natalie, this is an intimate process. In the same 2018 *Trackstarz* interview she says, "If I'm working with somebody I like, I have to love them, the person. Like, I have to be so inspired by whatever it is that they're already doing."

Both Preston and Natalie found paths to therapy that ultimately led to using their digital and physical platforms to inform and benefit the mental health of other digital Black Christians. Such strategies connect creatives through their intimate experiences with mental illness and by the development of collective pathways to healing and wholeness.

Selling the "New Black Church"

The Digital Work Week: Day 4

If I ever put out another album it'll be because of something @iammiketodd said in a sermon! 😅 Thank you for the conviction bredren!

@stitchfixmen #stitchfix And shout out to @carltonbanks5 for these fire images! #floodconference

—@beleafmel

Spent the morning with this dude, my brother and my Nihh @iammiketodd love you man! I'm So proud of you & the way you're serving and loving people here at home. Our city is changing because of you. I know my parents are in good hands with you / @wearetransformation family and that means the world to me ♡ between Theo and I on my Patreon Page link is in my bio.

—@natalielaurensims

The Digital Work Week: Day 5

Screened my project "Do you fear black men?" last night at @youtubespace LA and all my people came out! Also saw people that I admire in person. Being a #CreatorsForChange Ambassador is @youtube providing resources to us to create a thought provoking film. But honestly even without YouTube's initiative, I feel called to this effort. Everyone I know has a story that can help people see things from a different perspective. We need more people who are willing to document stories like these just to combat the hate. I'm honored to be on this years list. And I hope to continue to make content like this very soon!

Photos by: @dom_marcel

—@beleafmel

ALL SMILES! ISSA CELEBRATION

God is Good & We CANCER FREE! We partying all weekend because we Can!!!!!! 💃🏾💃🏾💃🏾🎉🎉🥂 #SomethingSomething happened in real life! I'm blown, excuse my language 😩

—@natalielaurensims

As noted at the outset, the aim of this book is to move beyond the Black Church in defining Christian expression for young Black adults. In the past, such approaches to the study of young Black people has meant chronicling what I call the "leaving/abandoning myth," the myth that young Black Christians are largely leaving or abandoning the Black Church is influenced by wider claims regarding the secularization of society. Yet, as Nancy Ammerman (2007) notes in *Everyday Religion*, secularization claims often rely upon surveys that only ask questions regarding formal church practices. In her assessment, "religion is bigger than the theological ideas and religious institutions about which typical surveys have inquired" (Ammerman 2007, 6). This assessment includes widely accepted surveys, such as that of the Pew Research Center regarding the "nones," those who check none or "unaffiliated" when asked questions regarding their religious practices. Yet, particularly for digital Black Christians, the "New Black Church" is defined not by a single box checked or unchecked, but by an infinite number of "and's."

Natalie practices both Eastern-influenced meditation and attends a multiracial church (which she helped establish) in Atlanta. Her Day 5 posts praising God for her father's cancer-free status is expletive laden, demonstrating a faith couched in language not normally sanctioned in a church environment. Yet Natalie's post exudes all the worship and praise of the church's liturgy. One can be both righteous and "ratchet," as the podcast title of popular digital Black Christian comedian KevOnStage (co-hosted with DoBoy) suggests. Digital Black Christians draw their "church" experience from multiple sources and meld these worlds together in their rhetorical choices. The common link in these "religiosities," as Ammerman (2007) calls them (here referring to what I call webwork), is often figures like Michael Todd. Like other creatives mentioned here, Todd was trained at a white evangelical seminary, Oral Roberts University. He was groomed by the university chaplain and church pastor Bishop Gary McIntosh to assume the pastorship of what was then Greenwood Christian Center. In 2015 the mostly Black congregation, under Todd's direction, became Transformation Church. Transformation now boasts over seven million weekly viewers and over seven thousand attendees at the church's location in Bixby, Oklahoma.

Todd's story helps to redefine exactly what we scholars mean when we say the "Black Church." The members of Greenwood Christian Center (now Transformation) had always been predominantly Black. Yet with Todd at the helm, their worship practices shifted toward contemporary gospel and hip hop and his sermons echo those of both Bishop McIntosh and the Black Church in which he was raised. Neo-Black churches like Todd's have gained a following and at times a measure of notoriety through popular online media buzz as a result of posts of their sermons.

Online machine learning technology, which provides algorithmic suggestions to users, has linked young Black and white Christians in a new and unexpected network. In October of 2017, thirty-nine-year-old Steven Furtick, a songwriter and popular white pastor of the multisite Elevation Church, was searching for one of his own sermons online when he came across a message by Michael Todd on YouTube. Refreshed and moved by his rhetorical approach, he quickly called Todd and later invited him to preach at Elevation Church. In April 2018, Todd preached a sermon titled "Marked" at Elevation Church. Both Todd and Furtick understood the significance of Todd's guest appearance at Elevation in raising Todd's profile and creating connections for Furtick with African Americans. Michael Todd's message regarding the personal promise that "marked" each believer reached twenty-six thousand or so members who attended that day, but also its well over one million views online. Since he appeared at Elevation Church, Todd's online viewership has nearly doubled in size.

In the wake of protests in Charlotte, North Carolina, following the 2016 police shooting of unarmed Black man Keith Lamont Scott, Furtick responded differently from several other white pastors in the Southern Baptist Convention of which he is a part. That he called on his mentor Bishop T. D. Jakes to discuss racial issues and that he admonished white congregates to "shut up and listen" to African Americans regarding their experiences of racial discrimination played well with Blacks in his congregation, who now number a third of Charlotte's Elevation Church attendees. Todd, and similar digital Black Christians' connections to such social justice–minded white evangelical pastors, signals the formation of new networks between young adult Black and white Christians. Much as digital discipleship linked Joseph Solomon to white Reformed theologians in the first decade of the millennium, the ever more refined process of algorithmic recommendations connected Todd and Furtick both digitally and physically. Signs are that such collaborative filtering will continue to create networks between the two racial groups in the future. Creatives like Natalie and Beleaf will be instrumental in the expansion of such networks through their joint connection to Todd.

For his part, Beleaf attends a multiracial church his home city of San Diego. Yet, as Day 4 demonstrates, it is also other church conferences, like that led by Michael Todd in Tulsa, Oklahoma, that have shaped his beliefs and thus his work networks. Both Beleaf and Natalie's connection to Todd demonstrates the vast and shifting network that is their Black Church. Being part of such networks ensures their access to bookings for shows, performances, and future collaborations. Yet these are more than strategic attempts at getting work; both Beleaf and Natalie have developed an intimate connection with Michael Todd.

Beleaf decided to end his career as an album-producing rap artist in 2018. He made this decision mostly because he felt undervalued in the digital economy. The meager return on his labor made him reconsider his approach to his work. Regarding a conversation with his wife, he said in our interview, "I asked her, 'How much is it worth for me to be away.' She said, 'Nothing. There's not an amount that can rationalize you being gone.' I said, 'That's it. I'm done.'" Creatives' online payments can range anywhere from zero to somewhere in the thousands. The financial devaluation of his labor led to some of Beleaf's bouts of depression. Yet, according to his Day 4 post, his association with Todd has him considering a return to album production. Digital and physical Black church connections through younger Christian leaders like Todd provide important and validating alternatives to the devaluation of Black life in the digital labor economy. This sense of being valued fuels creatives' work, as is clear in Beleaf's Day 4 post. Because he does the kind of work he is "called to," he further extends the digital Black Church network.

Natalie and Michael Todd both hail from Tulsa, Oklahoma. Their connection began well before their appearance together on Instagram. Back in 2017, Natalie began sharing her faith with her parents. They eventually decided to become Christians and joined Todd's church. The gratitude she extends to Todd in her Day 4 posts is important information for digital Black Christian onlookers. The Todd/Sims connection signals the importance of the two to one another and thus their importance as linked religious figures in their circle. Such information creates networks and informs onlookers' own creation of links and the likely possibility that Todd will be included in such networks through video views of his sermons. It is through such webwork that the new Black Church is formed among digital Black Christians. There is no telling whether such networks will last even through the day, having no authoritative body to package and promote them, yet they are made up millions of such loosely connected and/or disparate moments that happen to converge through similar uses of the handle @iammiketodd.

Regarding Day 5, Beleaf's posts exhibit a new Black Christian consciousness attuned to the same digital work as BLM. As an ethnographer of a constantly developing culture, I have had the privilege of watching growth, shifts, and changes in thinking among my guides. Particularly on the subject of what Black Christian activism should look like, their process of evolution must be noted. As the digital conversations shifted from Trayvon Martin to the Black Lives Matter movement, so too did creatives struggle to find language to reconcile their Christian belief with their Black identity. Beleaf's Day 5 post seeks to move this conversation along through a Creators for Change YouTube award he received. Each year YouTube, perhaps in response to criticism regarding its own algorithmic racism, provides artistic development and resources for an up and coming artist. Beleaf's project "Do You Fear Black Men?" promotes awareness of racism. While this is part of his "calling," he feels that as a Christian he names it neither as part of his faith, the current political climate, or Black Lives Matter. For many digital Black Christians, social justice appears on a frequency that is hard to map or locate among BLM activism, despite the clear influence of BLM on digital Black Christians. Which leads to an important consideration.

By this point in the book, the critical reader may wonder why this chapter, and this work as a whole, is not entering into the conversation about pervasive forms of injustice and people and groups associated with the same for digital Black Christians—people like Donald Trump, white nationalists, and other similar ideological currents. They—and Trump in particular—are deliberately decentered in this conversation, and are rarely mentioned in interviews (a deliberate attempt by digital Black Christians to avoid lending attention to Trump's rhetoric, policies, and social media presence). In our interview conversation, Beleaf says, regarding structural racism affecting Black people, "I understand, I'm supposed to care because I'm Black, and I do care. But at the same time, I can only do so much for my people. I feel like it does influence me. But at the same time, it's like I have to be very careful of what we're operating in. . . . because we're not dealing with only racial issues. . . . I think Trump is a manifestation of America." Digital Black Christians like Beleaf see such forms of racism and the current political crisis as only in part manifestations of racism. His allusions to Trump as revealing of America's larger problems hints at young Black Christians' beliefs that beneath racism are deeper issues of sin or separation from God. Beleaf is thus suggesting that one cannot become too concerned with social justice projects against racism, but must examine such movements in the context of Christianity. We also saw this rationale in the discussion of Jackie Hill-Perry's views, where I analyzed the phenomenon of *secondary Blackness*. Beleaf exhibits a similar worldview. He says as much in his discussion of how the digital context affirms racist constructs regarding Blackness, "I don't think I'm just a YouTuber . . . I can't even say that I'm Black anymore . . . society had to put me in a box that you're looking at me for my skin . . . My thing is, if my identity is hidden in Christ then Black is a secondary identity."

Such statements represent digital Black Christians' attempts to move toward discourse and projects that affirm their notions of divinity and self-worth in the digital arena. Some scholars have described this inaccurately as an apolitical stance on the part of young Black Christians, or worse, as a sign that they have been duped by white evangelicalism or white Christianity more broadly. That is not quite the case, however. A poem by Preston Perry titled "New Woke Christian" unpacks the complexity of young adult Black Christians' engagement with contemporary movements like Black Lives Matter (Legacy Disciple 2018). To an audience of mostly digital Black Christians at the 2018 Legacy Conference he recited:

> Is being woke only a trend for some of you
> like high top fades and ripped jeans
> which will one day go out of style
> are you riding the woke
> train to fit in?
> Is your
> heart really in love with justice?
> Be honest.
> Some of y'all ain't woke for real.
> Y'all just fighting sleep.
> Fear that
> you might miss out on the next hashtag. (Legacy Disciple 2018)

Perry's poem, together with the Day 4 and 5 posts, speak of a diverse new digital Black Church experience that connects digital Black Christians through Black millennial preachers popular online, notions of secondary Blackness, and BLM-inspired activism. Like gospel songs earlier in Black history, digital Back Christians confess, "This digital world is not my home" in an attempt to affirm their value amid racial undervaluing, turning the digital economy's monetary value claims on its head.

Working (Online) While Black and Female

The Digital Work Week: Day 6
As a proud supporter of the music industry both CHH & HipHop, I've Been reading these threads and thought I'd share my thoughts on #CHHSexism.
—@msnatalielauren

Black women always have to do an extra day of labor. The gendered dynamics of the digital labor economy require Black women to bear additional work responsibilities and to devise creative strategies to combat workplace discrimination. Along with the work of building one's own brand, meeting deadlines, and reaching new audiences, Natalie must also navigate the gendered realities of the digital labor economy. According to Mars Hicks (2017), these inequalities have been systematically built into the digital labor market. Considering the role of women in technology fields in Britain during the Second World War, Hicks exposes the fallacy of an unbiased meritocracy in tech. Instead, she argues that tech work was deliberately structured in such a way as to maintain a power dynamic in which women were barred from or not selected to fill certain positions, among them computer programming. In *Algorithms of Oppression*, Safiya Noble (2018) makes clear the resulting bias this creates for Black women through practices such as technological redlining. Natalie's experience mirrors these very realities of digital and physical racial-gendered bias in hip hop work. In describing her interactions with men, she notes, "the majority of the time I'm working with males and trying to maintain a level of respect without coming across as bossy. Men never have to worry about being seen as

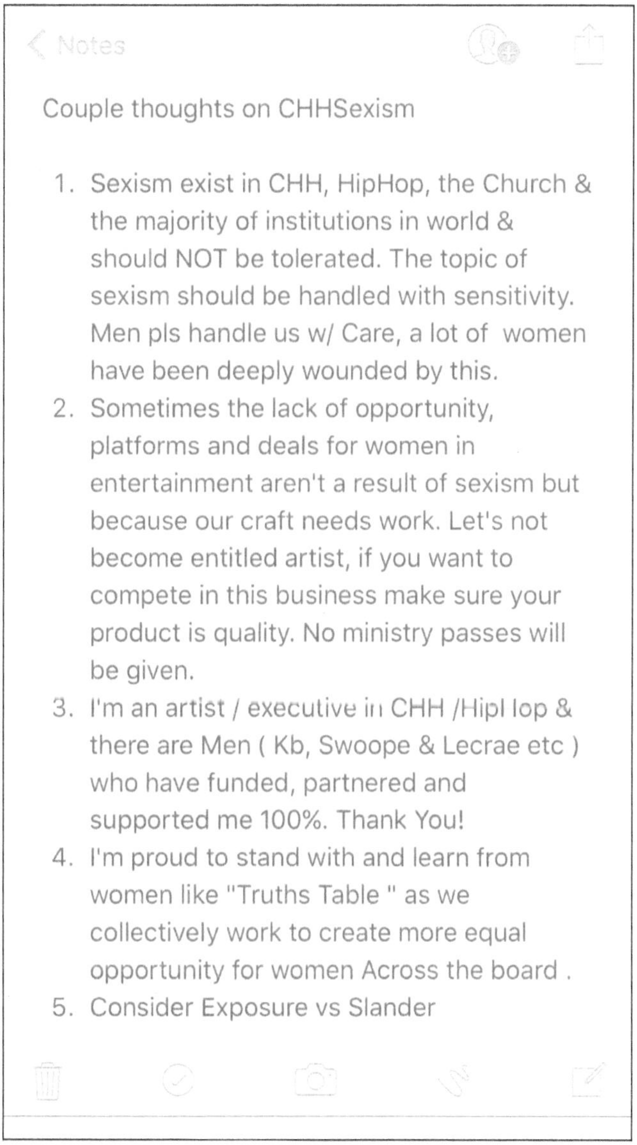

Couple thoughts on CHHSexism

1. Sexism exist in CHH, HipHop, the Church & the majority of institutions in world & should NOT be tolerated. The topic of sexism should be handled with sensitivity. Men pls handle us w/ Care, a lot of women have been deeply wounded by this.
2. Sometimes the lack of opportunity, platforms and deals for women in entertainment aren't a result of sexism but because our craft needs work. Let's not become entitled artist, if you want to compete in this business make sure your product is quality. No ministry passes will be given.
3. I'm an artist / executive in CHH /HipHop & there are Men (Kb, Swoope & Lecrae etc) who have funded, partnered and supported me 100%. Thank You!
4. I'm proud to stand with and learn from women like "Truths Table " as we collectively work to create more equal opportunity for women Across the board .
5. Consider Exposure vs Slander

Figure 4.1. Natalie Lauren Sims, Twitter post on her experience with #CHHSexism (Christian hip hop sexism), November 21, 2017.

bossy. Women aren't respected in the industry as much, so we have to work three times harder for credit and compensation."

In navigating hip hop circles, the labor of females requires an additional bullet point in their job description: they must be able to balance maintaining respect while assuaging male egos. It is telling that Natalie understands both the comparative difference in how males are perceived in the industry and what this will mean for how her labor is rewarded. Black women understand that they will routinely be required to work much more than their male counterparts in order to achieve "credit and compensation." This translates into unfair wage levels for Black female artists. In 2019, there were no women on the *Forbes* list of highest grossing hip hop artists. Just two female emcees broke the top twenty: Nicki Minaj and Cardi B at number twelve and thirteen, respectively (Greenburg 2019). And while Minaj out-positioned many of her other male counterparts, her ranking required significantly more artistic output and endorsement work. These realities in the wider hip hop arena are duplicated within Christian hip hop. This makes Natalie Lauren Sims's prodigious output and success in the industry an uncommon achievement.

The more common reality for most female creatives in Christian circles is one that more closely resembles the experience of Christina Bellizzi, who also goes by the name Cataphant online. The #CHHsexism (Christian hip hop) hashtag is her invention. Cataphant is the co-founder of YoungXLady, a group that promotes young Christian female rappers. Its roster has included, among others, Jamaica West.[8] On November 18, 2017, Cataphant posted a number of controversial messages regarding gender bias to her Twitter page (see Figure 4.1). She then called on other women to share their experiences using the #CHHSexism (see Figures 4.2 and 4.3). It was the height of the #MeToo movement and many similar religious hashtags appeared in support of the broader movement, such as #ChurchToo. It was only a matter of time before Christian hip hop, the physical and digital workplace for mostly young Christian males, had its own reckoning. Using the #CHHSexism, respected women in Christian hip hop like Butta P shared their own experiences and showed support for Cataphant. Butta P began as one third of the rap trio called Rhema Soul in Fort Lauderdale, Florida, in 2007. She helped ignite the career of notable male artists like GAWVI

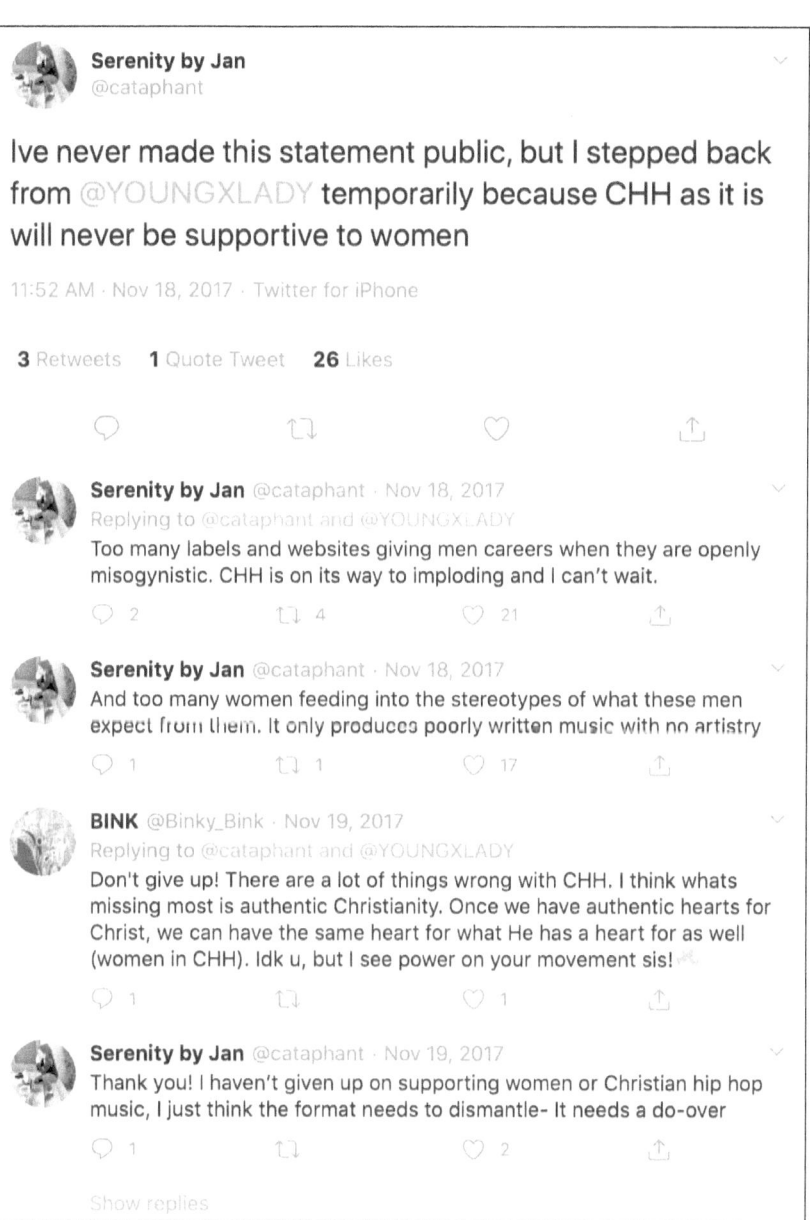

Figure 4.2. Catalina Bellizzi (@cataphant), Twitter post, November 18, 2017 (1 of 2).

(Gabriel Alberto Azucena), now a well-known producer on Reach Records, a subsidiary of Columbia Records. Four years prior to Cataphant's post, she too had spoken out against sexism in Christian hip hop spaces with a song titled "See Me."

Cataphant's hashtag was quickly picked up by other Christian female hip hop artists, telling their own stories of gender bias. Natalie's response to #CHHSexism offers balance, and mirrors her long-standing relationships with other top male artists. As an advocate for women, she encourages her male counterparts to deal sensitively with women. Conversely, she challenges female artists to produce quality content, as a response to the discrimination they face. She critiques the movement both by highlighting men who have supported her own projects (KB, Swoope, and Lecrae) and in the distinction she makes between exposure and slander.

Figure 4.3. Catalina Bellizzi (@cataphant), Twitter post, November 18, 2017 (2 of 2).

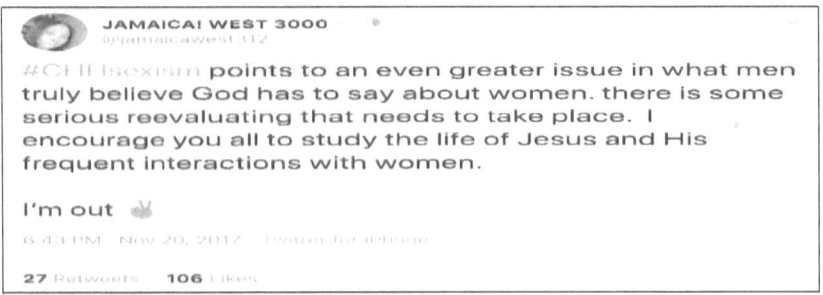

Figure 4.4. Jamaica West (@jamaicawest312), Twitter post, November 20, 2017.

Figure 4.5. Catalina Bellizzi (@cataphant), Twitter post, November 19, 2017 (1 of 2).

By choosing to "play both sides," so to speak, Natalie participates in a form of pretexting similar to what I described earlier in this volume in the work of Jackie Hill-Perry. By taking on parts of the culture through her discussion of her experiences, she is able to then offer a soft critique of it without risking her place in it. This inter-positionality is a continual situating affair for female creatives. In the online space, Natalie uses her platform and gender to complicate the #CHHSexism hashtag. It is not just men against women, she maintains. By acknowledging the presence of sexism amid allies and opportunities, Natalie privileges the role of humans and human networks in overcoming bias. This is in keeping with her person-centered approach to working in the digital economy. In our interview, regarding her work with a male counterpart, the rapper KB, she says, "KB and I wanted to have ownership. We wanted to provide

Figure 4.6. Catalina Bellizzi (@cataphant), Twitter post, November 19, 2017 (2 of 2).

opportunities for our people to be artistically, spiritually, and financially free and that comes with sacrifice and ownership. One day he realized that he couldn't pass down his catalogue of music to his kids because he didn't own it. I realized that I would always be a means to someone else's end. So, we started our own company."

The answer for Natalie has been "providing opportunities for our people." "People" here includes their friends, family members, and other artists who share their vision. While ownership requires both their participation and their exploitation in the digital labor market, Natalie sees this as a realignment of power. Through ownership, she extends equal footing to women and Black Christians in her network. For many female creatives like Natalie, such a racial-gendered project almost always occurs with the support and contribution of male allies. Rapper and producer KB is that person for Natalie. KB mirrors Natalie's belief regarding ownership in the 2019 track "DNOU2" (Don't Nobody Own Us) written, in part, by both Natalie and KB.

> Was trappin' out apartments
> Now I'm takin' off on Tarmacs

> Don't be driven by a contract
> Have your lawyer check the CARFAX (KB 2019)

While they employ the classic hip hop come-up narrative here, the lyrics penned by Natalie and KB move on to employee-related advice. They encourage younger Christian rappers to reconsider contracts that tether—and thus objectify—young Black bodies to a single record company. The comparisons of the modern labor economy for Blacks to historical slave economies is apparent in the repeated lines "Boy, don't nobody own us." This critique of the capitalist economy is situated within hip hop.

> Hip-Hop won't involve this
> Radio hasn't bought this
> Way, way too exhausted
> To tap dance for your profits (KB 2019)

The "this" referenced repeatedly in the lyrics is the artistic work and production of the writers. Hip hop, they argue, has no involvement or financial claim to either. Instead, the writers (Natalie and KB) privilege people over corporations, saying:

> I'm in love with my core fans
> Hold it down before the door slams
> Write free on my coffin
> Christ rules on my content
> Race, faith, and fashion
> Free sons and the daughters
> Free sons and the daughters (KB 2019)

Natalie Lauren Sims and KB reassign new meaning and thus value to creatives by locating them among the "free" sons and daughters of God. For Natalie in particular, this liberatory work is part and parcel of fighting gender discrimination. That this merges with similar goals of her male counterparts blurs the rich gender work at play here. Yet it reveals both the intersectional nature of Black women's oppression, and their multiple approaches to addressing such oppression through work alliances with their male colleagues.

Conclusion: Intimacy through Visibility and Valuation

In a digital labor economy that often devalues Black bodies, creatives employ a variety of strategies to gain visibility and restate their worth and sense of value in the workplace. This webwork includes packaging or branding their own struggle and come-up story, advocating mental health, creating opportunities and greater visibility for other creatives (i.e., "putting people on"), and finding creative ways of centering humans and the development of human networks.

The stories of Beleaf and Natalie demonstrate how such performances or "selling" creates high levels of intimacy with online viewers and fellow creatives. They mirror and reveal their audiences' own experiences. In addition to that, creatives like Beleaf and Natalie build intimacy by advocating for their own and other creatives' self-worth.

While this is an intentional and rewarding project, it has not been without its costs. Over the course of their development as creatives, digital Black Christians have struggled and sometimes failed to define their own value. Here, Beleaf's decision to end his rap career is telling. In a 2015 *Rapzilla* interview detailing her decision to work on Iggy Azalea's 2014 *The New Classic* album, Natalie described her later regret about the explicit content of the album and the fact that it was not aligned with her own Christian beliefs.

> I feared not making it. Afraid to take my own route, I often settled for what was given out of ignorance . . . When you've come from a low-income home, all [you] ever know is check to check and somebody throws a lot of money in your face, it's so easy to compromise for financial security. But the reality is, long after that money is gone, I still have to live with those decisions and the consequences . . . Now I'd rather take my chances and walk away from money. When I look back on what I've contributed to this industry, I want it to be an eternal impact—one that pushes people towards the reality that there's more to life than what they tell us. (Daniels 2015)

In highlighting her emergence from a "low-income home" and living "check to check," Natalie underscores the uneven way many creatives enter the digital labor market. Azalea's later rise to stardom also came in part through Natalie's and other digital Black Christians' early grooming of Azalea as a rapper. Natalie's role in Azalea's artistic development shows the role of Black women, in particular, as welcome surrogates for white female and male digital production, but often with little or far less compensation.

Yet Natalie's words also demonstrate the unique goals of digital Black Christians in the digital labor market. Her desire to "push people towards the reality that there's more to life than what they tell us" is a challenge to a capitalist economy, which values profit over persons. Instead Natalie favors the sensibilities of a woke economy. Her re-centering of a Christian ethic of human care and "eternal impact" offers followers and fans a new currency with which to acquire visibility and self-worth, one that is rooted in her notion of Christian divinity. It is also that insistence of Blackness onto the digital that Christiana Sharpe's work notes. The woke economies created by digital Black Christians refuse to allow their histories and existence to be overlooked and insist that they matter in the digital workforce as a right of Black Christian belief and practice.

5

Church

The Story of Jamaica West

> ERIKA: Do you have a church that you think of as your home church... I'm thinking of a physical structure, a place where you go to worship?
>
> JAMAICA:[1] ... it's so interesting that you bring this up because this is what the past year of my life has been about... I was raised in the Black Church. And as much as I come down on the Black Church due to a lot of hurt [and destructive] things happening, it's still in the church [that I found] home. It is very important to me, at least in this phase of my life, to have a church that I go to. Like a physical building where I go and pray in congregation with the saints, you know. There is something about it on Sunday morning, to go into the church and you see people of God and we all worship together in a building that we all say, "This is the church."... I do have a church in Chicago that I say, "This is my church building."
>
> ERIKA: So what's the name of the church that you attend regularly in Chicago?
>
> JAMAICA: It is called All Nations Worship Assembly.
>
> ERIKA: And is that church meaningful to you in your Christian walk?
>
> JAMAICA: Very meaningful... I just switched churches this year. [I] just started going there in June or July, I believe. Ever since I've been there it's been very meaningful.
>
> ERIKA: How is your current Black church experience different from or similar to the Black churches you grew up in?
>
> JAMAICA: My dad's church isn't a denomination... It was called the African American Spiritual Awareness Crusade. It was like [a] nondenominational [church], but very much focused on the Black experience in learning who the African American is in the image of God. And then he died. I went to church with my mother. At one point we were at another nondenominational church. The worship was very diverse. And we were at a [Church of God in Christ] church for a couple of years. You have the [church] mothers and, you know,

the ushers have the white gloves and things like that, which is really cool. And then I was also at a Pentecostal church and then [a] Baptist [church]. So my childhood in regards to Black Church denominations was very interesting.

And then, when I became an adult, I tried a Presbyterian church for some time and that was completely different, as well. And so now because I've been through so many different church experiences and because I studied them, where I am now is, of course, it's a Black church, but I see things a little bit differently.

The spiritual interiority of Jamaica's world mirrors wider shifts in young Black adult Christianity at the close of the first decade of the millennium. Jamaica West's move from Columbus, Ohio, to Chicago, Illinois, landed her in a hub of digital Black Christian meaning-making. Most of the creatives mentioned in this volume either lived or worked for a time in Chicago. Given creatives' affiliations with other Christian artists and white evangelical churches, many encountered and chose to participate in recent church plants in the city of Chicago. The church plants also mimicked many of the intimacies they were familiar with in their Black churches back home. The role of the urban church planting movement in reviving and reimagining the Black Church is significant. Church plants or house churches—small vibrant communities composed of mostly twenty and thirty-something Black Christians—harken back to the Black Church's roots in hush harbors—secret places where slaves would gather to practice religion. House churches in particular also denote the present shape of the Black Church with its digital and loosely constructed networks and multiethnic members that often obscure the Black Church nature of many digital Black Christian gathering spaces. Neo-Black churches headed by digital Black Christians offer a toned down yet still authentic performance of Black linguistic practices. That such pastors have developed international followings through social media signals the sort of webwork we have discussed.

In *The Location of Religion*, modern religion scholar Kim Knott (2005, 13) writes that "space or spaces are both material and metaphorical, physical and imagined." The Black Church exists in such liminal space for creatives like West, situated somewhere between the material and imagined, loosely connected by her own words and actions. Yet that liminal space is also racial space, as cultural geographer Katherine McKittrick (2006, 15) reminds us. Indeed, we cannot forget the interlocking forms of oppression and identity, "the social processes that make geography a racial-sexual terrain." McKittrick further observes that "Black matters are spatial matters." To enter and travel this terrain is to make apparent the way oppression is produced and built into the religious networks in which digital Black Christians take part.

Though it begins with Jamaica's own interiority, this chapter soon pans out to the wider geographies of Chicago, Atlanta, the "urban," All Nations Worship Assembly, and YouTube to begin a new mapping of this Black Church in the life of digital Black Christians like Jamaica. Through her story, we examine the relationship between creatives and the various kinds of physical churches led largely by digital Black Christians.

Jamaica West

Long before she appeared on the Passion for Christ Movement's (P4CM's) Rhetoric stage in California as an open mic performer, Jamaica West was already an avid writer and poet. Like female creatives Natalie Lauren Sims and Jackie Hill-Perry, Jamaica's work sprang from an attempt to deal with the trauma of her past. Born in Columbus, Ohio, in 1993, West was a victim of childhood molestation. This experience had a profound impact on her writing and performance style.

In her creative work Jamaica describes much of her childhood as dark—although, in interviews she remembers fondly her time as a child spent with her father prior to his passing. A self-professed hip hop head, West's father also served as the founding pastor of the African American Spiritual Awareness Crusade church. With the elder West at the helm, the church adopted a theology that celebrated and centralized Africa and African heritage in the Christian faith. In this climate, Jamaica developed her own love of Black people and culture, a love enhanced by her own and her father's shared love of East Coast rappers like Nas. Jamaica soon flowed into the creative arts, particularly poetry. As a teen, her writing reflected a growing interest in female emcees and spoken word artists. When it was time to apply to colleges, Jamaica knew she wanted to move far from Columbus to develop as an artist. Her acceptance to Columbia College's Poetics program in 2010 was her ticket out of Ohio and into the artistic oasis of Chicago. A developing spoken-word artist, she joined many other poets who trekked to the iconic Get Me High Lounge to perform and learn in the space where poet Marc Smith first began slam poetry. Columbia College's own campus offered Jamaica a number of other events and classes that provided her an essential space to flourish as an artist.

She used the opportunity of attending college to craft a bolder voice for herself through poetry. A mostly shy, 5' 7", dark-brown-skinned woman with chiseled features and of slender build, twenty-five at the time of our interviews, Jamaica is the youngest of all of the creatives studied here. Yet in terms of intellect and artistic ability, she is well ahead of her years. Our interviews are filled with her insights on women, Blackness, and hip hop. Her quirky sense of humor and bold stance on topics like sexism in white evangelical spaces are utterly compelling—which makes it easy to forget that not so long ago Jamaica struggled to find the courage to share her story of trauma. At Columbia College, though, she heard fellow students telling their own stories in prose. In time, she too found the courage to speak out—on behalf of others. Mostly, she was drawn to the darkest moments in her classmates' stories, she says. Their ability to locate and openly name their sites of trauma piqued her interest. While West still struggles to include her own story in her writing, she quickly developed a knack for speaking up for other women. When I learned that at her last church a young woman openly expressed interest in another male congregant, and some of the male elders laughingly scorned the woman for her desperate attempts "to get a man," I asked Jamaica if the treatment of the woman was ever addressed, she responded: "Oh, it was addressed because I bought it up!"

As the youngest of my interviewees, Jamaica is perhaps the most in flux. She continues to wrestle with whether she should pursue a professional career as an artist or move on to another occupation—an issue most older creatives I studied have already resolved. The early sexual assault Jamaica experienced is a trauma that remains unresolved in her writing and in our interview. Bouts of depression and suicide attempts plagued her early adulthood. In a post to Instagram in December 2018,

Jamaica writes about her first suicidal ideation at six years old and her continued struggle to overcome depression through medication and therapy.

The truly powerful part of her story, however, is her ability to roll this sort of darkness into a single seamless artistic meditation on Black women. In the poem "Black Girl Cinema" performed at the P4CM's Rhetoric 2015 spoken-word show (P4CM 2015), Jamaica uses "cinema" as a space to fully "see" and "be seen."

> Black women, Black girls
> somehow we became a mirage
> of personalities and wandering souls
> plastered on these bastard TV screens
> as the world applauded (*clapping*) our brokenness
> I know they watching our brokenness
> I know you're (*points to cameras/digital audience*) watching this brokenness

Jamaica first situates Black women outside of themselves. As an audience to their own "brokenness," she introduces mediatized productions of Black women to draw connections both to the global (the "world") perception of Black women and their own internalization of such perceptions. In locating Black female space outside of self and in the mediatized field of brokenness, Jamaica highlights the inescapable geographies of race and gender. To "see" how one's self is "being seen" is to reckon fully with the spatial construction of one's oppression. Jamaica thrust such a construct upon her listening audience by recalling familiar negative tropes:

> Over the years we may have become jigaboos and wannabees[2]
> but something tells me
> deep down inside
> our souls are still being
> raped by our masters and we still
> bearing they babies
> in the pit of our subconscious

Her reference here to "jigaboos and wannabees" is not only significant in its nod to Spike Lee's Black cinematic classic *School Daze*, but also for signaling the still-evolving history of Black women in America. Present Black womanhood continues to occupy historical space. She is yet "raped by . . . masters" and "still bearing they babies." Here the work of social theorist Henri Lefebvre can be brought to bear on the way "space is the product." Jamaica's linguistic strategy demonstrates how harmful depictions of Black women created the space in which she currently operates and not the other way around. The consideration of webwork continues here as Jamaica's words stretch across history and media images to form a composite of Black women's space. This networked space consists of both "metaphor and material." She closes with an embodied assessment of her physical space.

> . . . when
> they asked you at age 22
> "Jamaica West how does it feel to be a
> young black woman in America?"
> I tell them,
> "It feels like being murdered in a jail cell"
> I tell them
> "It feels like lies that don't make a noose around my neck"
> I tell them
> "It feels like my spine became a broken ladder"
> I tell them
> "It feels like my womb were with a poem for my unborn
> son who will be slain on the streets"
> I tell them
> "It feels like this poem"
> Empty.

The Black colloquialism to be "all up in" one's feelings applies here. With each repetition of "it feels like," Jamaica takes the listening audience *into* her America. In the end, she is living and bound by the emptiness of this space, even as she *is* the space. West's reading of the Black female self gives way to a reading of her *self* as/in America. Both the intimacy and introspection of this space also take shape in Jamaica's other work on romantic relationships.

In our interviews, her description of the power of both love and heartbreak as "making her" suggests a particular orientation toward the same sort of brokenness mentioned in "Black Girl Cinema." She recalls earlier moments of darkness as shaping her concerns around brokenness:

> [E]ver since my childhood I had a lot of dark times . . . because that was around the time when my father and my mother had gone through the divorce. And I saw my mom go through a lot of pain. I think it kind of changed me. And it made me very inquisitive about the power of love and the power of heartbreak. And it made me into something. It changed my life. And then I would hear my mother's story. And as I would get older she would tell me different things, different truths. And then I also saw stories of [other] women around [me]. . . . it is a major part of my art because it's something I'm still trying to figure out. I'm still trying to understand why does it [love and heartbreak] have the power that it does to completely change someone's world.

The female creatives portrayed in this book often depict their bodies as fragmented parts made whole in Christ. Jamaica's performance of this common trope allows space for sharing painful memories of past trauma. Yet we must treat Jamaica's work on the topic as more than a story of victimhood. Jamaica is doing the rich pretextual work of liberating bodies through her own bodily performance. An example of this is found in her poem "My Cleavage Is a Snare" (2015) performed at the Canvas conference hosted by Humble Beast Records (the recording label for both Propaganda and Jackie Hill-Perry, among others mentioned in this volume). As a performance piece, it can be viewed as a simmering pot of water. She begins in disarming calm (e.g., a joke, an accepted truth), but becomes clear that a hard truth is brewing just beneath the surface. The temperature increases as the audience realizes that Jamaica is speaking more of their stories than her own. At the poem's boiling point she paints a vivid portrait of what freedom looks like, for herself and for her listeners. Unlike in the work of Jackie Hill-Perry, Jamaica identifies her own body as a site of spiritual transformation, of healing and divinity. In discussing the sacredness of her own body and the purity politics surrounding women's clothing, she reminds us, "Hell / Mary carried her Christ / and ragged cloths of gold" (Solomon 2015).

Speaking of her choice to center women in this way she says, "I think that issues with women and in relationships ultimately . . . point to God, you know, and I think I've chosen issues of the woman and relationships almost because . . . that has been an epicenter . . . of who I am as a person, and how I've grown. And how I've seen God" (Solomon 2015).

Jamaica engages with other spaces—buildings, geography, landscapes—in light of how she has constructed her intimate religious space around Black women's history and emotional life. For creatives like Jamaica, urban spaces like Chicago and Atlanta connect to, replicate, and make material their interior religious space. Artist Torkwase Dyson notes in "Black Interiority: Notes on Architecture, Infrastructure, Environmental Justice, and Abstract Drawing" (2017) that "compositional movement (ways in which the body unifies, balances, and arranges itself to move through space) is a skill used in the service of self-emancipation within hostile geographies." Digital Black Christians view emancipation as a spiritual project. Emancipation being a form of migration, migration too becomes a spiritual act—in Jamaica's case, her migration to Chicago.

Chicago as Mecca

Jamaica did not come to Chicago in 2010 only to attend Columbia College. She was on a pilgrimage to Chicago. And what better place? Chicago has an extensive history of welcoming wearied Black migrants into any number of its storefront church, synagogues, temples, and other newly emerging spaces. Throughout the twentieth century it was the religious epicenter of groups like the African Hebrew Israelites, faith healers like Mother Lucy Smith, and the home of other health and wellness advocates like pastor and neuropathic Dr. Alvenia Fulton and her Fultonia Health and Fasting Institute. For a time, it was toward Chicago that Nation of Islam followers turned for prayer during its schism with traditional Muslim leaders. Chicago also remains a sacred site for its association with the passing of iconic Black youth. The gruesome funeral photo of the tortured and mutilated body of Emmett Till was taken at Roberts Temple Church of God in Christ in the city's well known Black neighborhood of Bronzeville, known as the "Black Metropolis." Contemporary instances of Black death fill my conversations with Joseph Solomon as he discusses the impact that the 2014 police shooting of LaQuan McDonald had on him and young Blacks living in Chicago at the time. Black death is pervasive and sacred in this city.

For all these reasons, Jamaica West's migration to this city can be thought of as quite religious. She describes it with an air of destiny, as the place she "had to be." Places that "call" creatives tell us as much about the place as it does about the creative. It is interesting to note, then, how many of the creatives portrayed here, like Jamaica, felt called to Chicago and later to Atlanta.

Chicago occupies a central place in this book's narrative as it is the space where Blackness, interlocking systems of oppression, and evangelicalism collide in the Legacy organization. The annual Legacy Conference brings together church leaders and youth to develop future urban ministries. Behind the conference is the larger body of the Legacy Fellowship Church, which plays an important role in the current orientation of the Black Church. The urban church planting movement of the latter half of the twentieth century is most responsible for Legacy's beginning.

In 2000 a few Chicago pastors returned from a conference on church planting held in London. They were energized by the words of noted Christian apologist Tim Keller, that "no one can reach a city by itself" (Chicago Partnership, n.d.). Joining a local movement of predominantly white churches seeking to plant ministries in the city, the pastors began the Chicago Partnership in 2009. One of its directors, Brian Dye, had already began this work through ministries like Inner City Impact and his own youth ministry training organization, Vision Nehemiah. Throughout the early years of the millennium, the Chicago church planting movement continued to infiltrate the heart of a mostly Black and Brown city through church plants and leadership training programs. However, their upper administration remains predominantly white, and given Keller's and other central figures' complementarian beliefs, also male. As such, this model of ministry has not been without its critics.

Signaling the pervasiveness and problems associated with this model, Christena Cleveland (2014) made waves in Christian circles with a blog post titled "Are You Starting an Urban Church Plant or PLANTATION?"

Cleveland contends that white suburban church planters, sometimes acting as masters, often replicated oppressive histories with their drive to establish inner city ministries. The plantation imagery used in her post was offensive to many, for it marked the urban space as both real and imagined sites of Black enslavement and white Christian hypocrisy. Cleveland used Buffalo, New York, as one example of the white suburban church planters' encroachment on the city. However, from my own research on young Black adults in Buffalo, New York, during this same period I know that Black churches retained a far more influential role than the speckling of suburban church planters that may have emerged during that time. In fact, the church planting movement, at least among the subjects of my study, were only minimally affected by this white-led movement through youth groups and other urban/suburban ministries during their childhoods. These white ministries were around much longer, yet I have found they had much less impact than Cleveland suggests. Some prominent urban Black churches in Buffalo, also out of a deep sense of calling, even moved to the suburbs to minister more effectively to a growing Black middle class. White Christian involvement in predominantly Black urban spaces tells the story of a much more complex pattern of religious migration. While it is easy to imagine white church planters as systematically overtaking the urban environment, in reality the loose networks described here made for tremendous variation in the urban mission field. This diversity ranged from fully Black-led efforts in some places to real-life versions of Cleveland's "urban church plantations" in others. Chicago was no different in that regard.

The Legacy Conference was an outgrowth of Vision Nehemiah, an organization created in 2003 by a young white man, then youth counselor Brian Dye (mentioned previously). Brian's mission was to train young adult leaders for urban ministry. In September 2011, Vision Nehemiah merged with GRIP Outreach for Youth, expanding both organizations' ministry to disaffected youth in Chicago's poorest urban areas. Jamaica West soon had several connections to the organization through her association with other creatives mentioned in this volume and Legacy's further growth into the church plant movement as one of a growing number of house churches. Of the many forms that a church plant can take, house churches are perhaps the most intimate. For a time, Jamaica West, far from home and in a much larger city than the one she was accustomed to, felt this was the sort of personal religious connection that she needed. The house church she attended consisted of a racially mixed group of mostly young single adults and families meeting regularly to break bread and study scripture. It was categorically different from the Black Church experience of "church mothers" and "white gloves" that she mentions having experienced earlier in her life. It was quite consistent, however, with earlier Black slave traditions of meeting in intimate secret locations—hush harbors. In such spaces, believers were free to engage with each other and their liturgical practices considered the Black body as sacred. Yet no one ever made that connection overtly.

Many white urban house or church planters often imagine their spaces like those of the early church as outlined in the Book of Acts. Acts describes how persecuted believers met in furtive locations, establishing small cells across the city to avoid capture, while simultaneously seeking to draw new believers to their ranks. This language, in predominantly Black urban communities in the present day, speaks to missionaries' sense of danger and fears due to gun violence and residents' disdain for Christian encroachment in their neighborhoods. Tropes of sexual depravity and Black monstrosity underlie such understandings of the urban space, however, as the church planter seeks to tame the wild terrain of the city. Yet emerging homegrown missionaries to the urban environment were not totally beholden to this model. Their awareness of the history of missional racism also balanced their approach to ministering to Black urban populations. Such young adult white church planters were pivotal in reshaping the rhetorical engagement of digital Black Christians with the Black Church. Though they omitted critical historical geographies of the hush harbors, they offered urban space for creatives to see themselves and their histories differently and thus to envision a new model for the Black Church.

Missionaries like Dye, who, though white, had grown up on Chicago's West Side, sought to overcome racist approaches to church planting through his full integration in the local community. He invited homeless Black youth to live with him and his wife, he held after school tutoring at his home, and fully immersed himself in the community. It is difficult to cast Dye as the traditional colonizer of Black space. Yet ministries like Dye's operated on the ground level. Loosely connected networks that embodied a certain local flavor were still largely guided, if only theologically, by white and male-led organizations like the deeply conservative Presbyterian Church of America, Acts 29, the Gospel Coalition, or Redeemer City to City. As Jamaica moved to other churches in this same network, she encountered this reality. In her religious movements in and around Chicago, she soon learned how much of a product this space was. This seemingly free and intimate church space in fact deliberately constructed geographies that mimicked the same structural forms of racism and sexism she had known for much of her life.

Joseph Solomon tells a similar story of experiencing racism in predominantly white small group settings prior to his arrival in Chicago. Like Jamaica and others, however, he felt "a calling" to the city. This came in the form of his association with the aforementioned Brian Dye. After several invitations from Brian, in 2015 Joseph finally decided to leave behind his life in Texas to work with teens at GRIP, a youth outreach partner of Brian's organization.

Then there is Perry Preston, a Chicago native, who was living in Atlanta in 2004. It was after a deadly shooting of a friend that he decided to change his life and move back to Chicago. Childhood friend Gary Brown, a former gang member turned seminary student at Moody Bible Institute in downtown Chicago, introduced Preston to Brian Dye. By 2009 Brian had come to have an intricate role in Preston's spiritual development, even guiding his decision to date Jackie Hill-Perry a year later. The two married in 2010 and lived together in Chicago before transitioning to Atlanta in 2017. He states,

> It was just perfect how God set it up, because Brian started to disciple me a couple weeks after I started pursuing Jackie . . . He walked with me through that whole process; talked to me about relationships, loving my wife as Christ loves the church. I was able to see, for the first time, a healthy marriage—a man who loved ministry, who loved discipling young men, at the same time as he served his wife. (Daniels 2018)

Whether through his youth organization, the Legacy conference, or their house church, as digital Black Christians encountered Dye and his ideas, their essential notion of the form and function of the physical Black Church shifted. No longer was it necessary to be in a predominantly Black Church to retain one's authentic Black religious practices.

Dye's intimate contact through discipleship with creatives decentered the essentiality of a physically located Black Church. While they may have retained some its beliefs and practices, the house church experience removed the need to identify with its physical geographies. Instead, the whole of the city of Chicago operated as a sacred site in which spiritual transformation could take place. Jamaica was moving through this geography in search of such transformation while creatives elsewhere were experiencing their own call to another urban mecca.

In 2009, at almost the same time that Preston and Jackie were beginning their courtship, a group of friends in Denton, Texas, were contemplating a bold move from their church Blueprint to plant another church in Atlanta, GA. Parts of this story have been shared earlier in discussing Lecrae's informal study with friend and Cross Movement Records rapper Ambassador. Nearby University of North Texas, which Lecrae attended until 2003, was a feeder school for two conservative Christian institutions in the area by the early millennium: Dallas Theological Seminary and Denton Bible Church. Lecrae was part of a group of young mostly Black artists and church planters who created a unique parachurch called Blueprint in Denton. When the founding pastor Dhati Lewis expressed a calling to start a church in Atlanta, twenty-four members uprooted their lives in Denton and followed him.

The move placed a racial spin on urban church planting. Dhati and the other church planters involved hoped to reverse the tide of Black urbanites absconding to white institutions to learn about urban evangelism. Instead, Dhati's goal was to "become the last generation of believers who have to leave the urban context in search of sound discipleship" (Blueprint Church, n.d.). Choosing instead a model of "indigenous disciple-makers," Blueprint Atlanta acknowledges its rootedness in Black cultural practices and seeks to incorporate this organically in the liturgy of the church. Yet, as with Legacy's continued Baptist and Presbyterian influence, so too mainline Baptist denominations continue to loosely influence the theology and leadership of the church. Blueprint, much like Denton Bible College, remains connected to the Southern Baptist Convention. While the convention in recent years has sought to atone for its past support of slavery and other racist practices, and several Black leaders have climbed its ranks, it remains a mostly white male-led convention, explicitly embracing complementarianism and barring women from the pastorate. The Blueprint Church website lists a number of male elders and pastors as well as female "Titus 2" leaders. The latter group are inspired by the New Testament book of Titus, specifically chapter 2 verses 3–5, which reads:

> Likewise, teach the older women to be reverent in the way they live, not to be slanderers or addicted to much wine, but to teach what is good. Then they can urge the younger women to love their husbands and children, to be self-controlled and pure, to be busy at home, to be kind, and to be subject to their husbands, so that no one will malign the word of God. (KJV)

The effect of such passages has been to circumscribe the roles of Black women in both white church spaces and even in predominantly Black churches like Blueprint. Far removed from Blueprint, Jamaica failed in many ways to escape these same geographies in Chicago even as she moved from church plants to other white-led churches. As she describes the treatment of women by male elders, she notes the way such policies police and limit female bodies. Through the loosely constructed networks of the church planting movement wherever she moved, the interiority of her religious life discussed earlier seemed to meet her.

Jamaica misses our first scheduled interview. When we finally connect she apologizes, explaining that she has just arrived back at her home in Chicago from Atlanta. She is working there now, both through a modeling agency and producing her own music. She is contemplating moving to Atlanta. But, she says after a long sigh, "We'll see what God says."

"God Told Me to Move to Atlanta"

Like Chicago, Atlanta has long been known as the "Black Mecca." It is shrouded with the same air of religious meaning. In the early years of this millennium it has also become an essential site for southern rap. The mid-1990s' creation of LaFace Records with artists like Usher and TLC earned Atlanta the title the "Motown of the South." Artists like Outkast and later TI, Ludacris, and Young Jeezy expanded Atlanta's profile as a major producer of hip hop's new sound. As an important site for

Figure 5.1. Jackie Hill-Perry and Preston Perry just prior to their move to Atlanta, GA. (Instagram post, November 29, 2017)

Black cultural production, for Blacks located elsewhere, Atlanta served as an important imaginary of freedom. As artists, the creatives studied in this book were deeply affected by what they heard and saw occurring in Atlanta in the early millennium period. They were able to link their spiritual desires with these physical geographies of freedom. Their "compositional movements" soon aligned the imagined space with the real space: nearly half of all of those documented in this volume have made the move to Atlanta (see Figure 5.1 for another example). Most make statements like Grammy Award–winning gospel artist and digital Black Christian Tasha Cobbs:

> Around 2006, God instructed me to move to Atlanta. It was one of those things where God is saying for you to do this but I didn't see it. I didn't want to leave my father. I was operating heavily in his ministry but God was telling me, "Tasha, it's time for you to move." (Cobbs 2014)

Cobbs took a job as a music minister with famed singer and pastor William Murphy III at dRream Church in Atlanta in 2006. A year prior to this, Lecrae headlined at the Legacy Disciple Conference in Chicago before heading back to Denton, TX. Only three years later, he too would fully relocate for the same reason as Tasha Cobbs.

Lecrae was instrumental in popularizing the Legacy Disciple Conference in Chicago. Several rappers of the 116 Clique (who later formed Reach Records) also stayed in Brian Dye's home. The same group provided the soundtrack to the church planting movement taking place in Denton, TX and in Chicago, IL. When Blueprint pastor Dhati Lewis moved to Atlanta, among those who moved with him were Lecrae, other members of the 116 Clique and Reach Records itself. From Texas to Chicago to Atlanta, creatives like Lecrae were both creating and extending new religious networks. In their artistic renderings and theological conversations, they signaled new ways and sites for doing and being the Black Church.

This early millennial wave of Black Church planters to "chocolate cities" like Atlanta further expanded digital Black Christians' Black Church to encompass urban ministry conferences, house and church plants, and even Reach Records. Notable in their language of "calling" and having a "heart for the urban context" is a desire to move freely and to be affirmed in their sense of sacredness. It also reveals a deep connection to other Black and brown bodies living in the same material and metaphorical geographies. They seek in their movement to "produce new space" for Black wholeness and value.

Soon Blueprint Atlanta began to support church plants or "sending churches." Natalie Lauren Sims served as one of the founding members of Cornerstone Community Church in west Atlanta, one such church plant. Natalie, already in Atlanta as a hip hop artist and as part of Reach Records, believed in her calling to the new church plant, as well. Record labels, hip hop music, and makeshift buildings formed an eclectic new religious geography that many among their ranks counted as a wholly new context, one quite different from the earlier Black Church, and an exciting project for many of them. Yet for this same reason, many within traditional Black churches, including those now affiliated with church plants like Blueprint, counted their church as part of the "Black Church."

Yet through its affiliation with the Southern Baptist Convention, this so-called new Black Church actually remains beholden to old geographies of oppression. It still consistently borrows from mainline white denominations' theologies, even while affirming racial justice. Its deep affiliation with these institutions and the challenge it faces in moving completely against the hetero-patriarchal white supremacy of white-led institutions evinces its particular failure to embrace women in leadership (i.e., as pastors or elders). In short, while such newer predominantly Black or multiethnic churches like Blueprint shy away from the term *the Black Church*, in this regard they are perhaps most like the Black Church in continuing to maintain such interlocking systems of oppression.

Digitized Pentecostalism: All Nations Worship Assembly

In our final interview, Jamaica West tells me that after attending multiethnic churches and predominantly white churches for a time, she now believes attending a Black Church is important to her. She attends All Nations Worship Assembly on the South Side of Chicago. The digital Black Christian world is sufficiently well connected that I wonder if I have heard of it before. It turns out that I have. More than a decade ago a friend of mine introduced me to a college student and youth pastor at his church. A decade later I lost contact with the friend, though we continue to share mutual acquaintances, like the college student, on Facebook. I learn that he was recently ordained as one of the Associate Pastors at the All Nations Worship Center in Atlanta. Coincidentally I learn that another acquaintance from my childhood, whose family fellowshipped at our church in Rochester, New York, recently began a church that is a part of the GATE Network (formerly The Global Fire Alliance). Like Pastor Mike Todd of Transformation Church mentioned earlier, he too studied at Oral Roberts University and for a time participated in ministry with Todd at Greenwood Christian Center. He traveled to Chicago in 2008 to learn more about Pastor Matthew Stevenson's network, The Global Fire Alliance, and soon joined. Since beginning his own church in Rochester, NY he has called Stevenson his "spiritual father" and is using digital media technology in similar ways to replicate Stevenson's prophetic ministry in his own city.

Prior to my interview request via Instagram, I had never met Jamaica West. Yet, through digital Black Christianity, we were deeply connected in the same network of people. Our digital connections made me think of the way online ties construct such overlapping networks that they bind digital Black Christians together in a multi-platform Black Church geography of sorts. The growth of All Nations Worship Assembly (ANWA), also led by Matthew Stevenson, and its mostly digital Black Christian audience, is also indicative of this fact.

As noted earlier in this chapter, many have voiced a call to the city of Chicago. In particular, ANWA has welcomed several such "migrants" from other states and churches after viewing online clips of its services and the pastor's sermons, to be a part of "what God is doing at All Nations." This church began in 2003 and now boasts over five thousand members. Yet it was between 2013 and 2015 that the church began to experience unprecedented growth, thanks in part to its increased online presence through social media and video-streaming apps like Periscope. Periscope was just a few months old when ANWA's Stevenson (2016) logged on with his first post "For Leaders Only!!!!! Dealing with IN-timidation!!!!!!!!!!" We have seen that young Black users were early adopters of digital technology, as internet scholar André Brock and feminist writer Feminista Jones (2019) have discussed particularly with regard to Black Twitter. When Twitter purchased and promoted the introduction of the new video-streaming site Periscope in March 2015, it was no wonder that Black Twitter users were some of its earliest subscribers. In the wake of police shootings, the rise of Black Lives Matter, and protests across the nation, many civil right activists like Deray McKesson used Periscope and other video-streaming apps to document their protest activities. With its "Go Live" button to begin recording, the liveness of Periscope was built into its design narrative from the beginning. And as media scholar Megan Sapnar Ankerson (2018, 233) notes regarding Periscope, "Design narratives don't just tell a story about the product; they inform the big picture, encompassing creation myths."

Created by Kayvon Beykpour and Joe Bernstein as a way to document their time in Istanbul during the Gezi Park protest, Periscope's design narrative touted its liveness as a "source of truth." That liveness also gave it an aura of impartiality. For digital Black Christians like Matthew Stevenson, such aspects of its narrative aligned deeply with their own efforts. The proliferation of evangelists, ministers, apostles, and other church-supported and non-ordained Black users operating as clergy has become so common that both derisive memes and how-to articles for clergy wanting to evangelize or monetize their Periscope activities or other digital live social media sites quickly began trending (see Figure 5.2).[3]

198 | CHURCH

Figure 5.2. Meme. (Unknown origin)

Like radio and television broadcasts in the previous century, what marked young Black religious users' approach to Periscope was their mission-driven attempts to "spread the Gospel" or the "Word." The aura of spirituality in its creation myth resonated with those doing religious work and with their own "me-centered" religious practices. While protest movements saw in Periscope a useful tool for "media witnessing" of communal forms of activism, digital Black Christians like Stevenson appealed to others of similar age and Black Church interests through personality-centered demonstrations of Black Church orality like preaching and prophesying. Dr. Matthew Stevenson has mastered this art by individually greeting each person as they join his Periscope live and by promising each one a word "for you" or voicing his desire to "share something with you from God." Many digital Black Christians, like Hill-Perry, in mimicking Black Church preaching participate in pretexting or "putting on" the Black Church. Digital Black Christians like Stevenson, operating as part of a new vanguard of Black Church leadership, invite their audience into a *virtual Black Church* space. The liveness of the Periscope moment mitigates distances of time and space to offer digital Black Christians a brief Black Church presence.

The feeling of such liveness—of feeling physically present through digital means and being digitally present at the physical meeting space—continues each Sunday morning at ANWA. Each of the three Sunday worship services at the second-floor, two-thousand-seat sanctuary is packed. The booming speakers can be heard on the ground floor of this sprawling, three-story converted Jewish temple. Just as noticeable are the friendly smiles, the care with which one of the ushers assists me in carrying my bags up the three flights of stairs and connecting me with a friend I am meeting at the service. This personal and warm treatment is intentional. In a Periscope video clip of the meeting posted by Matthew Stevenson in March 2016, Executive Director Martin Michael of ANWA Chicago can be heard telling leaders in a training meeting, "If we can be intentional about helping people . . . something like that will make people not care that we have three flights of stairs before they get to their seats . . . We don't want them to just watch the Periscope . . . we want them to actually come here and fellowship with us." The ANWA leadership seeks to construct a seamless internet-to-physical-location experience. This goal of connecting with people is perhaps most alluring to their young audience, which has become jaded by the lack of intimacy online. Learning from such examples, other contemporary Black churches that are thriving have captured a skill ANWA knows well and has worked hard to develop.

People's digital introduction to the ANWA organization generally occurs through Stevenson's messages. I first witnessed one such message, a Thursday-night sermon, a few years ago, on September 20, 2018. In the video, shared from a friend's Facebook page, Stevenson appears with a neat crop top streaked with orange on one side and a stylishly fitted button-down shirt and pants (YAM TV 2018). The razor-sharp lines of his beard and hairline match his equally precise diction as he walks the length of the stage prophesying and preaching in a style with which digital Black Christians who came of age with Black televangelists are most likely familiar. But his introduction to this audience, as it was for me, is now wrapped in social media soundbites shared from friends' pages, proclaiming "THISSS WORD!" or "This Word is for you!" Through Periscope and earlier social media encounters with Stevenson, several digital Black Christians like Jamaica West were drawn to this familiar and intimate experience. West notes that while her description of her earlier Black Church experiences is rooted in her aesthetic memories of "church mothers" and "white gloves," her decision to attend ANWA is motivated by how it makes her "feel." And you cannot help but feel something upon entering the main sanctuary.

The near darkness is broken up by a mixture of blaring lights from the front stage and a light production occurring throughout the worship portion of service, with fuchsia, blue, and yellow strobe lights. There is a faint smell of both marijuana and alcohol in the air as some in the audience struggle to resolve their Saturday night with their Sunday morning. The welcoming of visitors consists of a selfie break in which attendees are encouraged to snap a picture with people sitting near them and post it to Instagram with the hashtag #ANWA. I meet vlogger and writer Lamar Gibbs. He happens to be visiting Chicago for the Legacy Conference and publishes for Christian digital magazines. He tells me about his new web ministry, Thoughts of Redemption. Like Jamaica, Gibbs and much of the audience of more than two thousand are mostly in their twenties and almost exclusively Black. Surprisingly, however, the music is more Hillsong than Tasha Cobbs, very loud and very energetic. In other ways, as well, ANWA seems to vacillate in its liturgical decisions.

The service drifts between Black Church practices and white theology as the offering time approaches. The pastor encourages people not to tithe what they have, but to "tithe what you want." Hawk-like, Stevenson watches as the offering buckets are passed along the aisles. As noted earlier, digital Black Christians' disdain for prosperity Gospel preachers like Juanita Bynum and, in the past Bishop T. D. Jakes, seems to have escaped those gathered here. As he lifts up the buckets of their offerings, Stevenson leads the congregation in a chanting mantra popular among word-of-faith teachers:

> According to the word of God I declare that money cometh to the body of Christ and Money cometh to me for the sake of the Gospel. I call my church debt free. I have all that is necessary to completely pay all the buildings, properties, and equipment and do everything that God has called us as a church to do . . . We will reach the lost, help the believers walk in faith and victory by the preaching of the Gospel. I call myself

debt free and I proclaim I have the necessary finances to do everything God has called me to do with much in store to bless others. Father, I pray that by putting you first in my finances, giving my best in tithes and offerings, you are bringing me into my wealthy place. I call my house and all my property paid in full. I believe I receive raises and bonuses, sales and commissions, favorable settlements, estates and inheritances, interest and income, rebates and returns, discounts and dividends, checks in the mail, gifts and surprises, bills decreased and paid off. Thank you, Lord for meeting all my financial needs so that I have more than enough to give to your Kingdom. Money cometh to me now! You are bringing me into my wealthy place.

The Black Church's brief silence or criticism of prosperity-centered Gospels after the 2008 recession has evaporated. Now preachers like Stevenson introduce such theologies in a number of ways that digital Black Christians find largely acceptable. Stevenson trained for a time in white evangelical circles, as his theology shows. Yet, like many of those studied in this book, his encounters with racism have been jarring and may well be shifting his affiliations in such white evangelical circles.

Moreover, Stevenson and his co-pastor and wife Apostle Kamilah Stevenson continue to position themselves as powerful players in the Black Church world with savvy branding and business models. Unlike churches Jamaica has explored earlier, their Pentecostal roots allow for women in leadership. Of the churches discussed in this chapter, theirs is the only one that specifically promotes gender equality in its mission. On the other hand, Stevenson also became popular through sermon clips in which he degrades women and cites their physical appearance as responsible for "turning men gay." For digital Black Christians who grew up in Black Pentecostal or Charismatic settings, they find a deep familiarity within ANWA over and against white Southern Baptist and Presbyterian–influenced styles mentioned earlier. A number of apostolic traditions are not only known for ordaining women but for producing the sort of gospel sound that provides its own mapping of the Black Church throughout the twentieth century. ANWA delivers on this front, as well. The 2017 launch of their own recording label, Wells Media Group, received a Grammy nomination for the album *Worship at the Well,* volumes 1 and 2. Furthermore, ANWA recently hired Miranda

Curtis and Todd Dulaney as worship and fine arts pastors. The two are popular recording artists and were formerly worship leaders at Bishop T. D. Jakes's church. In the Black Church world, their move to Chicago signaled both the influence and vitality of the ANWA brand as well as the durability of gospel music (rather than hip hop) in physically located Black churches.

While this volume makes several connections to the way hip hop and social media are linked in digital Black Christians' lives, in churches like ANWA, hip hop remains mostly sidelined in worship practices. This is not a result of antiquated church leadership, as earlier works on the Black Church and hip hop have suggested, but a result of their appeal to integrate hip hop more fully into Black Church practices.[4] Digital Black Christians seem to compartmentalize hip hop's uses. They celebrate hip hop as a Black cultural expression, but seem content to leave it mostly absent from Black Church musical practices—a particularly strange fact given that ANWA is run by digital Black Christians. At times, hip hop's sensibilities and aesthetics show up in sartorial style and use of language among Stevenson and members of the congregation. But that is the exception. Typically, the Stevensons' sermon rhetoric is that of a traditional Pentecostal Black Church. It is only the dynamism with which the Stevensons are able to work across several digital platforms that is unique to the contemporary Black Church experience they provide. Hip hop is thus a dispensable garment. Beneath it lie timeless rituals of intimacy-building through which Black Church practices have both survived and thrived. This is Stevenson's biggest draw—the promise of divine intimacy through the Black Church experience. For such an encounter, as in the time of evangelists like D. L. Moody, evangelistically minded young Christians flock to Chicago. It has not been uncommon in recent years to hear of young Black Christians moving to Chicago to be closer to Stevenson and his ministry.

Jamaica West arrived in Chicago in 2012 to attend Columbia College, but soon became engrossed in the arts and poetry scene, affiliating with poets like Joseph Solomon, and with Jackie Hill-Perry and Preston Perry before their move to Atlanta. Like her fellow poets, it was ANWA and its reliance on both digital and traditional Black Church practices that drew Jamaica back to the Black Church. As I worshiped with other digital Black Christians that Sunday morning, it was evident that while ANWA had gone the way of most digital Black Christians with its heavy reliance on digital media technology, it still retained rhetorical practices, particularly for Pentecostal Black Church goers, that felt familiar, practices that had to do with the prosperity Gospel and with prophetic utterances like speaking in tongues.

This latter practice occurred at a number of points in the service I attended. Without provocation, everyone suddenly reverted to their "prayer language." Three prayers are given over the course of the worship portion of the service and three more prayers occur prior to the message; all promise "a breaking forth" or "good things" in the future. Such gifts of prophecy are central to the ministry. The expectation of the "Word" or words of prophecy promise personalized blessings for those in attendance. Later in the service Stevenson prophesies to two men in the congregation. One has a music career that will soon take off. The other, a twenty-something Latino man on the opposite side of the church, is called forward along with his wife and mother-in-law. According to Stevenson, this man has been telling his wife, "I expect you to leave. Everyone else does," because of his broken relationship with his mother since he was five years old and because of his past gang involvement. Lowering his voice to a raspy whisper, Stevenson draws out each word as he says, "But that's not who you are anymore." The accuracy of his prophecies is not so important to this audience. Indeed, during a 2017 Fire Conference Stevenson remarked to prospective pastors hoping to duplicate his success that "believability and credibility are more important than accuracy" (CookieTruth 2017). His power to name specifics about individuals is sufficiently authentic for a room of digital Black Christians often searching for such an authentic and intimate knowledge of self and the divine online. But such revelations of knowledge also serve another function.

If these prophetic utterances sometimes sound like titillating gossip, it is because they are, and in the prophetic circles online and in physically located spaces the spread of rumors, gossip, and even "disses" serves an essential role in extending the Gospel. Stevenson embodies the "rumor has it" appeal of his ministry with a Periscope profile that describes him as a husband, father, and the "the one they love to hate." On numerous occasions he has addressed his "haters" and rumors regarding him and his ministry. His haters include bloggers and social media personalities who have questioned his sincerity, verbal attacks, trendy clothing choices, or those he perceives as jealous of his accomplishments. One such digital figure is Larry Reid, the creator and host of the *Larry Reid Live Show*, a YouTube "live interactive digital entertainment news show" covering Black Church events and people. He routinely attracts upward of forty thousand viewers for his salacious accounts of Black Church celebrities like BeBe Winans, the Clark Sisters, and Kirk Franklin. His most popular episodes include interviews with celebs in the Black Church world who are willing to "spill the tea" on events and other celebrities of interests to Reid's viewers. Such episodes can reach well over five hundred thousand views. When covering Matthew Stevenson (as he has done on numerous occasions), Reid exclusively refers to him as "Maddy." Reid explains "I call him 'Maddy' because he's always fussing [in sermons], and then in [social media] comment sections he's pretty fussy, some of his posts are pretty fussy . . . Juanita Bynum-like" (Reid 2021). On August 14, 2018, another popular YouTuber, William Rogers, provided a recap of Stevenson's Facebook post earlier in the week, in which one commentor to Stevenson's Facebook post states, "He's no Apostle. He's an entertainer" (Rogers 2018). Stevenson quickly replied by calling the commentor "ugly" and stating that the Lord had revealed to Stevenson the commentor's porn addiction, financial troubles, and alcoholism. He closed his reply with "Be healed and get therapy" (Rogers 2018). In a widely shared sermon by Reid on August 12, 2018, Stevenson had followed up the earlier Facebook post by saying, "If ole boy write me again Imma tell him again he ugly!" He admonished his congregation not to attempt to offer any explanation or defense of his actions, adding, "If that makes you mad, I'll get to you soon . . . I don't care about offending you . . . if it ain't your flavor, change the channel" (Rogers 2018). This bit of gossip is just the tip of the iceberg for not only Reid's followers but several other Black Church YouTubers who have covered Matthew Stevenson's practices. Alleged scandals range from questions regarding his sexuality and affairs to misappropriation of funds and witchcraft. Like any good bits of gossip, the allegations are titillating and nearly impossible to substantiate. The digital contours of the Black Church are uniquely designed for the kind of "gossipy Gospel" on which digital Black Christians seem to thrive.

Another native of my hometown, social media entrepreneur Tipani Montgomery, released a number of Periscope and YouTube videos defaming the ministry of Stevenson on the grounds that, among other things, he and other church leaders created a culture of sexual impropriety following her 2017 departure from that church. She is not alone in posting tell-all videos and posts regarding Stevenson and ANWA. In 2016 Stevenson himself addressed the "Die Matthew Stevenson" Campaign that Vashon Dixon, an attendee of his Fire Conference, began to circulate on learning of Stevenson's opposition to the campaign of then-presidential hopeful Donald Trump. Dixon called on other—largely white—Christian Trump supporters to join her in a twenty-four-hour prayer vigil for the death of Stevenson.[5]

Such responses or disses to Stevenson and the ministry replicate other actions. When I attended their Sunday-morning service on July 15, 2018, one such incident occurred at ANWA, near the middle of Stevenson's sermon. A woman quickly began walking to the front of the sanctuary, loudly shouting accusations at Stevenson and promises that he would soon be exposed—for what is unclear, though given allegations ranging from verbal abuse toward women to sexual impropriety one need only take their pick. She was quickly intercepted by his security team and taken outside the sanctuary. Such ministry disses along with salacious rumors create an even broader network of meaning for digital Black Christians. For while you can put someone out of a physically located church, in the digital world you only further extend your connection to the excised member by commenting on it online. Online scandals and rumors are passed along through the network of various blogs and social media platforms, and tend to elicit other users' tales and experiences. These enlarge the Black Christians' network, linking them not necessarily as members in a particular church (indeed the notion of a church "member" is a fairly outdated, twentieth-century concept for many digital Black Christians in the twenty-first century) but as a series of digital and physically located events that continuously shift and change and are linked only through their linguistic practices. My last exchange with Jamaica West makes this apparent.

I tell Jamaica West I will be at her home church on Sunday. *Will I see you there*? She informs me that in the time since our last interview, she has begun attending a different church. In a bygone era, such flux would have indicated religious instability. While young adult Blacks attend church at much higher rates than their white counterparts, unlike previous decades there are still far fewer digital Black Christians overall signing their names on the roll books of American churches, making West's church practices much less of a phenomenon and more of a trend among digital Black Christians.[6] Just as routine are the mostly digital-only encounters I have had with each of the young Black Christians that I have studied over the past two years. Their faith consists of a fluid set of practices stitched together from online posts, podcast meetups, house churches, ministry conferences, and at times Black churches.

As the ANWA service closes and my friend and I flow out into the hall in the sea of younger Black Christians, we are met by those waiting to enter for the next service. The line wends its way down the staircase and nearly out of the door. The building itself is fairly unremarkable. The former home of the South Side Jewish Congregation, most of its stained glass windows have now been covered. The remaining rose window and Star of David point to a now-outdated concern with religious formality. Yet the signage and presentation I have just left behind moves toward the temporality of digital Black Christianity. In typical digital Black Christian fashion, no one seems to care or notice the contradiction or clash between old and new, formal and informal. Because as Jamaica, perhaps instinctively, notes in our interview, the Black Church is "home" whereas ANWA is just a "church building."

As I step out into the sunlight, someone suddenly grabs me by my elbow and takes my hand, helping me down the final long set of stairs outside. Looking up, I see a smiling face, and a young ANWA usher says, "You have a blessed day, ok?" Michael Martin's words ring true: "No one will care about the three flights up." A crowd of young Black worshipers gathers in a sweet reunion of laughter on the sidewalk below. They exchange lighthearted jokes, gossip, and greetings with passersby. Their benedictions go the way of Black Christians gathered at the end of church services end for more than a century. No one really does seem to care about the building. They are the building. And here and online, through their intimate fellowship with one another, digital Black Christians are building . . .

Conclusion

What might all of this mean, then, for the future of Black Church institutions? This chapter suggests two trends common to growing Black churches that seem likely to continue into the future.

First, *Black Church rhetorical traditions like prophesying and charismatic preaching will continue to provide important modes of intimacy-building online, particularly in the wake of COVID-19 and church closures, thus extending the digital network and nature of the Black Church into the future.* Churches like All Nations Worship Assembly led by thirty-something Dr. Matthew Stevenson makes clear from its website that "Our vision is to help usher mankind into unprecedented intimacy with God" (ANWA, n.d.). Despite the rumors and scandals that seem to pepper the ministries of all well-known American evangelists, Matthew Stevenson has weathered an online storm of scandals and response videos to create seven churches nationwide and he oversees several others as part of his GATE Network. Stevenson has proven adept in both building an online brand and responding to online detractors.

Second, *if the present is any indication, the saying "the future is female" may not apply to physically located Black churches.* It should not be lost on the reader that this chapter portrays Jamaica West in a crowd of exclusively male leaders. Even as she reveals the inner life of a digital Black Christian woman, the reality is that the location of religion beyond that interiority is mostly male. Female creatives continue to lean in to online spaces to remedy the discrimination they experience in physically located churches. All of the churches named in this chapter, with the exception of ANWA, either adhere to doctrinal statements forbidding women in pastoral roles or, for a myriad of other reasons, have consistently retained only male senior pastors. The story of Jamaica West drives home the historic and present role of progressive Black women as thought leaders in rebuilding and remaking the Black Church. Yet it also underscores the fact that just as in the past, there continues to remain too few opportunities for female leadership in senior positions in the Black Church. That predominantly Black churches like Blueprint Atlanta remain beholden to white-led institutions only promises that this reality will extend into the future, quite unfortunately. A final example drives this point home.

In July 2020, the East Atlanta pastor of Cornerstone Community Church (a parachurch of the Blueprint Church in Atlanta), John Onwuchekwa, one of the Southern Baptist Convention's rising stars, cut ties with the convention. Onwuchekwa cited convention members' support of Donald Trump and its inaction on issues of racial injustice. Southern Baptist Convention officials urged Onwuchekwa to return over $185,000 in grant funds given to his congregation to support the church plant. Onwuchekwa pointed to the SBS's long-standing involvement in the American slave trade as a far greater debt which the organization needed to attend to. The fallout between Cornerstone Community Church and the Southern Baptist Convention reveals why predominantly Black churches align themselves with such organizations despite a history of racial injustice: unmatched access to resources. Yet it also demonstrates the way religious space is made and remade, as digital Black Christians build their own networks of support.

Jamaica West moved across all of these geographies, locating her inner spiritual self in urban and physically located spaces. Like so many other creatives, from her writings, hip hop, the urban, Chicago, Atlanta, and ANWA, she stitched together an entirely new notion of what the Black Church is and its possibilities for spiritual self-renewal. She notes, "There are different things that I'm looking for . . . it's more . . . just about my individual relationship with God and how I feel." It is fitting that our interview ends there, then, with Jamaica "all up in her feelings." For, in the end, the physical Black Church is defined by her own intimate desires and pursuit of spiritual freedom. She asks,

> Am I welcome to have that freedom to have that relationship with Him in a church meeting? Can I lift my hands in the air? Am I free to do that in this church? Is the spirit of God encouraged in this church? Is prayer and passion for God? Am I [encouraged]? Am I affirmed in my identity as a woman? As an African American woman, is that affirmed? Those are things that are important to me.

Jamaica and other digital Black Christians have come to define the Black Church's geographies in its ability to answer these questions well. Their freedom is found in the range of possibilities such a Black Church offers for their movements and migrations across physical, digital, and interior spaces.

Epilogue

Generations "Birthed in Flickering Lights"

I want(ed) to anoint the next generation . . . but the Lord said the strangest thing to me. He said, "You cannot determine the next generation by age." Cuz I have some late bloomers who are just coming into their season, in the second phase of their life. And they're just now about to step into what they should have been into twenty years ago. And now that they're suddenly here, it's all starting to make sense." He said, "So don't call next by age, call next by opportunity." He said, "I want you to pray for the people that are on the verge of an opportunity that is about to be birthed in flickering lights!"
—T. D. Jakes, from the sermon titled "In Flickering Lights," March 8, 2020

Just as I was wrapping up my research, I came across a YouTube post of the sermon "In Flickering Lights" by Bishop T. D. Jakes (2020). It was in the midst of the coronavirus pandemic, when fears were still at a tremor and the government remained slow to acknowledge, let alone to respond to, the virus. Several physically located Black churches were divided on their approach. Despite warnings from the Centers for Disease Control, many Black churches chose to continue meeting in person. Memes quickly emerged from Black Christians either critical of believers for their lack of faith or confidently proclaiming their own faith and protection from the virus. Such memes proliferated on social media (see Figures E.1, E.2, and E.3). In truth, it was the same project that digital Black Christians had invested in for some time prior to the pandemic. As older church leaders and parishioners joined them online, the shift in polity, liturgy, identity, community—in short, all the things related in these pages—was worked out in real-time. In the process, both young

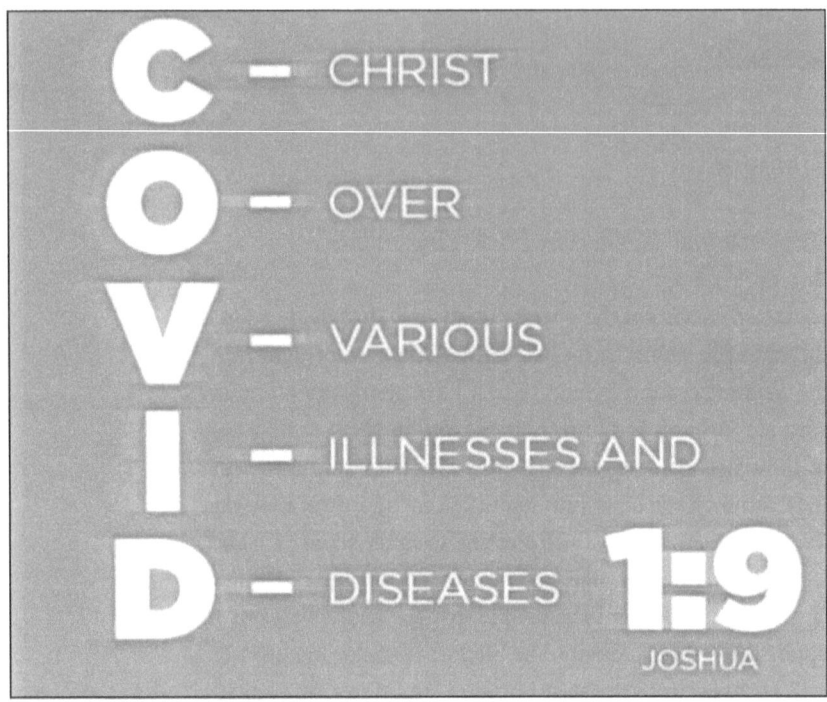

Figure E.1. Meme. (Unknown origin)

Figure E.2. Meme. (Unknown origin)

and older Black Christians met each other in the webwork of the new digital Black Church. They soon found that this church bore an uncanny resemblance to the century's old networks of the earlier Black Church.

"In Flickering Lights" captured the uncertainty Black believers of all ages were facing as many struggled to reconstitute their notion of the Black Church digitally. True to the design experience of social media platforms, I learned of this sermon through what Kristen Møller and Brady Robards (2019) call an "ephemeral mediated mobility"—the way online users swipe or scroll through (or "walk along") the internet, for any number of reasons, in search of content. Such mobilities inform and construct meaning, paths to knowing, and most importantly, the sort of webwork we do in building new networks. My own journey through "flickering lights" online exemplifies this point.

My point of departure was a March 10, 2020, YouTube video post to my Facebook newsfeed titled "Heather Lindsey & Cornelius Lindsey Corrected by Bishop TD Jakes! A Full Break Down of the Rebuke!" from the Facebook forum group Unfit Christian Congregation (UCC), a group with over four thousand members (Jakes 2020). A faithful observer of the Black Church (both during and outside of

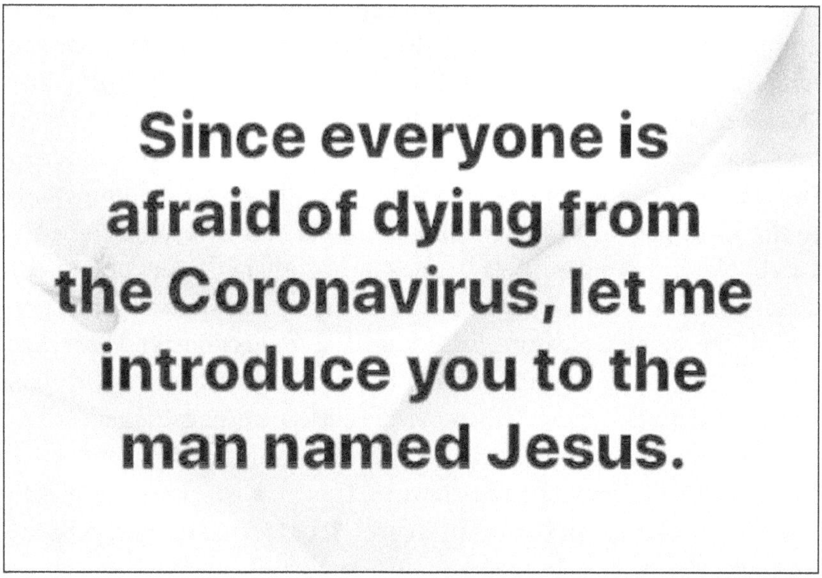

> Since everyone is afraid of dying from the Coronavirus, let me introduce you to the man named Jesus.

Figure E.3. Meme. (Church Funny, Facebook post, May 9, 2019) fieldwork), I clicked first on the link to the actual YouTube video, originally posted by Jaleceya Tate on March 9, 2020. Tate has produced a number of videos critical of both Heather and Cornelius Lindsey. The video under discussion has since been removed from the YouTube platform. Just prior to its removal, I viewed it; then I decided to move back over to Facebook, to Heather Lindsey's page, to consider her perspective on the event in question. This action required clicking on a video image of Bishop T. D. Jakes and the Lindseys on Heather Lindsey's fan page, posted by Heather on March 8, 2020 (Lindsey 2020b). In Heather's view, Jakes imparted a prophetic word and anointing on the popular Christian social media personality, thirty-eight-year-old Heather and her husband, thirty-four-year-old pastor Cornelius Lindsey, at the close of his "In Flickering Lights" sermon. Heather Lindsey is the founder of the Pinky Promise Movement, which boasts a membership of twenty-two thousand women. She has nearly four hundred thousand Instagram followers. Like her friend and fellow Atlanta resident Jackie Hill-Perry, in her teachings, books, and her online posts, Lindsey's message focuses on a traditional notions of Christian sexual purity.

While Heather may have written glowingly of this moment with Jakes, other young adult Blacks elsewhere on social media, like the UCC group where I encountered the video, viewed this encounter quite differently. The UCC member who posted the Jaleceya Tate YouTube video "Heather Lindsey & Cornelius Lindsey Corrected..." to the UCC Facebook page on March 10, 2020, considered Jakes's words to the Lindseys two days prior as a rebuke for their public failings. Most commentors to the UCC page read the encounter similarly. Members of the UCC Facebook forum immediately began sharing other critiques of Heather. She is generally disliked by forum members for her stance against premarital sex and oral pleasure, her evangelical connections, and her widespread digital influence and promotion of purity culture. On the other hand, UCC is beloved by its members for its frank discussions of sex and sexuality, its affirmation of LGBTQIA communities, and its celebration and critique of Black Church cultures. It is also well known for calling out popular Black Christian figures, like Jackie Hill-Perry, Kanye West, and John Gray. In the past, UCC founder Danyelle Thomas and other popular digital Black Christians have openly criticized Lindsey and her husband Cornelius Lindsey for their stance on complementarianism. The growing chorus of dissent against digital purity movement leaders can be viewed in digital Black Christians' artistic works, like Jamaica West's poem titled "Bury Cinderella" (2017). In the piece, Jamaica derides women who are,

> drown[ing] in . . . Victorian dating idolatry/ideologies,
> European beauty standards,
> extreme left ultra conservative politics,
> preach prophesy,
> turn your IG into a marriage ministry
> once you meet the perfect king
> and they'll praise your name.

In a blog post, *Red Lip Theology* podcast founder and digital Black Christian Candice Benbow (2017) describes purity workers as "Pinky Promise/Purity Circles/Wives-in-Training/Waiting Wives that take advantage of genuine desire and good intentions but are nothing more than spiritual pyramid schemes." Such critical responses to the Purity culture movement frame my walk through the Unfit Christian Facebook, March 10, 2020, member post and subsequent comments to the post. While critics of Lindsey revel in seeing Heather finally being "corrected" and "rebuked" by T. D. Jakes, in the words of Jaleceya Tate, Lindsey's own page post on March 8, 2020, accompanying Jakes's prophetic word and anointing of both Heather and Cornelius read differently to Heather (see Figure E.4). She views this moment as confirmation that she's been "on the right path all along" and as demonstrating that Bishop T. D. Jakes and Serita Jakes care for the "next generation" (Lindsey 2020b). It must be emphasized here that both Heather and many of the members of the UCC Facebook group can be counted among digital Black Christians. Yet as a group they are deeply divided about what they make of this moment, as it is ripe with multiple meanings and takeaways. And while I have presented points of common belief and practices throughout this volume, in the final analysis, digital Black Christians don't all agree and never will. Their voices are diverse and complex, and at times fragmented.

Figure E.4. Photos of Heather Lindsey and Cornelius Lindsey at the Potter's House with Bishop T. D. Jakes. (Heather Lindsey, Facebook post, March 8, 2020)

Viewing the attached clip leads me over to a March 9, 2020, post, regarding the same event, on Heather Lindsey's own Facebook page. There Lindsey recommends viewers of her page "go to @tphdallas and watch the FULL message" by Bishop T. D. Jakes (Lindsey 2020a). So I continue "walking through" to Jakes's home church, the Potter's House, online, where I view "In Flickering Lights" in its entirety.

In the spirit of full ethnographic disclosure, I have always been a fan of Bishop T. D. Jakes's homiletic prowess. A sign of a strange upbringing, I suppose, but my father and I often bonded over tapes and records of seminal Black preachers like Rev. B. W. Smith's "Watch Them Dogs" and "Who in the Hell Left the Gate Open?" Such sound technologies enlivened my notion of "good preaching" and in some ways underscore the earlier discussion regarding the function of preaching "sound" in contemporary digital Black Christians' use of hip hop, particularly by rappers like Lecrae. For me, Bishop T. D. Jakes's television appearances were a natural next installment in the earlier B. W. Smith preaching tradition.

If the reader finds it curious that a young Black girl in the South would make meaning of male voices whose sermons so centrally configured harmful gender views, that is a fair assessment. For as much as Jakes took on this tradition in a new age of media technology, he borrowed equally problematic portions of its theologies. I have used the aforementioned work of Jonathan Walton, Marla Frederick, and Tamura Lomax to discuss some of what has been and remains problematic about the tropes introduced by figures like Jakes. Such critiques demand careful attention when approaching any analysis of both the harm and healing his sermons have prompted. Despite necessary critiques of his ministry and messages, the act of ending a book with a discussion of Jakes is telling of his continued relevance to the Black Church, and more specifically, the tenor of present-day digital Black Christianity.

Although digital Black Christians like UCC members and purity movement leaders like Hill-Perry and Heather Lindsey disagree, both return to Jakes, either for his blessing or to criticize him. "That" Black Church is the intersection where both groups find meaning or "anointing" for the "next generation." As noted early in this volume, many scholarly publications and notable studies seek to define who Black millennials are. I have chosen instead to use the term *digital Black Christian* throughout, in order to cast suspicion on a term that emerged outside of the community of the young Black believers I have studied. Jakes takes on the same task in broadening the term *next generation*. In considering Bishop T. D. Jakes's message specifically, regarding "flickering lights," he associates "flickering" with uncertain or shifting times. For sure, this is a lively word in a time of a global pandemic. From the beginning of his sermon, he makes fluid the field of meaning for the listening audience by critiquing the term *millennial*. By the sermon's end, he includes everyone in his definition of the next generation. In essence, the moment—or what he calls the "opportunity"—defines the generation. Discarding earlier definitions of *millennial* that decenter or render young Black bodies and stories invisible, these desperate next-generation voices are all connected by the flickering light of our times. This much is true for me as well, as I have walked through the digital lives of young Black Christians and revealed my own history and religious memory. As messy, unfinished, and fraught with problems as this process is, through this webwork religious networks are constructed in the digital age for young Black Christians.

The story of Jakes, for better or worse, is an example of the way the webwork of the Black Church can define and reach a generation in more meaningful ways over and against institutions like white evangelical churches and the physically located Black Church or even widely accepted empirical studies, all of which derive their authority from racial and gendered histories of oppression. Yet none of these have ever achieved supremacy or universality in defining Black bodies.

Jakes's sermon reminds the reader of the liberatory work that the Black Church has always attempted, with varying degrees of success—the work of calling and moving oppressed persons toward a new definition and experience of self. This sort of calling is in itself a critique of the dominant social structure.

Charles Long described his own Black community as "a community signified by another community" (Jones and Hardy 1988, 259). This is how all such Black communities have historically been defined—in contrast or in response to white racist constructs. Lodged in the rhetoric of Bishop Jakes, as in so many others in the Black Church tradition, is an attempt to break free of those constructs and provide liberatory pathways, the "opportunity" Jakes speaks of, for the "next generation" to enact such breaking free as well. This is not unlike the pretexting or digital discipleship done by creatives discussed throughout this volume. It is even located in the conflicting readings of Jakes by Heather Lindsey and the UCC. This church is both problematic and beautiful in design. But this Black Church is also living, remaking, and being remade in this very moment.

By examining the religious practices of digital Black Christians online and in hip hop, I have attempted to strike a balance between the Black Church as traditionally conceived in the physically located practices of Black houses of worship and contemporary young Black Christians' digital practices. I have made a case for the study of digital Black Christians beyond Black churches as a way of highlighting their more discursive digital practices. By centering digital media technology and hip hop, I have highlighted the importance of relationships, identity, visibility, and valuation in distinguishing religious meaning-making among digital Black Christians. These four components of digital Black Christianity point to the emergence of an important though understudied aspect of the contemporary Black Church. Events like Joseph Solomon's immersion into digital discipleship or the therapeutic space created by Jackie Hill-Perry's YouTube poem "My Life as a Stud" together create a network of digital religious belief that signals new approaches to being a part of the Black Church tradition. In chronicling the contours of digital Black Christianity through their stories, I have sought to portray both the "why" and "what" of this complex and enthralling religious life, all the while pushing up against etic scholarly readings of digital Black Christians and instead constantly accounting for my own presence and position among those I studied.

The Black Church is of no less importance, nor should it be solely in opposition to the kinds of networks discussed throughout this book. The fact nonetheless remains that institutional Black churches' relationship with digital Black Christians is complicated by technology use. Though studies indicate that Black Christian internet users are just as likely as white evangelicals to use technology to view religious material (songs, sermons, religious podcasts), Black Protestant churches are far less likely to adopt technology in their church practices. Such trends point to larger realities of racial and wealth inequality in the United States. For example, in 2012, 73 percent of Black Protestant churches operated with a total income below $100,000, whereas only 53.3 percent of white conservative, evangelical, and fundamental churches had similar financial situations (Chavez, Anderson, and Eagle 2012). While Black churches may falter in terms of both access to and adoption of technology in religious services, they continue to retain higher numbers of younger Black congregants than white churches. This is due in large part to historic patterns of intimacy-building, as indicated in the rhetoric of Dr. Matthew Stevenson's work discussed earlier and Bishop T. D. Jakes's sermon. Even online, the Black Church references similar linguistic practices.

* * *

The narrative of the Black Church as a powerful institution remains an alluring one in both popular and scholarly circles. My goals for this work are far humbler than attempting to dismantle that Black Church, something so real and so fictive we have spent more than a century defending its borders and redefining its meaning. Yet this work does emphasize an important point for both scholars and also for practitioners and believers like myself, who remain invested in the Black Church as an institution.

Over here in the Black Church world, so much time has been spent talking about "what to do with the young folks" that many Black churches, struggling to retain younger congregants, have overlooked what the young folks are already doing! For my beloved Black Church friends, family, and colleagues, this book represents an attempt to describe ethnographically what the doing of religion looks like for young Black Christian folk. For this reason, the materiality of digital Black Christianity has mostly been described here as events, actions, and verbs to denote the ever-moving, shifting function of faith among digital Black Christians.

Given its own moves and movements, the Black Church tradition rooted in physically located experiences of whooping, shouting, or singing is thus not superseded. In fact, it forms the backdrop of each story told here, both in its early-life influence on digital Black Christians and in their revival of many of its practices online. It is kept alive even in digital Black Christians' critiques of its past and present activities and in their reworking of their own Black Christian identity. In people like Jakes, it is made ever more relevant in the intimacy derived from naming and renaming generations birthed in flickering times.

In considering the wider import of this book, in two ways this work moves beyond simply offering a fascinating portrait of young Black religious life in America. First, as the discussion of Lecrae's ethno-techno-biography attests, Black creative practices often emerge as new technologies of self, used to counter Black youths' marginalization. Such cultural practices in Blackness and the Black Church, as with religious technologies of the past (i.e., gospel music, wax sermon records), will overtake or be integrated into popular forms of religious expression. This book underscores the importance of knowing under what terms and by what route that process is taking place. Digital Black Christian culture is part of the global export of Black youth culture through hip hop. Through international poetry tours and sold out Christian rap shows across the Western Hemisphere, the interested reader witnesses the intellectual export of American digital Black Christian practices and beliefs around digital religious intimacy.

Second, perhaps the most salient feature of this work lies in the questions it raises about how we have traditionally viewed and thus studied young Black bodies. Statistics like those offered by the Pew Research Center regarding Black millennials remain insufficient as a full portrait of the beliefs and practices of this population (2009, 2015a, 2015b, 2021).[1] In raising such inquiries, this book holds up a lens for us to reexamine what we call "religion" and "church," and it calls forth a more imaginative view of them. That young Black Christians continue to create innovative ways of doing faith through online networks points to the emergence of a broader pattern in which digital usage greatly mediates forms of intimacy-seeking and intimacy-building in America. When we view the recent occurrences of temporal and digitally centered intimate encounters with the divine, like church services through the virtual game *Second Life*, Periscope preaching and patronage, Kanye West's pop-up Sunday services, and in the outbreak of the coronavirus, we recognize that faith declarations via memes and an uptick in digitally broadcast services mirror realities introduced here in the practices of digital Black Christians.

This book furthermore suggests a new direction in how we study people of faith of all ages and races, and in what constitutes "committed adherents." We must look more closely at the *relationships, identity formations, valuation*, and *visibility*-seeking that occur online, as these intimacies are intrinsic to many people's religious experience. Further, we do not fully capture the contemporary notion of the Black Church (or more broadly American Christianity) until we center the role of technology use in our analysis. The religious ground on which we stand is ever shifting. In outlining the intimacies that such technologies mediate and mediatize, this book implores us all—preachers, practitioners, and scholars alike—to catch up.

ACKNOWLEDGMENTS

The term *single-author volume* is quite misleading. So many people, conversations, and resources made this work possible. First, I'd like to wax Black Church for a minute and say "Lord, thank you for my life, health, and strength. Thank you that you did not make my last night's bed my cooling board." The rhetoric of the Black Church was brought home for me just last year. In the final months of writing, I suffered a heart attack. But God . . . ! So I pause first to say thank you, God, for being my sustainer in those moments of sickness and uncertainty and throughout this entire process.

I offer the deepest gratitude to my partner in poetry and life, Ntare Ali Gault. Your support makes my work possible. In the midst of all it, you made sure I always had "a room of my own" to grow, think, and write in. There is no one else I'd rather bounce ideas off of, fight for Black folks alongside, or to strategize with. Thank you for loving me well. Much gratitude goes to my little Hazel girl who reminds me why this work is important and that time spent away from the work reading books, playing music, and playing outdoors together will be part of the greatest legacy that I will leave with you. You quite literally came into being in the middle of this project. What a wonderful blessing you have been to our family ever since.

A special thank you goes to Angela Dillard, who offered me my first chance to engage with a real live Black religious scholar ! Your kindness and guidance during my time at NYU was everything. It is no overstatement to say that I would not have considered writing this book without you. I'll never forget our independent study on Black religion in America and our discussions on David Pickering's *Afro-American Jeremiad*. Other Black faculty who shaped my intellectual trajectory during that time include Bryonn Bain, Robin Kelly, and Emily Chang. Thank you.

During my time in the graduate program at Colgate Rochester Crozer Divinity School (CRCDS) I continued my development as a student of

Black religion. I count myself a product of its Black Church studies program (the first in the nation). As a child I attended preaching classes in the program with my father. It was there that I first saw Rev. B. W. Smith preach. Its halls have remained hallowed for me ever since that moment. Thank you to a few wonderful scholars who offered me the tools to develop a kind of Christian faith guided by both "head and heart." Thank you to Gay Byron, James Evans, Gail Ricciuti, Barbara Moore, and Christopher Evans. I am also especially thankful for Christopher Evans's class on American religious history, which I took at CRCDS, and for his service as a committee member for my comprehensive doctoral exams.

I offer deep thanks to my dissertation committee, consisting of Carl Nightingale, Jason Young, Greg Dimitriadis, and Anthony Pinn. Their insights were foundational to what later became this work. Carl Nightingale, thank you for guiding and supporting my earlier ethnographic work on young Black gospel rappers. Young Black voices are too often delegitimized and made invisible in the academy and out in the world. Through your advice and support you offered me critical space to speak of their experiences and my own. Thank you to Jason Young for seeing merit in digital ethnography long before I fully understood it as "a real thing." Along with agreeing to sit on my dissertation committee, I was privileged to take a class with Greg Dimitriadis. Greg was an impressive scholar. As these pages hopefully demonstrate, he was also influential to the way I approach hip hop ethnography. There were so many times in writing this volume that I wanted to email him to pick his brain. It still fills me with incredible sadness to think of his passing. But he left an incredible legacy in his publications and through his students. So very many thank-yous go to Anthony Pinn both for his rich body of work and continuous support.

Travis Terrell Harris read very early drafts of this work and added critical advice. Thank you, Travis. I offer deep gratitude to my first real professional family during my time at Hilbert College. I received generous support, wonderful conversations, and friendship from so many at the College. I will never forget my very first academic interview with Joan Crouse or the wonderful support from Christopher Holoman, Sharon Sisti, Kate and Ron Eskew, Maia Kapuszcak, Chris Gallant, Amy Smith, Megan Witzelben, Gordon Snow, Jenelle Lukasik, and Herb

Kauderer. Thank you to Cheyenne Jumanah, an advocate for students of color and a very dear friend. Thank you for making room for me in the academy. You are so deeply missed.

I extend thanks to my present institution in the persons of A.-P. Durand, Praise Zenenga, Bryan Carter, Alex Nava, Ken McAllister, Gennady Sare, the faculty of the Africana Studies Program, and my research assistants Ramatoulaye Mballo, Mija Alice Sanders, and Gertus van der Vyver. Your support has far exceeded a junior scholar's expectations. Thank you to Derrais Carter, Jerome Dotson, Tyina Steptoe, and Marya McQuirter, members of the Black Writing Group at the University of Arizona, for reading later chapters and offering wonderful resources and support. There are a number of scholars spanned across several other institutions with whom I have had the pleasure of engaging and who offered critical support and/or feedback during this process. Thank you to Elonda Clay, Daniel White Hodge, Mark Chavez, and Andre Johnson. I extend my gratitude to scholars in Black media and technology whose work has made room for my own, like Jonathan Walton, Tamura Lomax, Marla Frederick, Monique Moultrie, André Brock Jr., Ruha Benjamin, and Safiya Noble. There were two Black women preaching groups that cultivated my voice in the ministry while I lived in Buffalo, NY. They helped me think critically about gender, sexuality, and how one "makes" Black Church space. Thank you to Elder Sheila Wallace and the These Preaching Women Group, who welcomed and affirmed me. Once a week I (and Hazel!) joined this lovely group of Black women who loved to preach. Never have I felt so at home in the Black Church. Thank you to Rev. Rachelle Sat'chell Robinson for your friendship and for calling me to preach to, for, and about Black women when no one else was calling me to preach (outside of Youth Day and Women's Day programs). Much gratitude goes to Rev. Robinson's Deep Wells Ministries, Linda Brown, Barbara Campbell, and Stephanie Phillips. Thank you for our monthly breakfast (particularly the quiche) and for the laughter. They were a salve during this process. Our time together helped me see us (Black preaching women) better and enabled me to craft my own voice and vision in and beyond pulpit ministry. Other scholar/practitioners to whom I owe thanks are Black women like Melva Sampson for the rich treasure that is Pink Robe Chronicles and Danyella Thomas for the community and love exhibited in the Facebook forum group Unfit Christian

Congregation. In the midst of writing this book, I too was shifting, both physically (two cross-country moves!) and in thought. Their online work brought alive for me the expansiveness, essentiality, and beauty of the digital Black Church. Thank you to Jonathan Calvillo, Patrick Reyes, Darlene Hutto, Neichelle Guidrey, Candice Benbow, Joseph Solomon, Teddy Reeves, and (again) Melva Sampson for a lively and well-attended digital conversation titled "Gathering in the Moment: Mobilizing the Digital Black Church's Prophetic Witness" in the summer of 2020. In many ways, that discussion was the culmination of my work on digital Black Christians, and it provided me greater clarity and networks for thinking even more broadly regarding digital Black religion.

I am also grateful for both the caliber and consistency of support I received from NYU Press. I remember my freshman year of college at NYU, running my fingers along the new faculty books prominently displayed in the bookstore. Angela Dillard's first book was one that caught my eye. I was fascinated to learn both that NYU had its own press and that a Black woman was featured among its writers. All these years later it is quite special to me to join the ranks of its authors. Thank you to Jennifer Hammer for consistently providing superb feedback and guidance throughout this process. Much gratitude as well goes to Veronica Knutson for her assistance. Thanks to Ulrike Guthrie for her precise and excellent editing of my manuscript. She really is "the best in the business"!

I wish to acknowledge grant support from the Louisville Institute. The Institute's 2018–2019 First Book Grant for Scholars of Color allowed me to take a year off to finish interviews and begin writing. This work would not have been possible without its generous support. Thank you to the wonderful digital humanities folks at the CUNY Graduate Center in the persons of Lisa M. Rhody and Kalle Westerling. I was able to think through several elements of my work as part of the Digital Humanities Research Institute there.

My final thanks are reserved for family. Thank you to my church family, Elim Christian Fellowship, and especially to Bishop T. Anthony Bronner and Lady Linda Bronner for their early and sustained support of this work. I owe you a debt, Bishop! To all of the Black Church communities that have held me down and held me up in prayer throughout this process, I say thank you. Thank you to my longtime friends and sisters Shani, Doc, and Ting for supporting and loving me in more ways than there is ink left to mention. Suffice it to say I have been blessed to have your friendship throughout this process. Thank you to the Coffee family and the Haygood family, who really were the first Black Church I ever knew. To my in-laws McDaniel and Irene Gault, thank you for supporting this work in so many ways that these pages cannot fully contain.

I save the most precious gratitude for last. Thank you, Dad and Mom, for loving God and me with a fervor and authenticity that testifies to me still. In some small way I hope this work captures how much I love you and the One you first introduced me to. Much love.

NOTES

GLOSSARY

1. For more regarding the Black Church as a *tradition*, see Floyd-Thomas et al. 2007, xix–xxiv. On the African American rhetorical tradition, see Jackson and Richardson 2003. As does this volume, Jackson and Richardson's consideration of African American rhetoric relies on earlier conversations at the intersections of communications and Afrocentricity. Molefi Asante argues for greater inquiry into the rhetorical condition—"the structure, power pattern, assumed or imposed, during a rhetorical situation by the communicators"—of hierarchal discourse. See Asante and Atwater 1986. John B. Hatch argues in a similar vein that Gage Chapel's notion of *rhetorical synthesis* is not exclusive to elite classes or intellectual groups. Using Asante, he instead argues that Christian hip hop artists ("Gospel Gangstas"), through their inter-positionality, seek to reorder their position and identity in a fractured world in which they experience racism (Hatch 2002, 259). Taken together, these works demonstrate the historical flow of African discourse that continues to animate digital Black Christians' engagement with, and religious life within, the Black Church tradition as they build new online and offline identities.
2. Tricia Rose (1994) authored the first seminal scholarly text in hip hop studies. *Black Noise* signaled a turn in the academy. Prior to its publication, discussions of hip hop culture were largely viewed as marginal to Western musicology. In many scholarly circles and academic institutions, hip hop studies continues to experience a similar reception. However, Rose's initial work greatly legitimized hip hop scholarship.
3. Neil Howe and William Strauss are best known for their work on generational studies. The Strauss-Howe generational theory received wide popularity in the 1990s. Yet their theory—that each generation is guided by certain personalities (all white male figures) that define their age—has been met with criticism within some scholarly circles for its considerable omission of women, people of color, and the less affluent (Strauss and Howe 1991).

PREFACE

1. Trapper Keepers were a brand of decorative loose-leaf binder with several pockets and a Velcro closure. They were popular among school-age children, mostly in North America, in the 1980s and 1990s.
2. A reference to "To Zion," the fourth track on Lauryn Hill's debut album, *The Miseducation of Lauryn Hill* (1998). Hill's song was a nod to the Christian hymn,

"Marching Up to Zion." For a discussion of the rhetorical function of such Christian-centric songs, see Sorett 2009.

3. Over the course of the twentieth century, a number of scholars both expanded upon and critiqued earlier works regarding epistemology. Early twentieth-century philosopher Edmund Husserl argued for an examination of humans' lived practices as a site for the origin of phenomena. Foucault and other structuralists, however, saw particular historical periods as influencers in individual's epistemological assumptions. Human knowledge was not acquired *a priori*; it was structured by existing powers. See Foucault 2002. Post-structuralist Jacques Derrida, greatly influenced by Edmund Husserl, developed the notion of "deconstruction." Autoethnography, among other methodologies, owes much to both Derrida's and Foucault's approaches to epistemology. Autoethnography seeks to deconstruct the "order of things" by interrogating the "politics of [one's own] positionality" and of the assumed normative hierarchies imposed upon the research that overlook the author's own subjectivity and intersectionality. See Madison 2005. My own attempt at autoethnography seeks to lay bare the limits of knowledge, as Judith Butler argues any narrative "I" should. According to Butler, the autoethnographer's responsibility to the narrative is not fulfilled simply through "the conceit of a self fully transparent." Rather, "to take responsibility for oneself is to avow the limits of any self-understanding and to establish these limits not only as a condition for the subject but as a predicament of the human community" (Butler 2009, 83). In doing specifically hip hop ethnography, Greg Dimitriadis suggests a move away from biographical ethnography to Pierre Bourdieu's (2007) approach, in which the researcher becomes an "object of analysis." See also Dimitriadis 2015.

4. As a method, autoethnography has been roundly criticized for its hyper-focus on the individual, as well as for being overly romantic and nonanalytical. Yet, while providing critiques of the method, scholars have also offered useful trajectories for employing autoethnography in a researcher's work. Robin Boylorn, Mark Orbe, and Carolyn Ellis (2016) note the intersectional nature of human identity and explore the relationship between culture and communication out of this context. For criticisms of autoethnography, see Sparkes 2002; Delamont 2008. For another useful approach to autoethnography, see Jackson and Mazzei 2008.

5. A popular childhood rhyme used in hand-clapping games: "I met my boyfriend at the candy shop / He bought me ice cream / He bought me cake / He brought me home with a belly ache / Mama, Mama, I feel sick / Call the doctor / Quick, quick, quick / Doctor, doctor, will I die? / Count to five and stay alive / one, two, three, four, five / I'm alive!" The hand game creates a scene that is ripe with symbolism even as it serves as a duplicitous reminder for Black girls of both the intrigue of youthful sexual exploration and a cautionary tale regarding their bodies and premature motherhood.

INTRODUCTION

1. Jackie Hill-Perry was not immediately responsive to interview requests. All information contained in this book regarding her, including quotations, was culled from direct communication, sermons, speeches, her own writings (her autobiography, poetry, and rap songs), and online interviews.
2. Aitina Fareed-Cooke (AI), interview by author, June 27, 2018.
3. Jamaica West, interviews by author, November 20, 2017–July 22, 2018.
4. Propaganda (Jason Emmanuel Petty), interview by author, April 9, 2018.
5. Joseph Solomon, interviews by author, April 28–September 18, 2018.
6. Beleaf Melanin (Glen Henry), interviews by author, November 14, 2017–July 22, 2018.
7. Daniel Steele, interview by author, November 22, 2017.
8. Natalie Lauren Sims (formerly Suzy Rocks), interview by author, November 24, 2018.
9. The term *micro-celebrity* first appeared in the work of Theresa Senft. Tobias Ruin describes the micro-celebrity as one who is "famous to a niche group." Intimacy, according to Ruin, is intrinsic to their celebrity-hood. This work likewise argues that these intimacies allow for important networks or relationships to form among the digital Black Christians studied here and millions of other young Black Christians who they identify with and who follow them. See Senft 2013; Raun 2018; Marwick 2013.
10. Mia Lövheim and Heidi Campbell present similar arguments in their article detailing recent works in digital religion studies. In "Considering Critical Methods and Theoretical Lenses in Digital Religion Studies," they state that the concerns of sociologists and communication and media scholars intersect in their consideration of "social belonging, identity, and community" (Lövheim and Campbell 2017). Works like "Rethinking the Online-Offline Connection in the Study of Religion Online" (Campbell and Lövheim 2011) added a fourth oft-discussed topic in digital religion studies: an investigation of authority. Pauline Cheong's (2017) work on organizational practices and transnational authority expands this conversation. Such works require an investigation of the blended online-offline religious experience that adherents create through digital technology. I take such arguments as foundational for understanding one specific, though underexplored, group in digital religion studies; the same arguments, with important nuances, can be made for Black young adults, the Black Church, and technology.
11. Barry Wellman contends that twentieth-century communities once defined by affiliations, such as churches and neighborhoods, gave way to "personal communities." This idea has particular connections to studying the practices of online users, centered as they are around the personalities and prerogatives of the individual. Lee Raine and Barry Wellman (2012) call this "networked individualism." See also Urry and Larsen 2012.

12. For added interest, see also Granovetter's (1983) discussion on other theorists' use of his work on weak/strong ties.
13. In recent years, several scholars have troubled this topic in an attempt to redefine and theorize the boundaries of the "Black Church." From its origins in the title of W. E. B. Du Bois's book *The Negro Church* (1903), the term allowed religionists to circumscribe the Black Church's authority to include only educated middle-class men. Barbara Savage (2008) has noted that many venerable scholars, like Du Bois, Benjamin Mays, and Carter G. Woodson, viewed Black churches, collectively, as powerful social institutions. Black scholars of the early twentieth century hoped to harness Black churches' power to mobilize its congregants for racial equality. For political reasons, then, the idea of the "Black Church" was used to construct a denominational definition. This book, however, unhinges the Black Church from its physical pillar and post, situating it in the digital discourse of young adult Black Christians.
14. In *Map Is Not Territory: Studies in the History of Religions* (1978), Jonathan Smith notes in his discussion of "locative" maps, that the mapping of religion—and in this case the idea of—the Black Church—has always served an imperial function, in this case, of establishing and maintaining elitist and patriarchal authority. Indeed, Black churchmen greatly benefited from their inscribed roles within Black churches, serving in leadership positions equally denied to Black men and women in most other social institutions in America throughout much of the nineteenth and twentieth centuries. The Black Church was reified, mostly by Black churchmen and religious scholars, through its naming and by drawing lines around its borders, as revealed in locating the Black Church in the "seven major Black Protestant denominations" (the National Baptist Convention, the National Baptist Convention of America, the Progressive National Convention, the African Methodist Episcopal Church, the African Methodist Episcopal Zion Church, the Christian Methodist Episcopal Church and the Church of God in Christ). Through this process, as Savage (2008) notes, the Black Church became "an illusion and a metaphor that has taken on a life of its own." The Black Church then becomes a powerful signifier of multiple meanings within Black vernacular. It has taken on a life of its own in the continued scholarly and the often uninterrogated popular usage of it among contemporary Black Christians.
15. See Knott 2005. See also works like Angela Dillard's *Faith in the City* (2009), which constructs a view of the Black Church as a "powerful moral imperative" present in the 1960s in Detroit, Michigan's trade unions and in Black power ideology within the city. See also Evans 2008; and Pinn 2017.
16. From blog posts and online magazine articles to sermon anecdotes and parents gathered around a kitchen table, discussions of Black millennials abound. Their prowess with new media, their rejection of traditional notions of Black identity and respectability, their lack of economic security, their potential danger in interactions with law enforcement, the threat young Black bodies pose to white America, and their political activism through social media platforms and

hashtags like #BlackLivesMatter or #SayHerName are all topics of current discussion and mirror the findings of reputable studies widely discussed through print and digital news pieces. Yet when we turn to discussions regarding the religious beliefs and practices of Black millennials, we garner only well-worn assumptions.

The paucity of empirical work in this area has led many to believe two contradictory positions regarding the religious lives of Black millennials: (1) African American young adults remain connected to the Black Church; and (2) African American young adults are leaving the Black Church in droves. How can both of these facts be true? A short answer is that our present data on millennials' religion and religious identity is skewed, subject to a number of empirical challenges such as oversampling or what Monica Miller (2013) calls buffering transgressions—the reliance upon "thin and traditional measures of 'religiosity' defined by ancillary practices and institutional membership."

Because of these challenges in documenting religion more generally among millennials, there is tremendous difficulty when it comes to defining the Christian identity of Black millennials. As such, a study like the Pew Research Center's 2009 "Religious Portrait of African Americans" revealed that Black millennials were more likely to attend services at least once a week and pray daily. However, the study overlooks the number of African Americans between the ages of twenty-one and thirty-seven who may identify as Christian but choose not to attend church services regularly. Recently, Pew published new findings that offer greater latitude for documenting religious belief and affiliation among young adult Blacks (Pew Research Center 2021). There is more work to be done around the role and influence of digital technology and hip hop on the lived practices of young adult Blacks, however. To date, only Elonda Clay (2015) has highlighted this uninterrogated use in hip hop and religious studies focused on online practices.

17. danah boyd's (2008) term, *networked publics*, denotes "publics that are restructured by networked technologies." This includes the spaces created by networked technology and the fictive communities it creates through the meeting of people, technologies, and practices. boyd conceives publics more loosely, wishing to leave its terminology "messy." However, borrowing from Hannah Arendt, boyd includes publics as realities made concrete by the "the presence of others who see what we see and hear what we hear" (Arendt 1998). Such a notion of networked publics is used here to discuss the very public online spaces created by the the digital Black Christians studied here and several other young Black Christians who share their digital practices and/or connect with them in creating a loosely configured set of shared ideas, beliefs, and practices.

18. This is in keeping with works regarding lived religion by sociologists like Nancy Ammerman. See Ammerman 2007; and also Bender et al. 2012.

19. The National Center for the Study of Youth and Religion study, unlike many similar projects, more accurately reflects beliefs and opinions of Blacks between the ages of eighteen and twenty-three by including respondents proportionate to

their racial composition and importance of belief. As noted, this sample also includes a smaller age group among millennials. As mentioned in greater detail in the Terms section and in Chapter 2, this, I would argue is in better keeping with larger group studies, which seek to be representative of all young adults between twenty-one and thirty-seven, despite the rich diversity within the group.

20. See Cohen 2005. Making use of the National Center for the Study of Youth and Religion's findings regarding young adults' diverse attachments to religion, other studies have highlighted millennials' tendency to select and practice multiple religious beliefs online apart from their self-declared and publicly practiced religion. These "spiritual tinkerers" represent a few of Smith and Snell's (2009) categories.

21. A recent Nielsen report found that among millennials of all races, young Black adults are viral vanguards, "driving the use of mobile technology and closing the digital divide" (Nielsen 2016). Yet researchers of religion interested in young adult African American expressions of faith have often restricted their focus to Black churches or to other physical sites, overlooking the centrality of digital technology in young Black adult life.

22. Smith and Snell (2009) contend that committed traditionalists occupy a mere 15 percent of the overall emerging population of young adults between eighteen and twenty-three years of age.

23. This approach takes into consideration an important turn in cultural studies regarding capitalism and the study of subcultures. The late twentieth-century development of both digital technology and hip hop has occurred within patterns of consumer capitalism. Cultural theorists of the past often considered artistic work like reggae or hip hop as subcultural practices created in resistance to capitalism. While a meaningful analysis, it required a hyper-focus on spectacular practices of groups instead of the more mundane occurrences of a culture. In recent years, scholars have revisited such concepts. Many argue instead for theoretical possibilities beyond resistance to capitalism. Trading scholars' attention to the spectacular for an examination of everyday practices, theorists argue that marginal cultures may borrow from the dominant culture and may view themselves as not being "sub-anything" in creating meaning. Such a concept offers an important point of departure regarding how cultural readers make sense of artistic expression among young Black adults. Digital Black Christians borrow heavily from the dominant culture as they seek to construct a notion of Christian identity at times in contradiction to their Black identity or as they prioritize Christianity over racial identity. Socio-temporal worlds like those created around #SayHerName and digital podcasts like *Pass the Mic* also point to digital Black Christians' attempts at artistic production that move beyond physical space and place, such as print media that once defined theorists' notion of dominant culture and subculture. The world of Black youth art at hip hop's inception centered on just a few New York City neighborhoods. Today, hip hop artistic expression is lived in briefer moments, and is defined by much looser affiliations. Such loose attachments are digitally mediated and have significant

bearing on how digital Black Christians engage with the world. What is needed are studies both of emerging adult culture that consider the fluidity of cultures alongside staid and sometimes mundane practices, and of attempts at resistance that borrow from dominant practice and culture. Furthermore, a more useful approach to the study of youth and young adult cultures is one that both looks at the spectacular and that considers the connected and contextualized artifacts and sites that influence cultures. This work moves in that direction. See also Hodkinson 2015.

24. Many such discussions hold certain epistemological understandings regarding feminist thought. For instance, feminist theorists like Judith Butler and early scholars like Simone de Beauvoir and Kate Millet have written extensively on marriage as an extension of property rights formed in patriarchal social structures. The religious orientation of Black Christian young adults rests on a classical phenomenological approach to marriage, however. That is, marriage is viewed as a divine institution. Its paradigm conflicts with such feminist frameworks, which regard marriage as a social construct. This does not overlook the groundbreaking work (being) done by womanist scholars like Kelly Brown Douglas (1999), Delores Williams (1993), and others, as well as the trend of Black feminist/womanist scholars being more likely to offer nuanced religio-cultural criticism in general. Yet these conversations rarely intersect with the topics of Christian belief, youth and technology, and Black feminism. (For past and recent exceptions, see works like Kirk-Duggan and Hall 2011; Lomax 2018.) Also, even while arguing for greater inclusion of Black Christian frameworks in scholarly cultural analysis, other researchers often continue to use a social framework to describe the sacred practices of the group, absent their deeply spiritual understanding of the world. Fully defining and studying digital Black Christians requires linking these disparate conversations, as this work seeks to do.

25. I am attending here to the work of Monica Miller (2013). Miller takes issue with the way young Black people are often discussed as deviant in statistical analysis of religion. She argues instead for an approach that breaks down the sacred/secular binary in order to study the lived practices of young Black people.

26. Recent works like Tamura Lomax's *Jezebel Unhinged: Loosing the Black Female Body in Religion and Culture* (2018) reflect my own assessment regarding the need for more attention to Black religious practices, particularly for examining the lives of young Black adults. *Jezebel Unhinged* captures the centrality of Black religion in the lives of contemporary Black folk, namely Black women and girls, and argues for a focus on the Black Church in the scholarly analysis of Black women and girls. Yet my gaze is at once more narrowly and broadly defined. Narrow, in that I focus here on self-identified Christians through an ethnographic study. Broader, in that I move beyond the Black Church and textual analysis to online and non-church modes of Black religious practice and expression. Privileging as I do the lived practices of digital Black Christians, I move beyond the theoretical analysis of feminist/womanist thought that Lomax takes up, out into the "ugly"

and "messy" world of Black Christian millennial beliefs and practices, which she theorizes about through textual readings.
27. Statements and questions asked of Lecrae by the interviewer(s) centered on his Christian identity. Examples included: "Why they want you to mix with us sinners, I don't know." "You're a Christian rapper, right?" "Do you perform in clubs?" "Do you go to gentlemen's clubs?" This interview occurred two years prior to the publication of Lecrae's autobiography in which he writes, "In nearly every interview I do with the media, people struggle to talk about my actual music. Instead, they want to know if I smoke or drink or cuss. They ask if I feel weird around non-Christians. They want to know if I'm trying to evangelize people. I'm like a caged animal that people want to observe, but they aren't sure how close they can get" (Moore 2016c, 198).
28. In relating his own experience to mostly young hip hop readers, Lecrae writes, "If you're a Christian and you have a pulse, you probably know what I'm describing. It's like, you fit in, but you don't fully fit in. There is a sameness with those around you, but also a difference. You feel accepted by those around you, but not all the time or all the way" (Moore 2016c, 33).
29. See also Hoover and Emerich 2011.
30. This discussion regarding Lecrae reveals a larger disagreement regarding how Christians who rap should be identified. A blog post titled "We Just Lost One: Bye Lecrae" by *Truth+Fire* appeared on July 19, 2017, and was re-shared by Reformed pastor and rapper Shai Linne (Troutman 2017). Along with the release of his song "Reformed3," Linne set off a storm of debate online regarding Lecrae's beliefs and his alleged exit from Christianity. Linne later apologized for sharing the blog post, but maintained that Lecrae was in violation of several scriptures (Linne 2017).

Several articles, diss records, and heated online discussions accompanied by the hashtag #chhbeefs (Christian hip hop beefs) ensued. In an Instagram post, Christian rapper Datin criticized Lecrae's choice of words in an interview on the radio show *Sway in the Morning* (Moore 2017d). Lecrae agreed with interviewers that many Christian rappers had adopted their beliefs from "white evangelicalism (Ameri-Christianity) and not the authentic Eastern mindset of it. "You've [Christian rappers] adopted more of a nationalism than you've adopted a faith . . . It's making you hate your own kind, it's making you very condescending, making you self-righteous, making you feel like you're better than other people and not making you realize that grace is the only difference between me and somebody else" (Sarachik 2017c). Datin responded by saying: "It felt like Christian rappers were the nerdy little brother you [Lecrae] didn't want around your cool friends" (Sarachik 2017a).

These identity-centered discussions often have no clear winners or losers. Yet they demonstrate two points: the underlying suggestions of false-identity or deception that often permeate such digital discourse, and how such discourse joins digital Black Christians in common networks of belief. As Christian

rappers and other digital Black Christians wrestle together for naming rights, they further link their opposing camps.
31. For a few examples referenced elsewhere in this book, see Campbell 2010, 2012a; Pink et al. 2015; and Hoover and Echchaibi 2014.
32. The notion of socio-temporal worlds has been taken up in a number of recent studies. In *Table for One: A Critical Reading of Singlehood, Gender and Time* (2017), Kinneret Lahad takes as her field site web columns and blogs. Lahad does content analysis of common words used in describing single women in Israel. It is here indicative of the brief or fleeting communities that young adult Black Christians make through digital modes of communication.
33. Doreen Massey (2005) highlights the "event as place" in talking about the "constellation of processes" that go into understanding how a single event requires multiple acts. (For an example in this book of such an event, see Chapter 3's analysis of the Instagram discourse between Jackie Hill-Perry, Propaganda, and a white evangelical fan.) Pink et al. (2015) contend that examining an event as a place allows the researcher to better "understand both mundane and spectacular happenings as forms of event."
34. This approach is not without valid criticisms. In my own work, I am mindful of more recent articles like "Three Lies of Digital Ethnography" by Gabriele de Seta, in which the author expands on the notion of the field site to consider the "network of fieldsites" (de Seta 2020, 84). De Seta's approach to ethnographic "lies" is also a quite useful consideration for digital work. See also Fine 1993.
35. Since the 1990s, Elder Craig Lewis has received a nominal popularity in Black Church circles for his EX Ministries sermon series titled "The Truth Behind Hip Hop" on the sinful and cultic practices of Black celebrities. He claims to "expose" artists for their alleged devil worship and participation in a secret organization called the Illuminati. His rhetoric has gained currency among digital Black audiences interested in conspiracy theories.
36. This attends to the earlier categories posited by Elonda Clay (2011). Here it is taken up with greater specificity.
37. Yvonna S. Lincoln (1995) points to this as part of emerging commitments among contemporary qualitative researchers to establish "emergent relations with respondents, to a set of stances, and to a vision of research that enables and promotes justice" (277).
38. See also Marcus 1998.
39. For more on this method, see Anzul et al. 2003; and Lincoln and Guba 1985.
40. For more on this technique, see Creswell 2007, 271.
41. Creswell (2007) cites L. Edel, who uses the following question to sum up seeking reliability through this technique: "How has the [researcher] distinguished between reliable and unreliable witness? How has the researcher avoided making himself or herself simply the voice of the subject?" (214).
42. For a helpful breakdown of Lincoln and Guba's (1985) approach, along with other useful qualitative research practices, see also Müller and Ball 2012, 103.

1. TURNS

1. My own data collection reveals the persistent use of wording that mostly discusses Black millennial Christian practices as residing exclusively within an institutional Black Church context. Unlike how it appears in this volume, the traditions and institutional manifestations of the Black Church are often assumed to be one and the same in popular discourse. A Google data scrape of the words "Black millennial" and "Christian" revealed 1,230 unique instances entered in a one-year period. Consisting mostly of blog posts, opinion pieces, and social media site comments, in such data the most commonly related word was "Black Church."
2. While this has shifted to some extent since my initial research period, it is still significant to note that as of the year 2018, just logging a search for "Christian Black millennial," the first three retrievals exhibit tremendous diversity: Morgan Lee's "Why Black Churches Are Keeping Millennials" (2015), Luna Malbroux's "Why More Young Black People Are Trading in Church for African Spirituality" (2017), and Danyella Thomas's "Exodus: Why Black Millennials Are Leaving the Church" (2017). Each articles takes its research from the 2009 Pew Research Center study on all millennials. Only the *Christianity Today* article, in a quote from Thabiti Anyabwile, questions the oversampling of whites in the Pew Research study. Anyabwile points out, as I also indicate, that the Public Religion Research Institute study shows that Black Protestant losses of younger congregants has not been as steep as their white counterparts. However, in all three examples, the conversation remains situated around Black churches and defining young Black adult religiosity.
3. Monica Miller (2013) highlights similar assumptions of pathology that have stymied research conducted on Black youth and religion.
4. Many scholars at the dawn of hip hop scholarship quite appropriately responded to such conversations given claims lodged against both hip hop and Black youth culture that fell back on ideas of Black criminality. Works like *Black Noise: Rap Music and Black Culture in Contemporary America* (Rose 1994) and even later books like *The Hip Hop Generation: Young Blacks and the Crisis of African American Culture* (Kitwana 2002) are examples.
5. Acknowledging the value in these earlier works, they argue for a decentering of the Black pathology narrative in criminal justice works, in the study of empirical research on religion, in the racial codifying of biological conceptions of race in linguistics, and in "recovery" works in Black feminism, to name a few.
6. Writing of a similar tendency in how we understand Black men in particular, Simone C. Drake (2016, x–xi) says, "I am against crisis because not only is the discourse often rooted in patriarchal ideologies relying, for validation of their methods and rationale, on the subordination of Black women, but it also strips Black men and boys, including my own boys, of any inherent ability to act for and define themselves." I would include here not only Black males, but all young Blacks, here defined as digital Black Christians, whose capacity "to act for and define themselves" is often diminished in the literature.

7. This approach is guided by Daniel White Hodge's (2010a, 2016) work on the ethno–life history of Tupac and Lauryn Hill. Greg Dimitriadis (2009) likewise argues for an approach that considers the technological moments that shaped music, moving it beyond its collaborative and local performative nature.
8. In general, generational grouping in the twentieth century owes its inception to events surrounding the US Census of 1950. At the time of the 1950 US Census records, there was an uptick in birth rates following World War II. In 1951, *Washington Post* columnist and economist Sylvia Porter coined the term *baby boom* for the phenomenon of steadily rising birth rates. Hoping to take advantage of the phenomenon, marketing executives tailored several ads specifically to "baby boomers" throughout the sixties and seventies. There was a great monetary investment in the study of their likes and dislikes in an attempt to sell products to consumers born between 1946 and 1964. Widely successful marketing schemes for products like Swanson TV Dinners led marketing researchers to study the buying habits of successive age groups. It became even more advantageous for marketing researchers to coin their own names for later consumers. This attempt to shape the habits and thus buying potential of generational groups has relied partly on the census records, but also on market researchers' desire to sell products to particular groups. The currency of Strauss and Howe's generational theory among marketing firms further demonstrates this fact.
9. In a 2007 *Case Currents* article titled "Dispelling the Millennial Myth" authors Richard A. Hesel and Susan Basalla May take issue with Strauss and Howe's popular 2000 publication *Millennial Rising* for its poor methodology and overgeneralizations regarding the identity and habits of millennials.
10. Often, such bias is not deliberate. Instead, it represents more practical limitations of research. Racial minorities may be more difficult to find or identify for certain studies; as a result, white respondents are oversampled. In addition, questions that elicit similar responses among whites may be answered differently by other racial groups. If survey questions are phrased to anticipate certain kinds of phrasings or responses, or certain beliefs and practices, Black responses will tend to be improperly documented and evaluated. Wuthnow (2015) gives the example of a study that charted the religiosity of both Black and white respondents by measuring being born again, religious preference, and the degree to which respondents considered religion to be important to them. African Americans ranked only slightly higher than whites in their level of religiosity. Yet, in another survey, where other questions were used to chart religiosity and Blacks were oversampled, their religiosity was ranked as significantly higher than their white counterparts.
11. While highlighted for their creation of the term *millennial*, Strauss and Howe are not alone in excluding Black millennials in their analysis. Much has been written about them, but very few sustained studies of young Black adults have actually been conducted.
12. 83.1 million Americans are millennials, according to the 2015 US Census. A little more than forty percent of this group represents people of color, with 13 percent

identifying as African American. At a glance, this group can be described as mostly urban, less likely to be affiliated with a particular religion or religious organization, and more likely to face economic hardship than preceding generations. Yet there are important particularities regarding these statistics when it comes to Black millennials. US Department of Labor statistics indicate that unemployment rates for African Americans were substantially higher than whites or Latinxs between the ages of twenty and thirty-four (Rolen and Toossi 2018). Thus, Black millennials are also more likely to face poverty and workplace discrimination than are other groups. Regarding political engagement, African Americans between the ages of twenty-one and thirty-seven remain engaged. The success of Barack Obama in the 2012 election was due, in large part, to the turnout of young voters of color. Ninety-five percent of registered Black voters in this age bracket voted for President Obama. And if Black millennials had turned out in similar numbers in the 2016 election, Hillary Clinton's *What Happened?* quite possibly would never have been written.

Regarding religion, Black millennials are more likely to be connected to a particular religion and/or religious organization than their white counterparts. In the Higher Education Research Center's 2015 report on incoming freshman, as in prior years, African American students ranked lowest for non-affiliation with a particular religion than any other racial/ethnic group (Eagan et al. 2016). The Pew Research Center (2009) offers similar data for all African Americans. Taken as a whole, 83 percent of African Americans identify as affiliated with a particular religion. Among religions, Christianity in the form of historically Black Protestant churches ranks highest among African Americans of all ages, at 59 percent. However, Black millennials, while ranking higher in religious affiliation than their white or Latinx counterparts in the same group, appear to wane in comparison to Blacks within different age categories. Nineteen percent of African Americans under the age of thirty identify as unaffiliated in comparison to just 7 percent of African Americans sixty-five and older. These statistics reflect important current realities for digital Black Christians. See Pew Research Center 2009.

13. It is interesting to note that this is also the context in which he will ultimately spiral out of control, leading to depression, a suicide attempt, and institutionalization.
14. This can be read as more than an impression of Lecrae's writing style imposed by Jonathan Merritt. In latter rap songs like "Always Knew" (Moore 2017a) and "Facts" (Moore 2017c), he confirms similar sentiments regarding his white audiences' inability to fully understand the impact of figures like Tupac, Jay-Z, and Malcolm X on the lives of those who "grew up government fed."
15. For more regarding nuances in digital practices by age, see Wang, Sigerson, and Cheng 2019.
16. The sustained impact of *The Lion King* on young Black adult cultural memory and diasporic media is further viewable in the recent release of Beyoncé Knowles's *Black Is King* (2020).

17. In indicating the nuances with earlier post-structuralists' notions of simulacra, I wish to provide a different culturalist reading of young Black Christian culture. The digital Black Christians studied here often do not fully embrace the deconstructionist views of post-structuralists. Instead, digital Black Christians' representations, in their own estimation, do not leave them empty-handed—without an original. Their work is always meant to point back to a divine source. Yet there is a timelessness in deriving one's sense of history from an unknowable source, as God is believed to exist prior to time in their view. Digital Black Christians' imaginative tracing of history thus continues to move further back as multiple meanings are heaped upon an unending supply of historical moments. Additionally, digital Black Christians register their Blackness through their historical connections to past Black moments and figures. In this way, they often carry forward histories rooted in Black quests for freedom.
18. On February 4, 2014, on Facebook, Lecrae posted a picture of himself reading *My Bondage, My Freedom*, with the caption "Hangin out with Frederick Douglass." Status updates like this, along with Douglass quotes in interviews, formed the few public forums in which he discussed race or racial inequality as historical matters that only broadly informed contemporary social issues.
19. A 1989 *Village Voice* exposé on NWA chronicles the collusion of white evangelical organizations like Focus on the Family with local law enforcement to either halt or heavily police NWA performances at each tour stop (Marsh and Pollack 1989).
20. Examples include the following from a CNN interview by Don Lemon of popular basketball player LeBron James (2018): The fatal shooting of seventeen-year-old Trayvon Martin "hit a switch for me. From that point on, I knew that my voice and my platform had to be used for more than just sports."
21. Lecrae describes his grandmother, Big Momma, and her work on behalf of the poor in the border region of San Diego, CA. Yet, Lecrae's Christian development did not occur until college. Impact, the organization responsible for discipling him at their annual New Year's Eve event, as well as the church community and seminary with which he was initially associated as a new believer during this time, has deep white evangelical roots. While Black culture was evident in the embrace of the music, language, and fashion of the Cross Movement, rappers who first commissioned him at this event, in large part, the theology and Christian teaching remained contextually white (Moore 2016c).
22. Lecrae's Twitter post on July 4 was met with a flurry of criticism and support. One friend jokingly responded to Lecrae, "But we're still going to make money" along with an image of his "Welcome to America" t-shirt—a reference to a song on his upcoming album and a T-shirt then available on Lecrae's website.
23. Gone was the rap artist who said in 2016 regarding the police brutality of unarmed Blacks: "I don't see this as a Black-white issue. In India the Filipinos are being treated like they are less than human . . . I'm not focused on race, exactly. If Blacks in America are treated equally, I'll move on to the next group" (Boorstein 2016). By the following year, Lecrae had evolved and began doing "racial identity

development work," according to an interview with Christine Edmondson of *Truth's Table*. See Boorstein 2016; and *Truth's Table* 2019.

2. RACE

1. In my discussion with B. J. Thompson, one of the founding members of Reach Records and longtime friend of Lecrae, Thompson described some of those early moments with Lecrae ministering at detention centers as part of a broader network of young Black Christians' attempts at creating a new religious culture that spoke to urban Black youth culture in Dallas, TX. The theological conversations they embarked upon were also core to the Reformed theology that was at the center of Cross Movement Records. By the time Reach Records became its own successful label and began a movement of its own through the Unashamed Tour, these theologies and theologians that attended to a white construction of the Christian faith were central to their music. Thompson, personal communication, January 2018.

    Lecrae's 2008 song title "Don't Waste Your Life" was taken from the 2003 book by the same title written by Reformed theologian John Piper. And there were older stalwarts in white evangelical circles that Lecrae soon gravitated toward. His "D.O.G.'s—dead old guys," as he called them, included Charles Spurgeon, Francis Scheffer, and John Calvin.

2. The "college to (evangelical) Christian" connection cannot be overlooked. Lecrae writes in his autobiography that it was during his time in college at the University of Texas that he first decided to become a Christian. That decision was sparked by a Christian friend's invitation to a yearly retreat in Atlanta. He went to an event led by Impact, a college ministry serving African American students, participated in a Christian rap cipher, and saw prominent Christian rappers of the day, like Cross Movement. Lecrae recounts having a deeply transformative experience after one pastor's sermon. While the moment in 1998 represented a personal transformation for him, this was all quite routine for an Impact conference.

    In his autobiography, Moore does not address the implications of predominantly white-run religious institutions in his professional or personal development. However, in many ways Impact can be viewed as the Black wing of the larger Campus Crusade for Christ (now called Cru). Cru's conservative evangelical roots date back to the 1950s. Founded by husband and wife Bill Bright and Vonette Bright on the campus of the University of California–Los Angeles, its mission was to evangelize to college students. Over the next thirty years, the organization became a stalwart in Christian evangelical circles, attracting thousands of young adults through a program of simple and impactful alternatives to cultural movements of the day. Their Explo '72 event was given the nickname the "Christian Woodstock" by the press for its similarity to hippie culture. Yet its message was often meant to critique hippie culture, the sexual revolution, the Black Power Movement, more radical elements within the civil rights movement, and the anti-war protest movement. Through organizations like the Christian World Liberation Front, an organization begun by Cru on UCLA's campus, new Christian converts (mostly white, male former hippies) sought to respond directly to Berkeley's Liberation Movement.

Several student groups staged protests and sit-ins to demand a curriculum representative of its diverse student body. Students drafted an open letter to administrators which began: "WE ARE NOT WHITE. WE DO NOT WISH TO BE WHITE. WHAT IS GOOD FOR WHITE PEOPLE IS OFTEN WORSE THAN BAD FOR US" (see Berkeley Revolution 2021). It was a startling declaration of their Blackness and an attempt to steer their own course of study. However, the dynamics of race and racial history in America that ignited the Berkeley revolution were all but overlooked by the Christian World Liberation Front and the wider Campus Crusade for Christ. This became typical of how the Campus Crusade for Christ engaged with issues of race, either as part of the problem within a "sinful culture" or by completely overlooking the racial dynamics of larger social issues altogether. See Graduate Theological Union 2008.

It was not until 1991 that an African American missionary named Tom Fritz began the Impact Movement to reach African American college students in a racially relevant way. This was part of Cru's larger initiative to reach underrepresented racial groups that their organization have been engaged in for already forty years by that point. In that time, Cru had grown to encompass Family Life, which first gained notoriety through Bill and Vonette Bright's appearance on *Focus on the Family* TV show with James Dobson. In the 1980s, Cru galvanized its expanding forces along with other member organizations of the religious right. If African Americans were underrepresented in its ranks prior to the 1990s, it was because of its intentional political alliances, which firmly established it as a white Christian organization. To date, the conservative organization continues to compartmentalize racial issues and groups in its literature and public presence. It requires clicking on the link marked "urban" or visiting Impact's page directly to view issues specifically related to race. See Impact Movement, n.d.

3. Tamura Lomax (2018) describes Carlton Pearson's connections to influential Christian television broadcast networks like Christian Broadcasting Network (CBN), Trinity Broadcasting Network (TBN), Praise the Lord Network (PTL), and Daystar Television Network (DTN). Such networks catapulted Jakes to the national religious stage with his popular sermon "Woman Thou Art Loosed" (134). Such networks between white and Black Christians both reflected and influenced the linked theologies and shared spaces created between the generation of Black and white Christians online in the late twentieth century. See also Shayne Lee 2005.
4. See also Fanon 1967.
5. Unless otherwise indicated, all quotations from Propaganda in this chapter are from an interview by the author, April 9, 2018.
6. Unless otherwise indicated, all quotations from Joseph Solomon in this chapter are from an interview by the author, April 23, 2018.

7. As the first decade of the millennium ended, much like at its dawning, many in America remained attentive to race. At its dawn, works like Dinesh D'Souza's *The End of Racism: Principles for a Multiracial Society* (1995), captured both the *New York Times* number one spot and the imaginations of many who envisioned a post-racial future. A November 18, 1993, *Time* magazine cover story featured a racially nondescript woman (who somehow retained mostly European features), a computer-generated attempt at what "the new face of America" might look like, given immigration and the growing birth rate of multiethnic children, as identified in the most recent census. Yet, according to its own headlines that year and preceding years, race and racism would remain firmly entrenched in the American story. Cases like the shooting death of Amadou Diallo exhibited the long history of disproportionate violence used against unarmed Black men in America. In the wake of the bombing of the World Trade Center in 2001, the depth of American racial prejudice was revealed as Muslims, Arabs, and South Asians experienced intense ethnic profiling. Given this national climate, from op-ed pieces to scholarly books and journals, many commentators rightly scoffed at the notion of an end to race or racism. Yet by 2008 the presidential campaign and ultimate win of Barack Obama renewed the possibility in many minds of a post-racial society. In part, it was the likely suspects who trotted out well-worn visions of post-racialism, like Lou Dobbs and other well-known conservative pundits. In Black churches, many continued to argue that our nation had not moved past its own racism. Perhaps most famous was Jeremiah Wright's sermon cataloging American atrocities against several racial and ethnic minorities. Still, the conversations regarding race and racial justice in the early years of the Obama administration remained somewhat hopeful in these settings.
8. Elonda Clay (2011, 8) calls this a "performance of a hip hop aesthetic." Amiri Baraka's (formerly Leroi Jones's) definition of the "blues aesthetic" urgently maps onto the idea of the "performance of a hip hop aesthetic" as it relates to digital Black Christians. See L. Jones 1963; Cone 1992; Khabeer 2016.
9. At a time when other scholars and music critics sought to decenter Black music away from Black culture, Baraka (L. Jones 1963) argued that the blues aesthetic could only be understood in the context of Black culture and experience. He emphasizes the function of Black modes of performativity for digital Black Christians, the doing of hip hop as a way of being Christian, or even being hip hop in order to be Christian. See also Douglas 2012.
10. For Imani Perry (2004), realist narratives of "telling" and "being" support various toxic media representations and political agendas and reify stereotypes of Black urban life.
11. The African influence on apologetics in the early Christian philosophical school in places like Alexandria and/or the early Coptic church is rarely discussed in such seminary settings. This in itself is evidence of the widespread cultural bias in studies of Apologetics, as the parameters of essential apologetics is often drawn

around European thinkers with little attention to the much earlier African influence on their philosophies.
12. Talib Kweli (2012), writing in an online post about his artistic and spiritual development, relates a narrative shared by many digital Black Christian males who were deeply affected both by the biography of Malcolm X and its representation in Spike Lee's 1992 film about him. Kweli writes, "After reading about Malcolm's ultimate spiritual conversion towards the end of the book, I came to the conclusion that if Malcolm was right about everything else, he must be right about God. I did not decide to follow Islam at this time, but I decided that God must be real for a man like Malcolm to exist."
13. It was true that Oprah Winfrey had worked her way into the hearts of white women across the US through her hit syndicated talk show. The self-help guru offered advice to a generation of median-income white women anxious to hear titillating gossip on the stars or left reeling from sensational exposés on criminals, holy men, and even sitting presidents. In *Oprah: The Gospel of an Icon*, Kathryn Lofton (2011) argues that Oprah seeks to both transcend and embody her racial identity. At times, she calls forth her Blackness even while offering women spiritual alternatives beyond American Black religious traditions, as with Super Soul Sunday. Characterized by a her coupling of the "sassy Black woman" trope with business acumen, Oprah's empire was built through the watchful support of white women like the three sitting in Wolgemuth's apartment that late night. That Oprah, partly successful through scores of white women viewers like Wolgemuth, could easily be detached from her racial-context and offered a religious audience among white evangelicals was a logical conclusion. Their mission was to create a cadre of women with Oprah-like influence among Christians.
14. In an article titled "True Woman 1829," Mary Kassian (n.d.) aligns her True Woman Movement with the goals of the nineteenth century "cult" of domesticity. Kassian writes that when she learned the critique of this movement by feminist historians, "I had to smile, since I suspect that feminist historians will undoubtedly also call the modern-day True Woman Movement a 'cult.'"
15. Their "Statement of Faith" outlines the following positions:

- MEN AND WOMEN are both created in the image of God and are equal in value and dignity, but they have distinct roles and functions in the home and in the church.
- WE ARE CALLED as women to affirm and encourage men as they seek to express godly masculinity, and to honor and support God-ordained male leadership in the home and in the church.
- MARRIAGE, as created by God, is a sacred, binding, lifelong covenant between one man and one woman.
- WHEN WE RESPOND humbly and appropriately to male leadership in our homes and churches, we demonstrate a noble submission that honors God's Word and reflects Christ's obedience to the will of His Father.

- SELFISH INSISTENCE on personal rights is contrary to the spirit of Christ who humbled Himself, took on the form of a servant, and laid down His life for us. (Revive Our Hearts, n.d.-b).

16. Subrahmanyam, Greenfield, and Tynes (2004) provide foundational work on the topic through their study of 583 participants in an online teen chat room. See also Wright and Li 2011; and Quinn et al. 2012.
17. Given the sensitive nature of the following Instagram exchange and to reduce the focus on those who were not interviewed for inclusion in this book, the real name of @JimMann1985 has been excluded from the discussion.
18. See also Hendrickse et al. 2017, 92–100.
19. In a personal conversation, Christina Edmondson has shared that while two of the podcast members fall within the traditional definition of a "millennial," their audience often represents a cross section of young Black Christians in their thirties and forties who may or may not identify with the Reformed tradition.

3. BODY

1. Chapter 5 in this book demonstrates the way this pivot ultimately reflects a full rotation back to the institutional Black Church, with Black churches also being transformed by the new thoughts and ways of being Black and Christian offered by digital Black Christians.
2. The original article, titled "Gay Rights and Political Correctness: A Brief History," has mostly been expunged from online sources. See the following for versions of the original article still available and/or discussed: Schoenewolf 2005; Mock 2007.

4. WORK

1. Unless otherwise indicated, all quotations from Beleaf Melanin (Glen Henry) in this chapter are from interviews by the author, November 14, 2017–July 22, 2018.
2. Unless otherwise indicated, all quotations from Natalie Lauren Sims in this chapter are from an interview by the author, November 24, 2018.
3. *Def Poetry Jam* was a spoken-word poetry television series that aired on HBO from 2002 to 2007.
4. Patreon is an online membership platform that allows creators and artists to earn an income through subscriber contributions.
5. See Boardman and Alexander 2011; George and Lynch 2003; Shin et al. 2009.
6. Beleaf's story coincides with several of the stories regarding Black death discussed by Lecrae Moore in Chapter 2. The trauma and violence of urban life and family environ colors many of the stories of young Blacks. Lecrae's autobiography dedicates an entire chapter to discussing his descent into a depressive episode that ultimately landed him in a rehab facility. Later albums like *Rehab* (2010) tell this story, as well. As late as his 2017 album *All Things Work Together*, the rapper details his more recent bouts with depression in "Can't Stop Me Now":

> Last year I was feeling hopeless
> I just wanted it to end
> People stealing money from me, man
> I swear I thought that we was friends
> And I was so depressed, I was such a mess
> I couldn't shake it off (Moore 2017b)

7. Creatives also employ other protective strategies. This is discussed in Chapter 3 where I consider Jackie Hill-Perry's Instagram post and Propaganda's supportive response. In other ways, creatives seek to protect themselves. When I first meet Jackie Hill-Perry, I tell her that I have been trying to get in touch with her via email and Instagram to no avail. At the word *Instagram*, she begins shaking her head back and forth. "I don't check my Instagram." Like other Black Christian creatives, she has learned to expect a bevy of critical responses to her online posts (see Chapter 3).
8. Jamaica West was among those who commented on Cataphant's post on #CHHsexism. She tweets in response to Cataphant's original post on November 20, 2017: "#CHHsexism Points to an Even Greater Issue in What Men Truly Believe God Has to Say about Women. There Is Some Serious Reevaluating That Needs to Take Place. I Encourage You All to Study the Life of Jesus and His Frequent Interactions with Women. I'm out ✌"

5. CHURCH

1. Unless otherwise indicated, all quotations from Jamaica West in this chapter are from interviews by the author, November 20, 2017–July 22, 2018.
2. Jamaica West is here referencing the 1988 Spike Lee film titled *School Daze*, in which competing sororities square off over skin color. The two groups are referenced as the "Jigaboos" and the "Wannabees."
3. While this post has circulated widely on social media, it was perhaps most popularly shared by digital Black Christian and popular comedian KevOnStage.
4. See Kirk-Duggan and Hall 2011; Price 2012.
5. Many online references to the campaign have now been removed from social media sites following stiffer policies regarding hate speech. At the time of this writing, an archive of the events could be found on *The Old Black Church* blog (Ann Brock 2016).
6. See Pew Research Center 2021.

EPILOGUE

1. Just prior to the publication of this book, the Pew Research Center released its most expansive report on Black religion to date, the "2019–2020 Survey of Religion among Black Americans." While it takes into account the diversity of Black "nones" and offers an important look at religious involvement among young Black people, it fails to consider the role of technology in the religious phenomena that

it takes up. This is a particularly interesting oversight, in an otherwise timely report, considering that it was conducted, in large part, online. Yet the words "internet" and "online" appear only a few times in the whole report, and the digital's multiple modes of religious communication and its widespread impact on contemporary religion remain unaccounted for in the report (see Pew Research Center 2021). See also Hoover, Clark, and Rainie 2004 for an earlier study of faith online, though race is largely undiscussed in it.

REFERENCES

Ammerman, Nancy. 2007. *Everyday Religion: Observing Modern Religious Lives*. Oxford: Oxford University Press.

Ankerson, Megan Sapnar. 2018. "The Periscopic Regime of Live-Streaming." In *Appified: Culture in the Age of Apps*, edited by Jeremy Wade Morris and Sarah Murray, 227–36. Ann Arbor: University of Michigan Press.

ANWA (All Nations Worship Assembly). n.d. "Who We Are." Accessed May 2, 2019. http://allnationswa.com.

Anzul, Margaret, Margot Ely, Teri Freidman, Diane Garner, and Ann McCormack-Steinmetz. 2003. *Doing Qualitative Research: Circles within Circles*. New York: Routledge.

Apologetics with Preston Perry. 2019. "Who Gives a Black Man Permission to Feel? [An Ode to Uncle Stan] by Preston Perry for PIA 2019." YouTube, December 19, 2019. www.youtube.com/watch?v=NUWBDuzWMSE.

Arendt, Hannah. 1998. *The Human Condition*. 2nd ed. Chicago: University of Chicago Press.

Asante, Molefi Kete, and Deborah Atwater. 1986. "The Rhetorical Condition as Symbolic Structure in Discourse." *Communication Quarterly* 34 (2): 170–77.

Associated Press. 1989. "Bush Nominee for F.C.C." *New York Times*, November 22, 1989. www.nytimes.com.

Association of Internet Researchers. 2019. *Ethical Guidelines 3.0*. https://aoir.org.

Aupers, Stef, and Dick Houtman, eds. 2010. *Religions of Modernity: Relocating the Sacred to the Self and the Digital*. International Studies in Religion and Society 12. Leiden: Brill.

Barna Group. 2010. "Is There a 'Reformed' Movement in American Churches?" November 5, 2010. www.barna.com.

Baudrillard, Jean. 1994a. *The Illusion of the End*. Translated by Chris Turner. Stanford, CA: Stanford University Press.

Baudrillard, Jean. 1994b. *Simulacra and Simulation*. Translated by Sheila Glaser. Ann Arbor: University of Michigan Press.

Been Changed Magazine. 2014. "Lecrae Interview at The Breakfast Club Power 105 1 9 11 2014 YouTubevia torchbrowser com." YouTube, September 11, 2014. www.youtube.com/watch?v=inB-NImKlR4.

Beleaf (Glen Henry). 2014. "Suicide Roll." Track 8 on *Red Pills + Black Sugar*. Produced by Beleaf. Kings Dream Entertainment. Mp3.

Beleaf (Glen Henry). 2020. "Faith, Family & Foundation." Interview by TruthSeekah. Audio. 1:21:32. Accessed March 22, 2020. www.truthseekah.com.

Benbow, Candice. 2017. "What Shall We Say to These Things: The Implications of Black Women's Singleness." *Red Lip Theology* (blog), October 1, 2017. https://candicebenbow.com.

Bender, Courtney, Wendy Cadge, Peggy Levitt, and David Smilde, eds. 2012. *Religion on the Edge: De-Centering and Re-Centering the Sociology of Religion*. Oxford: Oxford University Press.

Berkeley Revolution. 2021. "The Third World Liberation Front." https://revolution.berkeley.edu.

Blair, Leonardo. 2018. "After Being 'Delivert' from Homosexuality, Andrew Caldwell Says He Now Has a Girlfriend." *Christian Post*, September 6, 2018. www.christianpost.com.

Blueprint Church. n.d. "Dhati Lewis." Accessed October 17, 2020. www.blueprintchurch.org.

Boardman, Jason D., and Kari B. Alexander. 2011. "Stress Trajectories, Health Behaviors, and the Mental Health of Black and White Young Adults." *Social Science & Medicine* 72 (10): 1659–66.

Boorstein, Michelle. 2016. "This Rapper Is Trying to Get His Fellow Evangelicals to Talk about Race. Not Everyone Is on Board." *Washington Post*, July 1, 2016. www.washingtonpost.com.

Bourdieu, Pierre. 2007. *Sketch for a Self-Analysis*. Cambridge, UK: Polity.

Bowler, Gerry. 2001. *God and the Simpsons: The Spirituality of Springfield*. Richmond, BC: Digory.

boyd, danah. 2008. "Taken Out of Context: American Teen Sociality in Networked Publics." PhD diss., University of California–Berkeley.

Boylorn, Robin M., Mark P. Orbe, and Carolyn Ellis. 2016. *Critical Autoethnography*. Vol. 13, *Writing Lives*. Walnut Creek, CA: Left Coast.

Breakfast Club Power 105.1. 2017. "Lecrae Talks *Blessings*, Bringing His Faith Into His Music, Keeping Family Off His Instagram & More." YouTube, March 3, 2017. www.youtube.com/watch?v=tgAu_hqluGU.

Broadman & Holman. 1996. *True Love Waits Bible: NIV*. Nashville: B&H.

Brock, André. 2012. "From the Blackhand Side: Twitter as a Cultural Conversation." *Journal of Broadcasting & Electronic Media* 56 (4): 529–49. https://doi.org/10.1080/08838151.2012.732147.

Brock, Ann. 2016. "The Attack against Apostle Dr. Matthew Stevenson Lll???" *The Old Black Church* (blog), August 23, 2016. https://theoldblackchurch.blogspot.com.

Broussard, Meredith. 2018. *Artificial Unintelligence: How Computers Misunderstand the World*. Cambridge, MA: MIT Press.

Buffardi, Laura E., and W. Keith Campbell. 2008. "Narcissism and Social Networking Web Sites." *Personality and Social Psychology Bulletin* 34 (10): 1303–14. https://doi.org/10.1177/0146167208320061.

Burrell, Jenna. 2009. "The Field Site as a Network: A Strategy for Locating Ethnographic Research." *Field Methods* 21 (2): 181–99. https://doi.org/10.1177/1525822 X08329699.

Butler, Judith P. 2009. *Giving an Account of Oneself*. New York: Fordham University Press.

Bynum, Juanita. 1997. "Dr Juanita Bynum No More Sheets." YouTube, March 9, 2014. https://youtu.be/rEsykPeRNyw.

Caliandro, Alessandro. 2018. "Digital Methods for Ethnography: Analytical Concepts for Ethnographers Exploring Social Media Environments." *Journal of Contemporary Ethnography* 47 (5): 551–78.

Campbell, Heidi A. 2010. *When Religion Meets New Media*. Media, Religion and Culture. Abingdon, UK: Routledge.

Campbell, Heidi A., ed. 2012a. *Digital Religion: Understanding Religious Practice in New Media Worlds*. New York: Routledge.

Campbell, Heidi A. 2012b. Introduction to *Digital Religion: Understanding Religious Practice in New Media Worlds*, 1–21. New York: Routledge.

Campbell, Heidi A., and Mia Lövheim. 2011. "Rethinking the Online-Offline Connection in the Study of Religion Online." *Communication & Society* 14 (8): 1083–96.

Carter, Earl. 2014. "Supt. Earl Carter Preaches Up a Revival at COGIC Convocation." Recorded at COGIC 107th Convocation in St. Louis, MO, November 9, 2014.

Chavez, Mark, Shawna Anderson, and Allison Eagle. 2012. "National Congregations Study, Cumulative Dataset (1998, 2006–2007, and 2012), Version 2." Cumulative data file and codebook. Durham, NC: Duke University, Department of Sociology. www.thearda.com.

Cheong, Pauline Hope. 2017. "The Vitality of New Media and Religion: Communicative Perspectives, Practices and Changing Authority in Spiritual Organizing." *New Media and Society* 19 (1): 25–33.

Chicago Partnership. n.d. "Our Vision." Accessed October 17, 2020. www.thechica gopartnership.com.

Christian, Barbara. 1985. *Black Feminist Criticism: Perspectives on Black Women Writers*. New York: Teachers College Press.

Clay, Elonda. 2011. "These Gods Got Swagger: Avatars, Gameplay, and the Digital Performance of Hip Hop Culture in Machinima." *Bulletin for the Study of Religion* 40 (3): 4–9.

Clay, Elonda. 2015. "#NOWTHATSRELIGIONANDHIPHOP: Mapping the Terrain of Religion and Hip Hop." In *Religion in Hip Hop: Mapping the New Terrain in the US*, edited by Monica Miller, Anthony Pinn, and Bernard "Bun B" Freeman, 87–95. London: Bloomsbury.

Cleveland, Christena. 2014. "Are You Starting an Urban Church Plant or PLANTATION?" *ChurchPlants*, November 20, 2014. https://churchplants.com.

Cobbs, Tasha. 2014. "#ChristopherHeron Chats with @TashaCobbs about Her Music & Her Ministry." Interview by Christopher Heron. Gospel Artists Interviews. *BlackGospel.com* (blog), March 10, 2014. https://blackgospel.com.

Cohen, Cathy J. 2005. "Black Youth Culture Survey." Chicago: Black Youth Project. www.blackyouthproject.com.
Coleman, Beth. 2009. "Race as Technology." *Camera Obscura* 24 (1): 177–207.
Collins, Patricia Hill. (1991) 2008. *Black Feminist Thought: Knowledge, Consciousness, and the Politics of Empowerment*. New York: Routledge.
Cone, James H. 1969. *Black Theology and Black Power*. New York: Seabury.
Cone, James H. 1970. *A Black Theology of Liberation*. New York: Lippincott.
Cone, James H. 1992. *The Spirituals and the Blues: An Interpretation*. New York: Orbis Books.
CookieTruth. 2017. "Church Planters Panel: Dr. Matthew L. Stevenson." YouTube, January 15, 2017. www.youtube.com/watch?v=epEQVK-gUYY.
Cooper, Anna J. (1892) 2017. *A Voice from the South: By a Black Woman of the South*. Chapel Hill: University of North Carolina Press.
Cooper, Brittney C. 2015. "Love No Limit: Towards a Black Feminist Future (In Theory)." *Black Scholar* 45 (4): 7–21. https://doi.org/10.1080/00064246.2015.1080912.
Cooper, Brittney C. 2019. *Eloquent Rage: A Black Feminist Discovers Her Superpower*. London: Picador.
Cressler, Matthew. 2017. *Authentically Black and Truly Catholic: The Rise of Black Catholicism in the Great Migration*. New York: New York University Press.
Creswell, John W. 2007. *Qualitative Inquiry and Research Design: Choosing among Five Approaches*. 2nd ed. Thousand Oaks, CA: Sage.
Crunk Feminist Collective. 2010. "Mission Statement." February 12, 2010. www.crunkfeministcollective.com/about/.
Daniels, David. 2015. "Christian Songwriter Natalie Lauren Maneuvers Working for Iggy Azalea, Lecrae." *Rapzilla*, February 4, 2015. https://rapzilla.com.
Daniels, David. 2018. "Preston Perry: Transformed By Discipleship." *Legacy Disciple* (blog), April 25, 2018. https://legacydisciple.org.
Davis, Angela Y. 1981. *Women, Race, and Class*. New York: Random House.
Day, Keri. 2017. "#BlackSkinWhiteSin: What Juanita Bynum Gets Wrong: Reflections from A Pentecostal Woman Preacher." *Feminist Wire*, February 13, 2017. https://thefeministwire.com.
Delamont, Sara. 2008. "Arguments against Auto-Ethnography." University of Leeds, January 14, 2008. www.leeds.ac.uk.
Demby, Gene. 2013. "The Truth behind the Lies of the Original 'Welfare Queen.'" *NPR*, December 20, 2013, www.npr.org.
Dent, Cristin. 2019. "PIA 2019 | I am here at the tour for the first time in INDIANAPOLIS." YouTube, September 10, 2019. https://youtu.be/dnRmGxC9pxI.
Denzin, Norman K. 1997. *Interpretive Ethnography: Ethnographic Practices for the 21st Century*. Thousand Oaks, CA: Sage.
Deparle, Jason. 1994. "From Pledge to Plan: The Campaign to End Welfare—A Special Report; The Clinton Welfare Bill: A Long, Stormy Journey." *New York Times*, July 15, 1994. www.nytimes.com.

de Seta, Gabriele. 2020. "Three Lies of Digital Ethnography." *Journal of Digital Social Research* 2 (1): 77–97. https://doi.org/10.33621/jdsr.v2i1.24.

Dever, Mark. 2014. "Where'd All These Calvinists Come From?" *9Marks*, June 18, 2014. www.9marks.org.

DeWitt, Amanda. 2013. "Lecrae: How God Brought Him from Searching for Significance to Serving His Savior. A Look at the Man, His Music, and His Message." *Dallas Family Magazine*, February 6, 2013. www.facebook.com/DallasFamilyMagazine/photos/211525032318780.

Diamant, Jeff, and Besheer Mohamed. 2018. "Black Millennials Are More Religious than Other Millennials." *Fact Tank*. July 20, 2018. www.pewresearch.org.

Dillard, Angela Denise. 2009. *Faith in the City: Preaching Radical Social Change in Detroit*. Ann Arbor: University of Michigan Press.

Dimitriadis, Greg. 2001. "Coming Clean at the Hyphen: Ethics and Dialogue at a Local Community Center." *Qualitative Inquiry* 7 (5): 578–97. https://doi.org/10.1177/107780040100700504.

Dimitriadis, Greg. 2003. *Friendship, Cliques, and Gangs: Young Black Men Coming of Age in Urban America*. New York: Teachers College Press.

Dimitriadis, Greg. 2009. *Performing Identity/Performing Culture: Hip Hop as Text, Pedagogy, and Lived Practice*. New York: Peter Lang.

Dimitriadis, Greg. 2015. "Framing Hip Hop: New Methodologies for New Times." *Urban Education* 50 (1): 31–51. https://doi.org/10.1177/0042085914563185.

Douglas, Kelly Brown. 1999. *Sexuality and the Black Church: A Womanist Perspective*. New York: Orbis Books.

Douglas, Kelly Brown. 2012. *Black Bodies and the Black Church: A Blues Slant*. London: Palgrave Macmillan.

Dove. 2020. "Real Beauty Campaign." www.dove.com.

Drake, Simone C. 2016. *When We Imagine Grace: Black Men and Subject Making*. Chicago: University of Chicago Press.

Drucker, Johanna. 2013. "Performative Materiality and Theoretical Approaches to Interface." *Digital Humanities Quarterly* 7 (1). www.digitalhumanities.org.

D'Souza, Dinesh. 1995. *The End of Racism: Principles for a Multiracial Society*. New York: Free Press.

Du Bois, W. E. B. 1903. *The Negro Church: Report of a Social Study Made under the Direction of Atlanta University: Together with the Proceedings of the Eighth Conference for the Study of the Negro Problems, Held at Atlanta University, May 26th, 1903*. Atlanta: Atlanta University Press, 1903.

Dyson, Michael Eric. 2008. *The Michael Eric Dyson Reader*. New York: Basic Books.

Dyson, Torkwase. 2017. "Black Interiority: Notes on Architecture, Infrastructure, Environmental Justice, and Abstract Drawing." *Pelican Bomb*, January 9, 2017. http://pelicanbomb.com.

Eagan, Kevin, Ellen Bara Stolzenberg, Abigail K. Bates, Melissa C. Aragon, Maria Ramirez Suchard, and Cecilia Rios-Aguilar. 2016. "The American Freshman: The

National Norms Fall 2015." Higher Education Research Institute & Cooperative Institutional Research Program. www.heri.ucla.edu.

Eisen, Lauren-Brooke, and Inimai M. Chettiar. 2016. "The Complex History of the Controversial 1994 Crime Bill." Brennan Center for Justice, April 14, 2016. www.brennancenter.org.

Evans, Curtis J. 2008. *The Burden of Black Religion*. Oxford: Oxford University Press.

Fanon, Frantz. 1967. *Black Skin, White Masks*. Translated by Charles Lam Markmann. New York: Grove.

Fine, Gary Alan. 1993. "Ten Lies of Ethnography: Moral Dilemmas of Field Research." *Journal of Contemporary Ethnography* 22 (3) (October): 267–94. https://doi.org/10.1177/089124193022003001.

Fiske, John. 1996. *Media Matters: Race and Gender in U.S. Politics*. Rev. ed. Minneapolis: University of Minnesota Press.

Floyd-Thomas, Stacey, Juan M. Floyd-Thomas, Carol B. Duncan, Stephen G. Ray Jr., and Nancy Lynne Westfield. 2007. *Black Church Studies: An Introduction*. Nashville: Abingdon.

Foucault, Michel. 1988. *Technologies of the Self: A Seminar with Michel Foucault*. Amherst: University of Massachusetts Press.

Foucault, Michel. 2002. *The Order of Things: An Archaeology of the Human Sciences*. London: Psychology Press.

Franklin, Kirk. 1997. "Stomp." *God's Property (featuring Cheryl James)*. B-Rite, Interscope. CD.

Franklin, Kirk. 2007. *Fight of My Life (featuring Da Truth)*. Produced by Kirk Franklin, James "Jazzy" Jordan, Carla Williams, and Jessie Hurst. GospoCentric. CD.

Frederick, Marla. 2015. *Colored Television: American Religion Gone Global*. Stanford, CA: Stanford University Press.

Friedman, Batya, and Helen Nissenbaum. 1996. "Bias in Computer Systems." *ACM Transactions on Information Systems* 4 (3): 330–47.

Fuchs, Christian. 2018. "Capitalism, Patriarchy, Slavery, and Racism in the Age of Digital Capitalism and Digital Labour." *Critical Sociology* 44, nos. 4–5 (July): 677–702. https://doi.org/10.1177/0896920517691108.

Gault, Erika, and Travis Harris, eds. 2019. *Beyond Christianity and Hip Hop*. New York: Routledge.

Geertz, Clifford. 1973. *The Interpretation of Cultures: Selected Essays*. New York: Basic Books.

George, Linda K., and Scott M. Lynch. 2003. "Race Differences in Depressive Symptoms: A Dynamic Perspective on Stress Exposure and Vulnerability." *Journal of Health and Social Behavior* 44 (3): 353–69.

Geyser, Werner. 2016. "How Much Do YouTubers Make? A YouTuber's Earnings Calculator." *Influencer Marketing Hub* (blog), November 27, 2016. https://influencermarketinghub.com.

Gjoni, Eron. 2013. Home page. www.thezoepost.wordpress.com.

Graduate Theological Union. 2008. "Inventory of the Christian World Liberation Front Collection." Accessed April 12, 2019. https://oac.cdlib.org.

Granovetter, Mark S. 1977. "The Strength of Weak Ties." In *Social Networks*, edited by Samuel Leinhardt, 347–67. https://doi.org/10.1016/B978-0-12-442450-0.50025-0.

Granovetter, Mark S. 1983. "The Strength of Weak Ties: A Network Theory Revisited." *Sociological Theory* 1: 201–33. https://doi.org/10.2307/202051.

Greenburg, Zack O'Malley. 2019. "Highest-Paid Hip-Hop Acts 2019: Kanye Tops Jay-Z To Claim Crown." *Forbes*, September 19, 2019. www.forbes.com.

Hall, Stuart, and Sut Jhally. 1996. "Race, the Floating Signifier." Transcript of video. Northampton, MA: Media Education Foundation. https://www.mediaed.org.

Hammonds, Evelynn. 2004. "Black (W)holes and the Geometry of Black Female Sexuality." In *The Black Studies Reader*, edited by Jacqueline Bobo, Cynthia Hudley, and Claudine Michel, 313–26. New York: Routledge.

Hanbury, Aaron Cline. 2017. "This Isn't the Same Lecrae." *RELEVANT Magazine* (blog), May 9, 2017. https://relevantmagazine.com.

Hansen, Collin. 2008. *Young, Restless, and Reformed: A Journalist's Journey with the New Calvinists*. Wheaton, IL: Crossway.

Hansen, Collin. 2019. "Still Young, Restless, and Reformed? The New Calvinists at 10." *9 Marks*, February 5, 2019. www.9marks.org.

Hardt, Michael. 1999. "Affective Labor." *boundary 2*, 26 (2) (Summer): 89–100.

Harrison, Anthony Kwame. 2009. *Hip Hop Underground: The Integrity and Ethics of Racial Identification*. Philadelphia: Temple University Press.

Haskins, Ron. 2008. "Making Work Pay—Again." *Brookings* (blog), September 15, 2008. www.brookings.edu.

Hatch, John B. 2002. "Rhetorical Synthesis through a (Rap)prochement of Identities: Hip-Hop and the Gospel According to the Gospel Gangstaz." *Journal of Communication and Religion* 25 (2): 228–67.

Hendrickse, J., L. M. Arpan, R. B. Clayton, and J. L. Ridgway. 2017. "Instagram and College Women's Body Image: Investigating the Roles of Appearance-Related Comparisons and Intrasexual Competition." *Computers in Human Behavior* 74:92–100. https://doi.org/10.1016/j.chb.2017.04.027.

Hesel, Richard, and Susan Basallia May. 2007. "Dispelling the Millennial Myth." *Case Currents*, February, 17–22.

Hicks, Mars. 2017. *Programmed Inequality: How Britain Discarded Women Technologists and Lost Its Edge in Computing*. Cambridge, MA: MIT Press.

Higginbotham, Evelyn Brooks. 1994. *Righteous Discontent: The Women's Movement in the Black Baptist Church, 1880–1920*. Cambridge, MA: Harvard University Press.

Hill, Lauryn. 1998. "Doo Wop (That Thing)." Track A5 on *The Miseducation of Lauryn Hill*. Produced by Lauryn Hill. Rufflehouse/Columbia Records. CD.

Hill, Marc Lamont. 2009. *Beats, Rhymes, and Classroom Life: Hip-Hop Pedagogy and the Politics of Identity*. New York: Teachers College Press.

Hill-Perry, Jackie. 2010. "MY LIFE AS A STUD by Jackie Hill OFFICIAL P4CM POET." PC4M. YouTube, March 19, 2010. www.youtube.com/watch?v=m70eWvF_hjo.

Hill-Perry, Jackie. 2012. "P4CM Presents JIG-A-BOO by Featured P4CM Poet Jackie Hill @JackieHillPerry." P4CM. YouTube, August 23, 2012. www.youtube.com/watch?v=ePsZNMJGMHs.
Hill-Perry, Jackie. 2014a. *The Art of Joy*. Produced by Humble Beast Records. Humble Beast. Mp3.
Hill-Perry, Jackie. 2014b. "Ode to Lauryn." On *The Art of Joy*. Produced by Humble Beast Records. Humble Beast. Mp3.
Hill-Perry, Jackie. 2018. *Gay Girl, Good God: The Story of Who I Was, and Who God Has Always Been*. Nashville: B&H.
Hodge, Daniel White. 2010a. *Heaven Has a Ghetto: The Missiological Gospel and Theology of Tupac Amaru Shakur*. Saarbrücken, Germany: VDM Verlag Dr. Müller.
Hodge, Daniel White. 2010b. *The Soul of Hip Hop: Rims, Timbs, and a Cultural Theology*. Westmont, IL: InterVarsity.
Hodge, Daniel White. 2016. *Hip Hop's Hostile Gospel: A Post-Soul Theological Exploration*. Leiden: Brill.
Hodkinson, Paul. 2015. "Contextualizing the Spectacular." In *The Borders of Subculture: Resistance and the Mainstream*, edited by Alexander Dhoest, Steven Malliet, Jacques Haers, and Barbara Segaert, 5–16. Abingdon, UK: Routledge.
hooks, bell. 1997. "Hardcore Honey: Bell Hooks Goes on the Down Low with Lil' Kim." *Paper*, May 1997. www.papermag.com.
Hoover, Stewart M., Lynn Schofield Clark, and Lee Rainie. 2004. "Faith Online." Pew Internet & American Life Project, in collaboration with the Lilly Endowment. www.pewinternet.org.
Hoover, Stewart M., and Nabil Echchaibi. 2014. "The Third Spaces of Digital Religion." Working paper, Center for Media, Religion and Culture, University of Colorado, Boulder, CO. www.colorado.edu.
Hoover, Stewart M., and Monica Emerich. 2011. *Media, Spiritualities and Social Change*. London: A&C Black.
Hsu, Wendy F. 2016. "A Performative Digital Ethnography." In *The Routledge Companion to Digital Ethnography*, edited by Larissa Hjorth, Heather Horst, Anne Galloway, and Genevieve Bell, 40–50. Abingdon, UK: Routledge.
Hurston, Zora Neale. 1928. "How It Feels To Be Colored Me." *The World Tomorrow* 11 (5) (May): 215–16.
Ibrahim, Awad. 2014. *The Rhizome of Blackness: A Critical Ethnography of Hip-Hop Culture, Language, Identity and the Politics of Becoming*. Toronto: Peter Lang.
Impact Movement. n.d. "Our History." Last modified 2018. https://impactmovement.org.
Indeep. 1982. "Last Night a DJ Saved My Life." Track 1 on *Last Night a DJ Saved My Life*. Written by Michael Cleveland. Becket Records. 12" LP.
Ito, Mizuko, Sonja Baumer, Matteo Bittanti, danah boyd, Rachel Cody, Becky Herr-Stephenson, Heather A. Horst, Patricia G. Lange, Dilan Mahendran, Katynka Z. Martínez, C. J. Pascoe, Dan Perkel, Laura Robinson, Christo Sims, and Lisa Tripp. 2010. *Hanging Out, Messing Around, Geeking Out: Kids Living and Learning with New Media*. Cambridge, MA: MIT Press.

Jackson, Alecia Y., and Lisa A. Mazzei. 2008. "Experience and 'I' in Autoethnography." *International Review of Qualitative Research* 1 (3): 299–318.

Jackson, John L., Jr. 2013. *Thin Description: Ethnography and the African Hebrew Israelites of Jerusalem*. Cambridge, MA: Harvard University Press.

Jackson, Ronald L., and Elaine B. Richardson. 2003. *Understanding African American Rhetoric: Classical Origins to Contemporary Innovations*. New York: Routledge.

Jakes, Bishop T. D. 2020. "In Flickering Lights." YouTube, March 8, 2020. https://youtu.be/oIYPTYqPJP4.

James, LeBron. 2018. "LeBron James' Journey from Childhood to NBA; Racism in the Free World." Interview with Don Lemon, CNN Tonight. *CNN*, July 30. http://transcripts.cnn.com.

Jason, Zachery. 2015. "Game Fear." *Boston Magazine*, January 15, 2015.

Jauregui, Joshua, Bjorn Watsjold, Laura Welsh, Jonathan S. Ilgen, and Lynne Robins. 2020. "Generational 'Othering': The Myth of the Millennial Learner." *Medical Education* 54:60–65.

Jenkins, Candice M. 2007. *Private Lives, Proper Relations: Regulating Black Intimacy*. Minneapolis: University of Minnesota Press.

Johnson, E. Patrick. 2003. *Appropriating Blackness: Performance and the Politics of Authenticity*. Durham, NC: Duke University Press.

Jones, Carolyn M. and Julia M. Hardy. 1988. "From Colonialism to Community: Religion and Culture in Charles H. Long's Significations." *Callaloo* no. 35 (Spring): 258–71. https://doi.org/10.2307/2930959.

Jones, Chelsey S. 2017. "Beleaf In Fatherhood Car Got Stolen." GoFundMe, April 11, 2017. www.gofundme.com.

Jones, Feminista. 2019. *Reclaiming Our Space: How Black Feminists Are Changing the World from the Tweets to the Streets*. Boston: Beacon.

Jones, Leroi. 1963. *Blues People: Negro Music in White America*. New York: William Morrow.

Jones, Robert P., and Daniel Cox. 2012. "Few Americans Use Social Media to Connect with Their Faith Communities." Public Religion Research Institute. www.prri.org.

Kassian, Mary. n.d. "True Woman 1829." *Girls Gone Wise* (blog). Last modified 2021. www.marykassian.com.

KB (Kevin Elijah Burgess). 2019. "DNOU2." Produced by KB. Independent. Mp3.

Khabeer, Su'ad Abdul. 2016. *Muslim Cool: Race, Religion, and Hip Hop in the United States*. New York: New York University Press.

Kirk-Duggan, Cheryl, and Marlon Hall. 2011. *Wake Up: Hip-Hop, Christianity, and the Black Church*. Nashville: Abingdon.

Kitwana, Bakari. 2002 .*The Hip Hop Generation: Young Blacks and the Crisis in African American Culture*. Black Thought and Culture. New York: Basic Civitas Books, 2002.

Knott, Kim. 2005. *The Location of Religion: A Spatial Analysis*. Sheffield, UK: Equinox.

Korzybski, Alfred. (1933) 1996. *Science and Sanity: An Introduction to Non-Aristotelian Systems and General Semantics*. 5th ed. New York: Institute of General Semantics.

Kuehn, Kathleen, and Thomas F. Corrigan. 2013. "Hope Labor: The Role of Employment Prospects in Online Social Production." *Political Economy of Communication* 1 (1) (May): 9–25. https://polecom.org.

Kweli, Talib (@talibkweli). 2012. "That One Time When I Was Atheist, and the Influence of Malcolm X." Tumbler blog post, September 9, 2012. https://talibkweli.tumblr.com/post/31221724835/that-one-time-when-i-was-atheist-and-the.

Lahad, Kinneret. 2017. *Table for One: A Critical Reading of Singlehood, Gender and Time*. Manchester, UK: Manchester University Press.

LandOfHipHop. 2015. "Chance the Rapper Interview." YouTube, March 4, 2015. www.youtube.com/watch?v=QSTB6iwhEao.

Lee, Morgan. 2015. "Why Black Churches Are Keeping Millennials." *Christianity Today*, January 30, 2015. www.christianitytoday.com.

Lee, Shayne. 2005. *T. D. Jakes: America's New Preacher*. New York: New York University Press.

Lee, Spike. 2016. *Michael Jackson's Journey from Motown to Off the Wall*. Produced by Spike Lee, John McClain, and John Branca. 40 Acres and a Mule Filmworks.

Legacy Disciple. 2018. "Storytellers: Preston Perry—New Woke Christian." YouTube, August 24, 2018. www.youtube.com/watch?v=gvdtfBi2pRA.

Lenhart, Amanda. 2015. "Teen, Social Media and Technology Overview 2015." Pew Research Center.

Lincoln, C. Eric, and Lawrence H. Mamiya. 1990. *The Black Church in the African American Experience*. Durham, NC: Duke University Press.

Lincoln, Yvonna S. 1995. "Emerging Criteria for Quality in Qualitative and Interpretive Research." *Qualitative Inquiry* 1 (3) (September): 275–89. https://doi.org/10.1177/107780049500100301.

Lincoln, Yvonna S., and Egon G. Guba. 1985. *Naturalistic Inquiry*. Thousand Oaks, CA: Sage.

Lindsey, Heather. 2020a. "So, ya'll asked for the video and I found it . . ." Facebook post, March 9, 2020. https://fb.watch/6bpI4YRBWg/.

Lindsey, Heather. 2020b. "Ummm about this weekend . . ." Facebook post, March 8, 2020. www.facebook.com/MrsHeatherLindsey.

Linne, Shai. 2017. "Shai Linne: Dear CHH." *Rapzilla*, August 12, 2017. https://rapzilla.com.

Lofton, Kathryn. 2011. *Oprah: The Gospel of an Icon*. Berkeley: University of California Press.

Lomax, Tamura. 2018. *Jezebel Unhinged: Loosing the Black Female Body in Religion and Culture*. Durham, NC: Duke University Press.

Lorde, Audre. (1984) 2007. *Sister Outsider: Essays and Speeches*. New York: Crossing.

Lövheim, Mia. 2012. "Identity." In Campbell 2012a, 41–56.

Lövheim, Mia, and Heidi A. Campbell. 2017. "Considering Critical Methods and theoretical Lenses in Digital Religion Studies." *New Media & Society* 19 (1): 5–14. https://doi.org/10.1177/1461444816649911.

Madison, D. Soyini. 2005. *Critical Ethnography: Method, Ethics, and Performance*. Thousand Oaks, CA: Sage.

Malbroux, Luna. 2017. "Why More Young Black People Are Trading in Church for African Spirituality." *Splinternews*, December 18, 2017. https://splinternews.com.
Marcus, George E. 1998. "Ethnography in/of the World System: The Emergence of Multi-sited Ethnography." In *Ethnography through Thick and Thin*, edited by George E. Marcus, 79–104. Princeton, NJ: Princeton University Press.
Markham, Annette. 2006. "Ethic as Method, Method as Ethic." *Journal of Information Ethics* 15 (2): 37–54.
Marsh, Dave, and Phyllis Pollack. 1989. "When Christian America and the Cops Went Insane over N.W.A., Rap, and Metal." *Village Voice*, October 10, 1989. www.village voice.com.
Martin, Lerone A. 2014. *Preaching on Wax: The Phonograph and the Shaping of Modern African American Religion*. New York: New York University Press.
Marwick, Alice E. 2013. *Status Update: Celebrity, Publicity, and Branding in the Social Media Age*. New Haven, CT: Yale University Press.
Marx, Karl. (1862–63) 1969. *Theories of Surplus Value*. London: Lawrence and Wishart.
Marx, Karl. (1867) 1894. *Das Kapital: Kritik der politischen Oekonomie; herausgegeben von Friedrich Engels*. Vol. 3, *Der Gesamtprozess der kapitalistischen Produktion*. Hamburg: Verlag von Otto Meissner. https://doi.org/10.3931/e-rara-25739.
Mase [Mason Bethel]. 2004. *Welcome Back*. Produced by The Movement, Rick Rock, Tyrice Jones, Chad Hamilton, and Brass 'n Blues. Bad Boy. CD.
Massey, Doreen. 2005. *For Space*. Thousand Oaks, CA: Sage.
McKittrick, Katherine. 2006. *Demonic Grounds: Black Women and the Cartographies of Struggle*. Minneapolis: University of Minnesota Press.
Miller, Daniel, and Don Slater. 2001. *The Internet: An Ethnographic Approach*. Oxford, UK: Berg.
Miller, Monica R. 2013. *Religion and Hip Hop*. New York: Routledge.
Mock, Brentin. 2007. "Anti-Gay Organization NARTH Publishes Essay on Gay Rights and Political Correctness." Intelligence Report, January 16, 2007. www.splcenter.org.
Møller, Kristian, and Brady Robards. 2019. "Walking Through, Going Along and Scrolling Back: Ephemeral Mobilities in Digital Ethnography." *Nordicom Review* 40 (1): 95–109. https://doi.org/10.2478/nor-2019-0016.
Moore, Lecrae. 2004. *Real Talk*. Produced by Reach Records. Reach Records. CD.
Moore, Lecrae. 2010. *Rehab*. Produced by PK, CheeseBeats, Benjah, Street Symphony, Alex Medina, G.P., Kajmir Royale, Joseph Prielozny, Justin Boller, G. Roc, J.R. Reach Records. MP3.
Moore, Lecrae. 2012. "Rise." Track 7 on *Church Clothes*. Produced by 9th Wonder. Reach Records. Mp3.
Moore, Lecrae. 2016a. "The Pains of Humanity Have Been Draining Me." *HuffPost*, October 20, 2016. www.huffpost.com.
Moore, Lecrae. 2016b. "Sidelines." Track 4 on *Church Clothes 3*. Produced by Joseph Prielozny. Reach Records. Mp3.
Moore, Lecrae. 2016c. *Unashamed*. Nashville: B&H.

Moore, Lecrae. 2017a. "Always Knew." Track A1 on *All Things Work Together*. Produced by Alex Media et al. Reach Records and Columbia Records. Mp3.

Moore, Lecrae. 2017b. "Can't Stop Me Now (Destination)." Track C3 on *All Things Work Together*. Produced by Alex Media et al. Reach Records and Columbia Records. Mp3.

Moore, Lecrae. 2017c. "Facts." Track A2 on *All Things Work Together*. Produced by Alex Media et al. Reach Records and Columbia Records. Mp3.

Moore, Lecrae. 2017d. "Lecrae Freestyles Live + Speaks on Balancing Music with His Marriage." Interview by Sway Calloway, Sway Universe. YouTube, March 2, 2017. www.youtube.com/watch?time_continue=954&v=Uj9lkmiMOpM.

Morgan, Joan. 2000. *When Chickenheads Come Home to Roost: A Hip-Hop Feminist Breaks It Down*. New York: Simon and Schuster.

Morgan, Joan, and Mark Anthony Neal. 2006. "A Brand New Feminism: A Conversation with Joan Morgan and Mark Anthony Neal." In *Total Chaos: The Art and Aesthetics of Hip Hop*, edited by Jeff Chang, 233–44. New York: Basic Civitas Books.

Moultrie, Monique. 2017. *Passionate and Pious: Religious Media and Black Women's Sexuality*. Durham, NC: Duke University Press.

Müller, Nicole, and Martin J. Ball. 2012. *Research Methods in Clinical Linguistics and Phonetics: A Practical Guide*. Guides to Research Methods in Language and Linguistics Series. Oxford, UK: Wiley-Blackwell.

NBC 12 News. 2015. "'I Don't Like Mens No More' Viral Sensation: I Still Have Desires." *NBC-WWBT News*, February 26, 2015. www.nbc12.com.

Neal, Mark Anthony. 2014. *Songs in the Key of Black Life: A Rhythm and Blues Nation*. New York: Routledge.

Nielsen. 2016. "Nielsen 2016 Report: Black Millennials Close the Digital Divide." October 17, 2016. www.nielsen.com.

Noble, Safiya. 2018. *Algorithms of Oppression: How Search Engines Reinforce Racism*. New York: New York University Press.

Orsi, Robert A. 2010. *The Madonna of 115th Street: Faith and Community in Italian Harlem, 1880–1950*. New Haven, CT: Yale University Press.

Perry, Imani. 2004. *Prophets of the Hood: Politics and Poetics in Hip Hop*. Durham, NC: Duke University Press.

Petchauer, Emery. 2009. "Framing and Reviewing Hip-Hop Educational Research." *Review of Educational Research* 79 (2): 946–78. https://doi.org/10.3102/0034654 308330967.

Pew Research Center. 2009. "A Religious Portrait of African-Americans." January 30, 2009.

Pew Research Center. 2015a. "America's Changing Religious Landscape." May 12, 2015.

Pew Research Center. 2015b. "U.S. Public Becoming Less Religious." November 3, 2015.

Pew Research Center. 2016. "Gig Work, Online Selling and Home Sharing." November 2016.

Pew Research Center. 2021. "Faith among Black Americans." February 16, 2021.

P4CM (Passion for Christ Movement). 2015. "Jamaica West—Black Girl Cinema | RHETORIC 2015." YouTube, November 13, 2015. www.youtube.com/watch?v=_gKV7zu32HI&t=97s.

Pinder, Sherrow O. 2015. *Colorblindness, Post-Raciality, and Whiteness in the United States*. New York: Springer.

Pink, Sarah, Heather Horst, John Postill, Larissa Hjorth, Tania Lewis, and Jo Tacchi. 2015. *Digital Ethnography: Principles and Practice*. Thousand Oaks, CA: Sage.

Pinn, Anthony B. 2017. *Varieties of African American Religious Experience: Toward a Comparative Black Theology—20th Anniversary Edition*. Minneapolis: Fortress.

Price, Emmett. 2012. *The Black Church and Hip Hop Culture: Toward Bridging the Generational Divide*. Lanham, MD: Scarecrow.

Propaganda. 2012. "Precious Puritans." Track 2 on *Excellent*. Produced by Beautiful Eulogy. Humble Beast Records. Mp3.

Propaganda. 2017. "I Hate Cats." Track B8 on *Crooked*. Produced by Daniel Steele. Humble Beast Records. Mp3.

Quinn, Amy, Bonka Boneva, Robert Kraut, Sara Kiesler, Jonathon Cummings, and Irina Shklovski. 2012. "Teenage Communication in the Instant Messaging Era." In *Computers, Phones, and the Internet: Domesticating Information Technology*, edited by Robert Kraut, Malcolm Brynin, and Sara Kiesler, 201–18. Oxford: Oxford University Press.

Rainie, Lee, and Barry Wellman. 2012. *Networked: The New Social Operating System*. Cambridge, MA: MIT Press.

Raphelson, Samantha. 2014. "From GIs to Gen Z (Or Is It IGen?): How Generations Get Nicknames." *NPR*, October 6, 2014. www.npr.org.

Rapzilla. 2010. "Lecrae at Legacy Conference 2010." YouTube, July 30, 2010. www.youtube.com/watch?v=YMCx5SH4Zvs.

Rapzilla. 2016. "Phanatik on His Ministry Post-Cross Movement and New Books." YouTube, August 31, 2016. www.youtube.com/watch?v=6w-kAICz8OU&feature=emb_logo.

Raun, Tobias. 2018. "Capitalizing Intimacy: New Subcultural Forms of Micro-Celebrity Strategies and Affective Labour on YouTube." *Convergence* 24 (1): 99–113.

Rawson, Katie, and Trevor Muñoz. 2016. "Against Cleaning." *Curating Menus* (blog), July 6, 2016. www.curating-menus.org.

Reid, Larry. 2018. "Matthew Stevenson Responds to His Critics about His IG Clapback." *Larry Reid Show*. YouTube, August 12, 2018. https://fb.watch/6bkUaNm2eN/.

Reid, Larry. 2021. "Discussing Your Viral Posts and Jamal Bryant Picture and Matthew Stevenson's Video . . ." *Larry Reid Show*. YouTube, May 24, 2017. https://youtu.be/L38NJHmc-c0.

Revive Our Hearts. 2018. "True Woman '18 (Session 1)." Facebook, September 27, 2018. www.facebook.com.

Revive Our Hearts. n.d.-a. "About." Accessed April 12, 2019. www.reviveourhearts.com.

Revive Our Hearts. n.d.-b. "Statement of Faith." Accessed April 12, 2019. www.reviveourhearts.com.

Richardson, Alissa. 2020. "The 'Good News': How the Gospel of Anti-Respectability Is Shaping Black Millennial Christian Podcasting." *Fire* 6 (1): 67–97.

Robehmed, Natalie. 2019. "At 21, Kylie Jenner Becomes the Youngest Self-Made Billionaire Ever." *Forbes*, March 5, 2019. www.forbes.com.

Rogers, Walter B. 2018. "Matthew Stevenson Calls a Man Ugly on Social Media . . ." YouTube, August 14, 2018. www.youtube.com/watch?v=lsWQ7IylQ4E.

Rolen, Emily, and Mitra Toossi. 2108. *Blacks in the Labor Force*. US Bureau of Labor Statistics, February 2018. www.bls.gov.

Rose, Tricia. 1994. *Black Noise: Rap Music and Black Culture in Contemporary America*. Middletown, VT: Wesleyan University Press.

Rose, Tricia. 2008. *The Hip Hop Wars What We Talk About When We Talk About Hip Hop—And Why It Matters*. New York: Basic Civitas Books.

Rutgers University. 2015. "Percussive Pedagogies with the Crunk Feminist Collective." YouTube, April 9, 2015. www.youtube.com/watch?v=aciIBnl2K-E&t=571s.

Samie. 2012. "The Breakfast Club Power 105.1 Interview with Kendrick Lamar." YouTube, June 6, 2012. www.youtube.com/watch?v=i_JSvcbMqlU&list=RDOov944xegAI&index=7.

Sampson, Melva L. 2017. "#BlackSkinWhiteSin: No Redemptive Quality: Black Women's Bodies, Black Church and the Business of Shame." *Feminist Wire*, February 14, 2017. https://thefeministwire.com.

Sampson, Melva L. 2020. "Digital Hush Harbors." *Fire* 6 (1): 45–66.

Sarachik, Justin. 2017a. "Datin Addresses Lecrae Not Defending Christian Rap, Lecrae Responds." *Rapzilla*, March 4, 2017. https://rapzilla.com.

Sarachik, Justin. 2017b. "Lecrae's 'All Things Work Together' Opening Week Numbers Are In." *Rapzilla*, October 2, 2017. https://rapzilla.com.

Sarachik, Justin. 2017c. "Lecrae Speaks To Sway About 'White-Evangelicalism' & Hot 97 About Chance The Rapper." *Rapzilla*, March 2, 2017. https://rapzilla.com.

Savage, Barbara. 2008. *Your Spirits Walk Beside Us: The Politics of Black Religion*. Cambridge, MA: Harvard University Press.

Schoenewolf, Gerald. 2005. "Gay Rights and Political Correctness: A Brief History." NARTH, April 4, 2005. www.narth.com.

Senft, Theresa M. 2013. "Microcelebrity and the Branded Self." In *A Companion to New Media Dynamics*, edited by John Hartley, Jean Burgess, and Axel Bruns, 346–54. Oxford, UK: Wiley-Blackwell.

Sharpe, Christina. 2016. *In the Wake: On Blackness and Being*. Durham, NC: Duke University Press.

Shin, Sunny Hyucksun, Erika Edwards, Timothy Heeren, and Maryann Amodeo. 2009. "Relationship between Multiple Forms of Maltreatment by a Parent or Guardian and Adolescent Alcohol Use." *American Journal on Addictions* 18 (3): 226–34. https://doi.org/10.1080/10550490902786959.

Simpson, Dave. 2017. "Sugarhill Gang: How We Made Rapper's Delight." *Guardian*, May 2, 2017. www.theguardian.com.

Sims, Natalie Lauren. 2019. *Meditate*. Produced by Swoope. Ngrooves (on behalf of Rostrum Records). Mp3.

Smith, Christian, and Patricia Snell. 2009. *Souls in Transition: The Religious and Spiritual Lives of Emerging Adults*. Oxford: Oxford University Press.

Smith, Jonathan Z. 1978. *Map Is Not Territory: Studies in the History of Religions*. Studies in Judaism in Late Antiquity 23. Leiden: Brill.

Solomon, Joseph. 2015. "My Cleavage Is a Snare | @jamaicawest312 @chaseGodtv." YouTube, May 20, 2015. www.youtube.com/watch?v=eLHcQx1vw_E&feature=youtu.be.

Solomon, Joseph. 2016. "I'm So Black Christian | @whatisjoedoing @jamaicawest312." YouTube, April 25, 2016. www.youtube.com/watch?v=ujnolG1VV9o.

Solomon, Joseph. 2018. "Shadow of a Doubt." Presented at the Legacy Conference. Live Performance, Moody Bible Institute, Chicago, IL, July 18, 2018.

Sorett, Josef. 2009. "'Believe Me, This Pimp Game Is Very Religious': Toward a Religious History of Hip Hop." *Culture and Religion* 10 (1): 11–22. https://doi.org/10.1080/14755610902786288.

Sparkes, A. C. 2002. "Autoethnography: Self-Indulgence or Something More?" In *Ethnographically Speaking: Autoethnography, Literature, and Aesthetics*, edited by Carolyn Ellis and Arthur P. Bochner, 209–32. Walnut Creek, CA: AltaMira.

SSEXBBOX. 2017. "On Inequality Angela Davis and Judith Butler in Conversation." YouTube, May 22, 2017. www.youtube.com/watch?v=-MzmifPGk94&t=1281s.

Stevenson, Matthew. 2016. "Dr. Matthew L Stevenson III: 'Sneak Peak!!! ANWA Training!!! My Executive Pastor! Michael Martin.'" PSCP. www.pscp.tv.

Strachan, Owen. 2012. "Reflecting on Propaganda's Fiery 'Precious Puritans' Rap Song." *Thought Life* (blog), September 26, 2012. www.patheos.com.

Strachan, Owen. 2013. "Hip-Hop Theologians and Preachers: The Artists Most Shaping the Movement." *Christianity Today*, May 3, 2013. www.christianitytoday.com.

Strauss, Anselm, and Juliet M. Corbin. 1998. *Basics of Qualitative Research*. Thousand Oaks, CA: Sage.

Strauss, William, and Neil Howe. 1991. *Generations: The History of America's Future, 1584 to 2069*. New York: Morrow.

Strauss, William, and Neil Howe. 1997. *The Fourth Turning: An American Prophecy—What the Cycles of History Tell Us about America's Next Rendezvous with Destiny*. New York: Crown.

Strauss, William, and Neil Howe. 2000. *Millennial Rising: The Next Great Generation*. New York: Vintage.

Subrahmanyam, Kaveri, Patricia M. Greenfield, and Brendesha Tynes. 2004. "Constructing Sexuality and Identity in an Online Teen Chat Room." *Journal of Applied Developmental Psychology* 25 (6): 651–66.

Tedashii (Tedashii Lavoy Anderson). 2011. "Dum Dum." Featuring Lecrae. Track 14 on *Backlight*. Written by Charles Cornelius, Lecrae Moore, and Tedashii Anderson. Produced by GeeDA. Reach Records. Mp3.

Tesfamariam, Rahiel. 2015. "Why the Modern Civil Rights Movement Keeps Religious Leaders at Arm's Length." *Washington Post*, September 18, 2015. www.washingtonpost.com.

Thomas, Danyella. 2017. "Exodus: Why Black Millennials Are Leaving the Church." *Unfit Christian* (blog), May 11, 2017. www.unfitchristian.com.

Trackstarz. 2017. "Interview: Trackstarz on New Lecrae Album and Insight on CHH Industry." *Wade-O Radio Video Channel*. YouTube, December 6, 2017. www.youtube.com/watch?v=uQ3jNeIK390.

Trackstarz. 2018. "Natalie Lauren at Flavor Fest 18—Interview." YouTube, October 11, 2018. www.youtube.com/watch?v=qvTPKEP3sRs&t=167s.

Troutman, Constance. 2017. "We Just Lost One: Bye Lecrae." *Truth + Fire* (blog), July 19, 2017. www.truthandfire.com.

Truth's Table. 2018. "Behind the Book: *Gay Girl, Good God* with Jackie Hill-Perry." Interview by Christina Edmondson and Ekemini Uwan. August 18, 2018. MP3. 58:46. https://podcastrepublic.net.

Truth's Table. 2019. "Facts about Lecrae." Interview by Christina Edmondson. Produced by Joshua Heath. February 17, 2019. MP3. 50:00. https://soundcloud.com.

Turner, Patrick. 2010. "Hip Hop Versus Rap: An Ethnography of the Cultural Politics of New Hip Hop Practices." PhD diss., Goldsmiths, University of London. http://research.gold.ac.uk.

Urry, John, and Jonas Larsen. 2012. *The Tourist Gaze 3.0*. London: Sage.

Wade-O. 2017. "Lecrae Responds to Datin, Explains Aha Gazelle Signing and Not Being a Christian Rapper." YouTube, March 20, 2017. www.youtube.com/watch?v=Lp24ovXAWZU&t=28s.

Walton, Jonathan L. 2009. *Watch This! The Ethics and Aesthetics of Black Televangelism*. New York: New York University Press.

Wang, Hsin-Yi, Leif Sigerson, and Cecilia Cheng. 2019. "Digital Nativity and Information Technology Addiction: Age Cohort versus Individual Difference Approaches." *Computers in Human Behavior* 90 (January): 1–9. www.sciencedirect.com.

Ward, Earlise, Jacqueline C. Wiltshire, Michelle A. Detry, and Roger L. Brown. 2013. "African American Men and Women's Attitudes toward Mental Illness, Perceptions of Stigma, and Preferred Coping Behaviors." *Nursing Research* 62 (3): 185.

Welcome 2 Church. 2014. "WATCH: Man Gets Delivered from Gay Homosexuality (I DON'T LIKE MENS NO MORE!)." YouTube, November 12, 2014. www.youtube.com/watch?v=L_Fqn2HJ1gk.

West, Jamaica. 2017. "Bury Cinderella." YouTube, October 24, 2017. www.youtube.com/watch?v=JLoDn1byLBI.

Williams, Delores S. 1993. *Sisters in the Wilderness: The Challenge of Womanist God-Talk*. New York: Orbis Books.

Wright, Michelle, and Yan Li. 2011. "The Associations between Young Adults' Face-to-Face Prosocial Behaviors and Their Online Prosocial Behaviors." *Computers in Human Behavior* 27 (5): 1959–62. www.sciencedirect.com.

Wuthnow, Robert. 2015. *Inventing American Religion: Polls, Surveys, and the Tenuous Quest for a Nation's Faith*. Oxford: Oxford University Press.

YaleUniversity. 2018. "Yale Town Hall Conversation with Lecrae." YouTube, September 13, 2018. www.youtube.com/watch?v=1Fcq5eaJ6vI.

YAM TV. 2018. "Dr Matthew Stevenson Says Men in Church Turn Gay Because of Fat Women." YouTube, October 1, 2018. www.youtube.com/watch?v=l4-iXZlFXSQ.

INDEX

abstinence, 35
activism, Black Christian, 168, 170, 198
adults, young Black, 50–51
aesthetic, hip hop, 79, 242n9
African American rhetorical tradition, 227n1
African American Spiritual Awareness Crusade, 180, 182
"Against Cleaning" (Rawson and Muñoz), 25
Algorithms of Oppression (Noble), 170
#AllLivesMatter, 66
All Nations Worship Assembly (ANWA), 180, 196–97, 199–202, 206, 207
All Things Work Together (*ATWT*), 63, 66–67
"Always Knew," 238n14
Ambassador, 80
American Academy of Religion's Critical Approaches to Hip Hop and Religion, xxii
Ammerman, Nancy, 165, 231n18
Anomaly, 63
Anti-Drug Abuse Act (1986), 114
ANWA. *See* All Nations Worship Assembly
anxiety, 162, 163
Anyabwile, Thabiti, 106
apologetics, 80, 242n11
Art of Joy, 109, 132
Association of Internet Researchers, 22
Atlanta, 193–96
ATWT. *See All Things Work Together*
Authentically Black and Truly Catholic (Cressler), 6

autoethnography, xxiv, 228nn3–4
Azalea, Iggy, 149, 178–79

baby boomers, 237n8
Bain, Bryon, xix
Beleaf in Fatherhood (YouTube channel), 30–31, 146
Beleaf Melanin. *See* Henry, Glen
belief, spectrum of, 8
Bellizzi, Christina (Cataphant), 172, *173*, 174, *174*, 175, *175*
Benbow, Candice, 213
Berkeley's Liberation Movement, 240n2
Bernstein, Joe, 197
Bethel Deliverance International Church, 3
Beykpour, Kayvon, 197
bias, racial, 47–49
"Bias in the Computer System" (Friedman and Nissanbaum), 25
Bible: Book of Acts, 190; Titus, 193; TWL, 114
Black American Christianity, 74
Black bodies, 107–8, 114–16, 134, 135, 218–19; capitalism and, 140, 141; fetishizing of, 118; stereotypes of, 141; work of, 141. *See also* Black female body
Black Christian activism, 168, 170
Black Christian female body, 107–8
Black Christians, xx, 5; ethnography on, 8–9; millennial, 41–42, 236nn1–2; webwork, 27; young, 11–12, 13, 14. *See also* digital Black Christians

265

The Black Church, xi, 5, 6, 7, 41, 106; Blueprint Church and, 195–96; digital Black Christians and, 216, 217–19; family connections of, 76–77; Hill-Perry and, 127–29, 137; hip hop and, 133, 216; history of, 230nn13–15; millennials leaving, 41–42; new, 163–70, 195–96; racism and, 118; rappers rejected by, 82–84; sexuality and, 124–25; Solomon on, 86; technology and, 2, 219; as tradition, 227n1 (glossary); West, J., on, 180–81, 208
Black churches, x, 207–8, 218, 230n13; Neo-, 165, 181. *See also specific Black churches*
Black culture, media and, 54
Black digital religion, 20–27
Black fatherlessness, 52, 56, 57, 58–59
Black female body, 119, 130, 131–33, 135; Christian, 107–10; digital Black Christian, 113–21; hip hop portrayal of, 116–17; hypersexualization of, 116; stereotypes on, 116; West, J., and, 186–87
"Black Girl Cinema" (West, J.), 184, 186
"Black Interiority" (Dyson), 187
Black Is King, 238n16
Black Lives Matter (BLM) movement, 62–63, 138–39, 168
Black men, 35, 164, 236n6; depression and, 160–61; incarceration of, 35
Black militancy, xxi
Black millennials, xxiii, 49–51, 230n16, 237nn11–12
Black modesty, 117
Black Muslims, 19
Blackness, 19, 53, 86, 102–3; Christianity and, 55; digital Black Christians and, 239n17; Hill-Perry and, 133, 134; hip hop and, 79; queer, 121–22; secondary, 169, 170; technology and, 43; on television, 57; troubling, 93–94, 104
Black Noise (Rose), 129, 227n2
Black Panthers, 59
Black pathology, 42, 236n5

Blacksheep t-shirts, 34
Black spirituality, 6, 7
Black Twitter, 101, 197
Black women, 185–86, 207; online working, 170–77
Black youth, criminalized depictions of, 53, 236n4
Black Youth Project, 50–51
BLM. *See* Black Lives Matter
blogs, 81
Blueprint Church, 192–93, 195–96
body work, 112
Book of Acts, 190
boom box, 44
boyd, danah, 231n17
Boyd-Pates, Tyree, 67
Boy Erased (film), 122
broadcasting, religious, 73–74
Brock, André, 26, 101
brokenness, 186
Broussard, Meredith, 55
Brown, James, 58
Buffalo, New York, xxi
"Bury Cinderella" (West, J.), 213
Bush, George H. W., 113–14
Bush, George W., xx–xxi, 77
Butler, Judith, 228n3
Butta P, 172–73
Bynum, Juanita, 107, 108–9, 118–20, 148

Cable Act (1992), 114
Caldwell, Andrew, 126–27
Calvinism, 82, 87
Campbell, Heidi, 14
Campus Crusade for Christ (Cru), 240n2
"Can't Stop Me Now," 244n6
capitalism: Black bodies and, 140, 141; resistance to, 232n23; woke, 142
Carter, Bryan, 21
Carter, Earl, 127
Carter, Tony, 106
Castile, Philando, 66
Cataphant. *See* Bellizzi, Christina

INDEX | 267

celebrity: Instagram culture of, 151; micro, 2, 229n9
Chance the Rapper, 12
Chandler, Damita, 148
chaseGodtv (Solomon YouTube channel), 81–82
CHH. *See* Christian hip hop
#chhbeefs (Christian hip hop beefs), 234n30
#CHHSexism, 9, *171*, 172–74, *174–75*, 245n8
Chicago, 187–93, 202
Chopra, Deepak, 162
Christian, Barbara, 108
Christian hip hop (CHH), xviii, 60, 77, 79–80, 90; sexism within, 9, *171*, 172–75; white men and, 88; women portrayed in, 133
Christian hip hop beefs (#chhbeefs), 234n30
Christianity: Black American, 74; Blackness and, 55; hip hop and, xviii, 9, 60, 77, 79–80; Moore, L., and, 234nn27–28, 239n20; online, 66; social justice, 99; white, 63–64, 73
Christianity Today (magazine), 93
Christian rap, 80, 90, 234n30
Christians, xi–xii; Black millennial, 41–42, 236nn1–2; college to, 240n2; conservative, 60–61; white, 59, 66, 189. *See also* Black Christians; digital Black Christians
Christian television networks, 241n3
Christian unity, 60
Christian World Liberation Front, 240n2
Christian youth culture, 35
Christology, 80
churches: Latinx, 105; leaving, xxi, 81–82; Neo-Black, 165, 181; online, 85; switching, 206. *See also* Black Church, The; Black churches
church planting, 188–89, 190, 193, 195
Clay, Elonda, 19

Cleveland, Christena, 188–89
Clinton, Bill, 114, 115
CMR. *See* Cross Movement Records
Cobbs, Tasha, 194–95
codes, for data collection, 27
college, to Christian, 240n2
Collins, Patricia Hill, 108
"Colored People," 77
Colored Television (Frederick), 108
Colson, Charles, 61–62
committed traditionalists, 8, 232n22
conscious hip hop, 143–44
conservative Christians, 60–61
conservative evangelicals, 99
conversion therapy, 122–24
Cooper, Brittany, 132
coping mechanisms, 156
Cornerstone Community Church, 195
coronavirus. *See* COVID-19 pandemic
Corrigan, Thomas, 139
counseling, marriage, 158, 160
COVID-19 pandemic, 40, 207, 209; memes on, 209, *210*, 211, *211*
Creative RX, 163
creatives, xii, 20, 21–22, 24, 27–39; discipleship and, 72–73; female, 207; labor value and, 139–40; online, 142–45; protective strategies of, 245n7
Cressler, Matthew, 6
criminalized depictions, of Black youth, 53, 236n4
Critical Race and Digital Studies Syllabus, 25
critical race theory, 14
critical technocultural discourse, 26
Cross Movement Records (CMR), 78–81, 90
Cru. *See* Campus Crusade for Christ
cultural expression, 79
culture, 218; Black, 54; Christian youth, 35; hip hop, xxii; Instagram celebrity, 151
Cure for Love (film), 122
Curtis, Miranda, 201–2

"Damn. Damn. Damn." meme, 57
data-collection, 236nn1–2; on millennials, 49–50; for study, 26–27
data mining, 27
Davis, Angela, 139, 157
DC Talk, 77–78
death, 53–54, 56; Black, 58–59, 64–65, 68, 188, 244n6; in media, 64–65
Dedoose, 24–25
Def Poetry Jam (TV show), 143, 244n3
Denton Bible Church, 192
"Depressed," 157
depression, 238n13, 244n6; Black, 152–57; Black men and, 160–61
Dever, Mark, 82–83, 84, 87
Diallo, Amadou, 242n7
digital Black Christians, xii, xv–xxvii, xxiv, 2–7, 12, 38; Black bodies and, 121; The Black Church and, 216, 217–19; Blackness and, 239n17; BLM and, 138–39; CMR and, 79; digital religion studies and, 14; female, 100–101; hip hop and, 14–27, 54; identity of, 129, 232n23; Jakes and, 215; labor of, 142–46; *The Lion King* and, 56–57; lived practices of, 8–9; movement of, 34; multidimensionality of, 98; older, 46; origins of, 42–43, 51; podcasts by, 106, 145; scholarship on, 7; social media and, 93; technology and, 14–27, 46, 54–55; white evangelism and, 104; YouTube and, 121–35. *See also* study, digital Black Christians
digital discipleship, 73, 105
digital ethnography, xii, xxii, 9–14
digital hip hop, 2
Digital Humanities Institute, 26
digital labor, 145, 178
digital narrative, 158
digital religion, 14, 39, 68
digital religion studies, 229n10
digital tagging, 25

digital technology, 54–56, 157; millennials and, 232n21; Moore, L., and, 65–66
digitized Pentecostalism, 196–206
Dillard, Angela, 230n15
Dimitriadis, Greg, 18, 237n7
discipleship, 71–72, 80–81, 90; digital, 73, 105
discrimination: gender, 177; workplace, 170
"Dispelling the Millennial Myth" (Hesel and May), 237n9
Dixon, Vashon, 205
DJ Wade-O, 36, 37, 37–38, 63
"DNOU2" (Don't Nobody Own Us), 176–77
Dollar, Creflo, 74
"Don't Stop 'til You Get Enough," 43
"Don't Waste Your Life," 240n1
doo wop music, 117
"Doo Wop (That Thing)," 117
Douglas, Kelly Brown, 124
Douglass, Frederick, 59, 239n18
Dove Soap campaign, 142
Drake, Simone C., 236n6
dress, styles of, 110, 115
Drucker, Johanna, 94
D'Souza, Dinesh, 242n7
Du Bois, W. E. B., xi, 230n13
Dulaney, Todd, 202
"Dum Dum," 38
Dye, Brian, 28–29, 190–92
Dyson, Torkwase, 187

East Coast rap, 45
East Coast/West Coast feud, 78
economies, woke, 141–42
Edmondson, Christina, 244n19
Eleft, Holly, 95
Elevation Church, 166
Elim Christian Fellowship, xxiii
emotional labor, 149
The End of Racism (D'Souza), 242n7
enslavement, 26, 135, 189

"ephemeral mediated mobility," 211
epistemology, xxiii–xxiv, 228n3
equality, of women, 10
ERACE Foundation (Eliminating Racism and Creating Equality), 77
erasure. *See* racial erasure
erotic repression, 118, 119
ethics, 21
ethnography, xxiii–xxiv; auto-, xxiv, 228nn3–4; on Black Christians, 8–9; of Black digital religion, 20–27; digital, xii, xxii, 9–14; hip hop, 12, 18–19, 228n3; justice-centered digital, 21
evangelism, 77, 81; conservative, 99; televangelism, 74. *See also* white evangelism
event, as place, 235n33
Everyday Religion (Ammerman), 165
Excellent, 91
exnomination, 74–75, 77
exodus, from Church, 81–82

"Facts," 238n14
faith, race and, xx
Faith in the City (Dillard), 230n15
family connections, of Black Church, 76–77
Fareed-Cooke, Aitina (AI), 32
fashion trends, 115
fatherhood, 146, 152
fatherlessness, Black, 52, 56, 57, 58–59
female creatives, 207
feminism, 95, 233n24
feminist thought, 10, 233n24
feud, East Coast/West Coast, 78
finances, 200–201
Floyd, George, 40
Focus on the Family, 239n19
"follow the thing" methodology, 22–23
Foucault, Michel, 54–55, 228n3
The Fourth Turning (Strauss and Howe), 48
Frederick, Marla, 22, 108

The Fresh Prince of Bel-Air (TV show), 56
Friedman, Batya, 25
Friendship, Cliques, and Gangs (Dimitriadis), 18
Fritz, Tom, 240n2
"From the Blackhand Side" (Brock), 101
Furtick, Steven, 166

Gamergate controversy, 98–99
gay community, 128–29
Gay Girl, Good God (Hill-Perry), 110, 132, 133–34
gay rights, 244n2 (chap. 3)
gender, 58; discrimination against, 177; inequalities and, 170; questioning, 123
gender dynamics, 139
gender normativity, xviii
gender roles, 96, 99
generational theory, 48–49, 227n3, 237n8
generational wealth, 151
Generations (Strauss and Howe), 47–48
Gibbs, Lamar, 200
gig work, 145
Global Fire Alliance, 196
glory, 83
God, 135; praying to, 148; sovereignty of, 83
GoFundMe, for Beleaf, 30–31
Gomez, Betsy, 96
Good Religion, 146
Good Times (TV show), 57
Gospel Gangstas, 90
gospel music, Southern, 147
gospel rap, xviii, xxi, 88
Granovetter, Mark S., 4
guides, 20, 24, 27
gun violence, 160

Haddon, Deitrick, 148
Hall, Stuart, 94
hand-clapping games, 228n5
Hansen, Collin, 81, 82, 87
hashtags, 9

healing, 148
health, mental, 64, 155, 162–63
health care, access to, 155
Heaven's Mentality, 78–79
Henry, Glen (Beleaf Melanin), 1, 24, 30–32, 66, 138, 139; on depression, 154–55, 156–58; early life of, 146–47; post by, 149–51, 152–53, 163–64; Todd and, 166–67
Hesel, Richard A., 237n9
heterosexuality, 122
Hill, Lauryn, 1, 58, 116–17, 237n7
Hill-Perry, Jackie, 9–13, 30, 81, 135, 229n1; Black Church and, 127–29, 137; Blackness and, 133, 134; early life of, 113; on Hill, 117, 121; Instagram post by, 97–100, 102–4, 136–37; at Legacy Conference, 100–101; Perry, P., and, 191, *194*; sexuality and, 107, 109–10, 112, 123–24, 133; wearing hip hop, 129–30, 131, 133, 135; on YouTube, 122–23, 124–31. *See also* "My Life as a Stud"
hip hop, xii–xiii, xvii, xix, 1, 6; aesthetic of, 79, 242n9; ANWA and, 202; Black Church and, 133, 216; Black female bodies portrayed in, 116–17; Blackness and, 79; Christianity and, xviii, 9, 60, 77, 79–80; conscious, 143–44; digital, 2; digital Black Christians and, 14–27, 54; dress style of, 115; Hill-Perry wearing, 129–30, 131, 133, 135; media and, 44; Petty on, 89–90; religion and, 17–18; as resistance, 232n23; technology and, 7, 14–27, 46–47; on television, 46. *See also* Christian hip hop (CHH)
hip hop culture, xxii
hip hop ethnography, 12, 18–19, 228n3
hip hop scholarship, 227n2
Hip Hop's Hostile Gospel (Hodge), 16
hip hop writing, 18
HIV, 120
Hodge, Daniel White, 16, 237n7
Holy Ghost, xvi

homosexuality, 123, 125–27
honest lie, 14
"housewifization," 139
Howe, Neil, 47–50, 227n3
"How Many Licks," 116
Hsu, Wendy, 94
Hurston, Zora Neale, 53
Husserl, Edmund, 228n3
hypersexualization, of Black female body, 116

iconography, Christian, 34–35
"I Hate Cats," 69, 70
illness, mental, 155–58
Impact Movement, 240n2
"I'm So Black Christian," 3–4, 5–6, 67–68
incarceration: Black male, 35; rate of, 114
Indeep, 38–39
individualism, networked, 229n11
"In Flickering Lights," 209, 211, 212, 214, 215
Instagram, 5, 93, 149–50; celebrity cultures on, 151; Hill-Perry post on, 97–100, 102–4, 136–37; Solomon post on, *33*
internet, xxi–xxii; role of, 84–86
The Internet (Slater and Miller), 7
intimacy, 2–3; through identity, 135–37; through relationships, 104–6; through visibility and valuation, 178–79
Iraq war, xx
Ito, Mizuko, 142

Jakes, T. D., 74, 118, 166, 209, 212, 213–16, *214*
James, LeBron, 239n20
Janette . . . ikz's. *See* Watson, Janette
Jenkins, Candice, 141
Jenner, Kylie, 151
Jesus, 72
Jezebel Unhinged (Lomax), 233n26
"Jig-a-boo," on YouTube, 131–35, 136
Johnson, Patrick, 19
Jones, James Earl, 56, 57

Jones, Sarah, xix
Jon Jon Traxx, 149
justice-centered digital ethnography, 21

Kassian, Mary, 95, 243n14
KB, 175–77
Keller, Tim, 188
Kennedy, John F., 48
KevOnStage, 165
Khabeer, Su'ad Abdul, 19
King, Martin Luther, Jr., 48, 58, 59, 61
Kirk Franklin and the Family, xvii
Knott, Kim, 181–82
Korzybski, Alfred, 5
Kuehn, Kathleen, 139
Kweli, Talib, 243n12

labor: Black online, 145–46, 167; digital, 145, 178; digital Black Christian, 142–46; emotional, 149; value of, 139–40
Lahad, Kinneret, 235n32
Lamar, Kendrick, 6, 12
language, xvi
Latinx churches, 105
Latinx community, 89
law enforcement, 115; white evangelism and, 239n19
Lawrence, Martin, 58
Lefebvre, Henri, 185
Legacy Disciple Conference, 28–32, 33, 36, 37, 70; creation of, 188, 189; Hill-Perry at, 100–101; Moore, L., at, 194–95
lesbianism, 97, 121, 132
Lewis, Dhati, 192, 195
Lewis, Elder Craig, 235n35
LGBTQIA folk, 121, 124, 127, 130; pretexting and, 111–12
liberation, spiritual, 110
lie, honest, 14
Lincoln, Yvonna S., 235n37
Lindsey, Cornelius, 212–13, *214*
Lindsey, Heather, 212–14, *214*
Linne, Shai, 80, 234n30

The Lion King (film), 56–57, 238n16
lived religion, 231n18
The Location of Religion (Knott), 181–82
Lofton, Kathryn, 243n13
Lomax, Tamura, 108, 233n26, 241n3
Lorde, Audre, 133
"I Love to Praise Him," 147
Lövheim, Mia, 14
lyricism, 16, 80
Lyricist Lounge, 144

The Madonna of 115th Street (Orsi), 11–12
Malcolm X, 59, 61, 243n12
Mann, Jim, 98–99, 100, 102–4, 244n16
Mannheim, Karl, 49
Map Is Not Territory (Smith), 230n14
marriage, 233n24; counseling for, 158, 160; of Watson, J., 29–30
Martin (TV show), 58
Martin, Trayvon, 59, 62, 65, 92, 239n20
Marx, Karl, 154
masculinity, xviii, 58
Mason, Eric, 52
Massey, Doreen, 235n33
Matheson, David, 122
May, Susan Basalla, 237n9
McGee and Me (comic book), 114
McIntosh, Gary, 165
McKittrick, Katherine, 182
McSweeny, Michelle, 26
media, 40, 55, 120; Black culture and, 54; Black death in, 64–65; hip hop and, 44; Moore, L., and, 64–65
Medicaid, 116
meditation, 162–63, 165
memes, 197, *198*; on COVID-19 pandemic, 209, *210*, 211, *211*; "Damn. Damn. Damn.," 57
men: Black, 35, 160–61, 164, 236n6; white, 81, 82, 83, 88
mental health, 64, 155, 162–63
mental illness, 155–58
Merritt, James, 52

Merritt, Jonathan, 52
method of study, for survey, 24–27
#MeToo movement, 172
micro-celebrity, 2, 229n9
militancy, Black, xxi
Millennial Rising (Strauss and Howe), 48
millennials, xiii, 8, 16–17, 215, 232n20; Black, xxiii, 49–51, 170, 230n16, 237nn11–12; Black Christian, 41–42, 236n1–2; Black Church left by, 41–42; data collection on, 49–50; demographics of, 237n12; digital technology and, 232n21; origins of term, 46, 47–50, 237n11
Miller, Daniel, 7, 16
Miller, Monica, xxii, 233n25, 236n4
Minaj, Nicki, 172
minorities, racial, 237n10
misogyny, 129
modesty, xviii; Black, 117
Møller, Kristen, 211
Montgomery, Tipani, 205
Moody Bible Institute, 28–32
Moody Publishers, 96
Moore, Jessica Care, xix
Moore, Lecrae Devaughn, 12–13, 28–29, 38, 41–42, 58–60; *ATWT* by, 63, 66–67; Black death and, 68, 244n6; Blueprint in Denton and, 192; Christianity and, 234nn27–28, 239n21; CMR and, 78; on college, 240n2; on depression, 156–57; digital technology and, 65–66; early life of, 43–46, 51–52, 53; at Legacy Disciple Conference, 194–95; media and, 64–65; racial-religious identity of, 61–64, 66–68, 239n18, 239n23; Shakur and, 51–52, 53; Thompson on, 240n1; twitter post by, 65, 239n22; writing style of, 238n14; at Yale University talks, 63–64
motherhood, single Black, 56
Moultrie, Monique, 108, 112
MTV, 44–45
Muñoz, Trevor, 25

music, writing, 148–49. *See also specific genres*
Muslim Cool (Khabeer), 19
Muslims, Black, 19
"My Cleavage Is a Snare" (West, J.), 186
"My Life as a Stud" (Hill-Perry), 81, 109, 122, 124, 137, 217; comments on, 125–27; on YouTube, 124–31

National Association for Research and Therapy of Homosexuality (NARTH), 123
National Center for the Study of Youth and Religion study, 8, 231n19–232n20
The Negro Church (Du Bois), xi, 230n13
Neo-Black churches, 165, 181
networked individualism, 229n11
networked publics, 231n17
networks, xiii, 4–5
new Black Church, 163–70, 195–96
"New Woke Christian" (Perry, P.), 169–70
Nicolosi, Joseph, 123
1979, 43–44
Nissanbaum, Helen, 25
NoBigDyl, 34
Noble, Safiya, 26
"No More Sheets" (Bynum), 109, 118–19, 120
Ntare, xxii
Nu Nation, xvii

Obama, Barack, 77, 95, 237n12, 242n7
"offline," 17
The Old Black Church blog, 245n5
116 Clique, 195
online, 138, 219, 229n11; Black labor, 145–46, 167; Black women working, 170–77; blogs, 81; Christianity, 66; churches, 85; creatives, 142–45; interactions, 32; mentorship, 121; offline life and, 98; racial erasure, 103; religious identity, 14; scandals, 205; sermons, 166; white evangelism, 85

Onwuchekwa, John, 208
oppression: systemic, 93; of women, 177
Oprah (Lofton), 243n13
orality, 198
Oral Roberts University, 74
Orsi, Robert, 10–11

PAIR (Personal Assessment of Intimacy in Relationship) model, 105
pandemic. *See* COVID-19 pandemic
participant selection, for study, 21–24
Passionate and Pious (Moultrie), 108
Passion for Christ Movement (P4CM), 9, 29, 30, 81, 122, 124
pathology, Black, 42, 236n5
Patreon, 151, 244n4
patriarchy, 10
P4CM. *See* Passion for Christ Movement
Pearcey, Nancy, 62
Pearson, Carlton, 74, 241n3
Pentecostal church, xv, 201
Pentecostalism, digitized, 196–206
people of color, 48, 99
performativity, racial, 19–20
Performing Identity/Performing Culture (Dimitriadis), 18, 56
Periscope app, 197, 198–99
Perry, Imani, 79, 242n10
Perry, Preston, 35, 158, 159–61, 169–70, 191, *194*
Personal Assessment of Intimacy in Relationship. *See* PAIR
Personal Responsibility and Work Opportunity Reconciliation Act (1992), 116
Petty, Jason Emmanuel (Propaganda), 1, 69–71, 75, 88, 91–93, 102–4; early life of, 89; on hip hop, 89–90; poster for, *71*
Pew Research Center, 50
Phanatik, 78–79
PIA. *See* Poets in Autumn
place, event as, 235n33
"Planet Rock," 47
planting, church, 188–89, 190, 193, 195

podcasts, by digital Black Christians, 106, 145
poetry, xxii, 33
Poets in Autumn (PIA) Tour, 34–35, 158–59, 161
police brutality, 40, 92, 156, 239n23
politics, study on, 50–51
poster, for Propaganda, *71*
post-racialism, 242n7
Potter's House, 17
power, race and, 103
prayer, 148
preachers: Black millennial, 170; rappers as, 92–93
preaching, 214; digital, *198*, 199; on sexuality, 120
"Precious Puritans," 88, 91–92
pretexting, 110–12, 129–30, 136, 175
prison industrial complex, 115
privilege, white, 151
The Problem of Generations (Mannheim), 49
process, to product, 149–52
prohibition, sexual, 120
Propaganda. *See* Petty, Jason Emmanuel
prophecies, 203–4
Prophets of the Hood (Perry, I.), 79
protective strategies, of creatives, 245n7
Protestantism, liberal, 73
PTSD, 160
publics, networked, 231n17
Puritanism, 91–92
purity, sexual, 113, 212–13

Queen Latifah, 35
queer Blackness, 121–22
Quinn, Zoe, 99

RAAN. *See* Reformed African American Network
race, 93–94, 104; faith and, xx; post-racialism, 242n7; power and, 103; in *Unashamed*, 52–53

racial bias, 47, 48–50
racial divide, 59
racial erasure, 74, 75, 77, 82, 86; online, 103; Solomon on, 87–88
racial identity, 53
racial justice movements, 10, 62–63, 138–39, 168
racial minorities, 237n10
racial performativity, 19–20
racial-religious identity, of Moore, L., 61–63, 66–68, 239n18, 239n23
racial solidarity, 62–63
racism, 73, 74, 92, 112, 118, 242n7; church planting and, 188–89, 190; structural, 168–69, 191; systematic, 64; systemic, 155; white, 64, 118, 141, 216
rap music, xvi–xvii, xxi; Black Church rejecting, 82–84; Christian, 13, 80, 90; East Coast, 45; gospel, xviii, xxi, 88; Reformed, 82; on television, 44–45
Rapper Da Truth, 37
rappers: Christian, 234n30; as preachers, 92–93
Rawson, Katie, 25
Reagan, Ronald, 116
Real Talk, 60
rebranding strategies, 157–58
Red Couch (podcast), 92
Reformed African American Network (RAAN), 106
Reformed movement, 84–86; Calvinism and, 82, 87
Reformed rap, 82–83
Reformed theology, 81–82, 86, 87, 90–91, 105–6
Reid, Larry, 204
relationships, intimacy through, 104–6
religion, 165, 232n20, 233n26; Black digital, 20–27; Black millennials and, 230n16; digital, 14, 39, 68; digital-religious practices, 39; hip hop and, 17–18; lived, 231n18

Religion and Hip Hop (Miller), xxii
religiosity, study on, 237n10
religious identity, 7; of digital Black Christians, 129, 232n23; online, 14
repression, erotic, 118, 119
Robards, Brady, 211
Rose, Tricia, 47, 55, 129, 227n2
Ruin, Tobias, 229n9

sadness, selling, 152–57
Salt-n-Pepa, xvii
Sampson, Melva, 136
San Diego, California, 46
scandals online, 205
School Daze (film), 185, 245n5
Scott, Keith Lamont, 166
secondary Blackness, 169, 170
Senft, Theresa, 229n9
September 11, xix–xx
sermons online, 166
de Seta, Gabriele, 235n34
sexism, 112, 191; Christian hip hop, 9, *171*, 172–75
sexual assault, 183–84
sexual identity, 30
sexual impropriety, 205
sexuality, 97, 99, 107–9, 118–19; Black Church and, 124–25; hetero-, 122; homo-, 123, 125–27; preaching on, 120; UCC and, 212–13
Sexuality and the Black Church (Douglas), 124
sexual prohibition, 120
sexual purity, 113, 212–13
"A Shadow of a Doubt" (Solomon), 76
Shakur, Tupac, 51–52, 53–54, 58, 78, 237n7
sharecroppers, Black, 65, 66
Sharpe, Christina, 140–41, 179
"Sidelines," 58
sign/signifier theory, 75
Sims, Natalie Lauren, 2, 66, 138, 147–49, 176–77; Azalea and, 178–79; on

#CHHSexism, *171*, 172, 175; posts by, 150–52, 153–54, 164, 170; on religion, 165; on therapy, 162–63; Todd and, 166–68
Sinclair, Madge, 56, 57
single Black motherhood, 56
#sjw. *See* social justice warrior
Slater, Don, 7, 16
slavery, 35
Smalls, Christopher "Biggie," 53, 78
smartphones, 22
Smith, Christian, 8
Smith, Jonathan, 230n14
Snell, Patricia, 8
social justice, 10, 59, 66, 67, 98–99, 103
Social Justice and the Gospel Statement, 10
social justice Christianity, 99
social justice warrior (#sjw), 98–99
social media, 4, 6, 7, 93, 100, 211. *See also* Instagram; Twitter
social networking, 85
socio-temporal worlds, xxiii, 232n23, 235n32
solidarity, racial, 62–63
Solomon, Joseph, 1, 3–4, 5, 31, 32–33, 191; on Black church, 86; discipleship and, 72, 80–81, 105; early life of, 75–77; Instagram post by, 33; performance by, 36; Propaganda and, 69–71; on racial erasure, 87–88; white evangelism and, 74, 84–85
Souls in Transition (Smith and Snell), 8
Southern Baptist Convention, 52, 117, 195–96, 208
Southern gospel music, 147
sovereignty, of God, 83
spectrum, of belief, 8
spirit, body and, 111
spirituality, Black, 6, 7
spiritual liberation, 110
spoken word, xix, xxiv–xxvii, 111, 144
"The Spoken Word" class, xix

Star Trek (tv series), 47
Steele, Daniel, 2
stereotypes, 242n10; of Black bodies, 141; of Black female body, 116
Stevenson, Kamilah, 201
Stevenson, Matthew, 196, 197, 198, 199–205, 207
Strachan, Owen, 91–92
strategies: rebranding, 157–58; therapeutic, 158–63
Strauss, William, 47–50, 227n3
strong ties, 4
structural racism, 168–69, 191
Stuckey, Allie Beth, 99
study, digital Black Christians: data-collection for, 26–27; method for, 24–27; participant selection, 21–24; on political, 50–51
styles, xvi; of dress, 110, 115, 127
success, 149–50
suffering, Black, 68
suicide, 53, 147, 153, 157–58, 183–84
"Suicide Roll," 157–58
supremacy. *See* white supremacy
systematic racism, 64
systemic oppression, 93
systemic racism, 155

Table for One (Lahad), 235n32
tablet, writing, xv
tagging, digital, 25
Tate, Jaleceya, 212, 213
Taylor, Linda, 116
technology, 85, 217; The Black Church and, 2, 219; Blackness and, 43; digital Black Christians and, 14–27, 46, 54–55; hip hop and, 7, 14–27, 46–47. *See also* digital technology
Telecommunications Act (1996), 45, 120
televangelism, 74, 108, 136
television: Blackness on, 57; Christian networks on, 241n3; fatherlessness on, 56; hip hop on, 46; rap music on, 44–45

"That's Why We Pray," xvii
theology, Reformed, 81–82, 86, 87, 90–91, 105–6
therapeutic strategies, 158–63
therapy, 160–63; conversion, 122–24
Thesis, 80
Thompson, B. J., 240n1
"Three Lies of Digital Ethnography" (de Seta), 235n34
Titus 2 leaders, 193
TLW. *See* True Love Waits
TLW Bible, 114
Todd, Michael, 165–68
tongues, speaking in, 203
traditionalists, committed, 8, 232n22
Transformation Church, 165
Trapper Keepers, 227n1 (preface)
trauma, 155, 157; of life challenges, 152, 184, 186; workplace, 140
troubling Blackness, 93–94, 104
True Love Waits (TLW) campaign, 113
True Woman Conference, 94–98
"True Woman 1829" (Kassian), 243n14
True Woman Movement, 243nn14–15
Trump, Donald, 168–69, 205, 208
"The Truth Behind Hip Hop" (Lewis, E.), 235n35
Truth's Table (podcast), 66, 128–29, 131, 244n19
Truth Wins Out, 123
The Tunnel Rats, 90
twin towers, xix–xx
Twitter, 24–25, *173*, *174*, *175*, *176*; Black, 101, 197; post by Moore, L., 65, 239n22

UCC. *See* Unfit Christian Congregation
Unashamed (Moore, L.), 13, 43, 52–53
Unfit Christian Congregation (UCC), 211–13
unity, Christian, 60
University of Arizona, 21

video-sharing, 7
violence: exposure to, 155–56; gun, 160; against women, 132, 133
Violent Crime Control and Law Enforcement Act (1994), 114
visibility and valuation, intimacy through, 178–79
Vision Nehemiah, 188, 189
Voices of Unity, 148

Walkman, 44
Walton, Jonathan, 25, 108
Watch This! (Walton), 25, 108
Watson, Janette (Janette . . . ikz's), 3, 29–30, 81
Watson, Matt, 29–30
weak ties, 4
wealth, generational, 151
Weaver, Jason, 56
web applications, 26–27
webwork, 2, 19–20, 27, 178; Black Christian, 27
wedding, of Watson, J., 29–30
welfare, 115–16, 118
West, Jamaica, 1, 3–4, 18, 32, 33–34, *174*, 180–81; ANWA and, 200, 205–6; on The Black Church, 180–81, 208; Black female body and, 186–87; "Bury Cinderella," 213; Chicago and, 187–93, 202; early life of, 182–84
West, Kanye, 19
white Christianity, 59, 63–64, 66, 73, 189
white evangelism, 5, 13, 60, 62–63, 73, 103; digital Black Christians and, 104; exnomination and, 75; law enforcement and, 239n19; Moore, L., and, 66; online, 85; Solomon and, 74, 84–85
white men, 81, 82, 83; Christian hip hop and, 88
whiteness, 74, 75, 92, 95–96
white privilege, 151

white racism, 64, 118, 141, 216
white supremacy, 13, 92, 195–96; exnomination and, 74–75; resistance to, 19
white women, 95–96, 243n13
Williams, Andwele, 143, 144
Winfrey, Oprah, 95, 243n13
woke capitalism, 142
woke economies, 141–42
Wolgemuth, Nancy, 95, 96–97, 133–34
"Woman, Thou Art Loosed" conference, 118, 119
womanhood, Black, 185
women, 48, 193; CHH portrayal of, 133; digital Black Christian, 100–101; equality and, 10; oppression of, 177; violence against, 132, 133; white, 95–96, 243n13. *See also* Black female body; Black women
workplace discrimination, 170
workplace traumas, 140
Worship at the Well, 201
Worth the Wait (YouTube series), 29–30

writing style: hip hop, 18; of Moore, L., 238n14
writing tablet, xv

Xpressions Taboo Tour, 3

Yale University, Moore, L., talks at, 63–64
Yezzianity, 19
Yo! MTV Raps (TV show), 44–45
Young, Restless, and Reformed (Hansen), 82
Young, Restless, and Reformed Movement, 81, 93
young Black adults, 50–51
young Black Christians, 11–12, 13, 14
YoungXLady, 172
YouTube, 3, 5, 29–31, 154–55; digital Black Christians and, 121–35; Hill-Perry on, 122–23; "Jig-a-boo" on, 131–35; "My Life as a Stud" on, 124–31; Solomon on, 72; as therapeutic, 161–62

Zaragoza-Petty, Alma, 92
Zimmerman, George, 92

ABOUT THE AUTHOR

ERIKA D. GAULT is a scholar, poet, and ordained elder whose justice-centered work blends research, art, and religion to advocate for the rights of young Black people. Gault is currently Assistant Professor in the Africana Studies Program at the University of Arizona. Her recent publications include a co-edited volume titled *Beyond Christian Hip Hop: A Move towards Christians and Hip Hop*.

www.ingramcontent.com/pod-product-compliance
Lightning Source LLC
Chambersburg PA
CBHW020356080526
44584CB00014B/1040